Labour Law and Industrial Relations in Central and Eastern Europe
(From Planned to a Market Economy)

Labour Law and Industrial Relations in Central and Eastern Europe (From Planned to a Market Economy)

Bulletin of Comparative Labour Relations 31 - 1996

Editor: R. Blanpain
Guest Editor: L. Nagy

Contributors:

H. Barancova
M. Belina
S. Ghimpu
S. A. Ivanov
P. Koncar
V. Mrachkov
L. Nagy
A. Ravnic
M. Sewerynski
A. Ticlea

1996
Kluwer Law International
The Hague / London / Boston

Published by Kluwer Law International
P.O. Box 85889
2508 CN The Hague
The Netherlands
Tel.: 31-70-3081500
Fax: 31-70-3081515

Sold and distributed in the USA and Canada by
Kluwer Law International
675 Massachusetts Avenue
Cambridge, MA 02139, USA
Tel.: 1-617-354-0140
Fax: 1-617-354-8595

Sold and distributed in all other countries by
Kluwer Law International
P.O. Box 85889
2508 CN The Hague
The Netherlands

Library of Congress Cataloging-in-Publication Data

Labour law and industrial relations in Central and Eastern Europe
    from planned to a market economy / editor, R. Blanpain ; guest
    editor, L. Nagy.
        p.   cm. -- (Bulletin of comparative labour relations ; 31)
     ISBN 9041102981 (pbk. : alk. paper)
     1. Labor laws and legislation--Europe, Eastern. 2. Industrial
relations--Europe, Eastern. 3. Capitalism--Europe, Eastern.
4. Labor laws and legislation--Europe, Central. 5. Industrial
relations--Europe, Central. 6. Capitalism--Europe, Central.
I. Blanpain, R. (Roger), 1932-   . II. Nagy, Lajos, 1926-
KJC2855.L318 1996
344.47'01--dc20
[344.7041]   96-36287

Printed on acid-free paper

ISBN 90411-0298-1

This volume is up-to-date as of 31 March 1995.

Kluwer Law International incorporates the publishing programmes of Graham & Trotman Ltd, Kluwer Law and Taxation Publishers and Martinus Nijhoff Publishers.

iv

Table of Contents

A Comparative Overview

László Nagy

I. INTRODUCTION

This present volume is intended to provide a view of ongoing changes in legal regulation and industrial relations in the Central and Eastern European countries (henceforth CEEC). A few general remarks seem to be appropriate by way of introduction.

Prior to the socialist political and economic systems, the CEEC were states with democratic and market economy structures developed to differing extents. These structures were done away with in the first years of socialist transformation. Starting from 1949 and the early 1950s, the political, economic, and social systems of these countries were uniformly characterized by the omnipotent direction of the party, a planned economy, and a corresponding centralized legal regulation and administration. In the 1960s, some countries, such as Czechoslovakia and Hungary, started economic reform experiments. In the 1980s these were coupled with politically significant trade union action, for instance in Poland. These experiments and activities contributed to a certain relinquishing of economic centralization but had virtually no impact on political power. Therefore, the collapse of the socialist block at the turn of 1989-1990 meant that the establishment of new democratic states and market economy mechanisms in the CEEC was a new task to carry out. There were two indications of the difficulties that lay ahead: First, the nearly 50 years – or in the case of some countries even more – of socialism destroyed the earlier existing state and economic mechanisms to such an extent that a simple restoration of those had become practically impossible. Even if such restoration would have been possible, the restored old structures would have been out of touch with the world, which in the meantime had undergone profound political, economic, and social changes. Consequently, the present day transformation of the CEEC has to be done against the benchmark of today's Western political, state and economic mechanisms. The task is multifaceted: a dictatorial system has to be replaced by a democratic one, where freedom of association and speech, as well as equal opportunities for citizens are a norm. This level playing field includes the rule of law and creation of its institutions. It also means a transformation of the economy in order to obtain a predominantly private ownership and to put in place the market mechanism institutions. The difficulty and complexity of the transformation stems from the fact that the above requirements are not separable from each other; life produces them in their interrelationship. The second indication of a difficult transition is that a well-orchestrated transformation takes vision, experience, and time. The West took centuries of gradual development and occasional conflicts to arrive at the present-day political, administrative, and economic standards. These standards allow for a concert of state institutions, legal regulation, and socio-economic background. By contrast, the CEEC had only an extremely short period of time, a few years. In addition,

1

the past decades allowed for no theoretical foundations to be laid, or even less, for practical experiences to be accumulated by well-established organizations, or parties, that would steer the transformation and equip it with foresight and resources. Consequently, institutions are to be shaped, and laws are to be made under circumstances wherein the underlying living conditions are only taking shape and the course of development is not quite clear. For instance, labour codes and bankruptcy acts had to be hammered out at a time when the market economy was hardly functional and established. In this present volume the reader will find more examples of this kind.

The above hardships are essentially the logical outcome of history – of overall political, social, and economic backwardness. But there is more: one precondition of transformation in the CEEC is that their economies should be functional. Unfortunately, the beginning of transformation coincided with two events that considerably hindered, rather than helped, the process. One was recession in the Western countries. It has slowed down the influx of capital into the CEEC, discouraged interest in privatization, and hardened exports to the West. The other was the implosion of the Soviet Union in 1991, which has practically done away with Central and Eastern European exports to that enormous market. The above two factors have strongly held the CEEC back, rendering the course of transformation much more difficult and in some cases loading it with conflicts.

II. HISTORY OF THE CEEC SINCE 1989

Transformation has a strong impact on labour law and industrial relations. In this respect we distinguish between three time periods in the history of the CEEC since 1989.

a. The first is from 1989 to 1990, (or to 1991/1992 in the countries where the phenomenon started later). In these years:
  - Legal regulation was limited to amendments considered to be most urgent for transformation. Basic laws, e.g., labour codes, were not repealed. Amended were regulations related to collective agreements, establishment and cessation of labour relations; the right to strike was acknowledged.
  - Significant changes started in the trade union movement. The unions of former times shifted the focus of their activity on safeguarding worker interests.
    Organizational frameworks were altered. The homogeneity of unions was over: trade union pluralism appeared in most countries. Because of the lack of basis for comparison, it was extremely difficult to determine what is the social background of the various unions. The situation brought about a fierce, mostly politically charged in-fighting of the various trade union groupings.
  - Although the legal terms of collective bargaining were in place, in practice it was rather rare, one reason being the above unclear situation of the unions. Much more important was the lack of adequate partners on the employer side, either at branch or at corporate level. New employer organizations appeared, but their background and support base remained uncertain. State company managers lacked interest, and, primarily, decision making powers, in conducting substantive bargaining. This was aggravated by the economic uncertainty or bankrupt condition of the bulk of such companies. In some countries the government tried to promote collective bargaining. In Hungary, for instance, the government initiated an interest reconciliation council which comprised union and employer

organization representatives. There were similar solutions in Slovenia and Romania.

- Unemployment appeared as a new phenomenon. It was expected prior to transformation as an inevitable corollary of the market economy, but was thought to be a transitory phenomenon to subside following the transition.

b. The second period is 1991-1992 and 1993 for Eastern European countries. Its features are:
  - New regulations and labour codes were made to replace earlier amendments in most of the countries of the region. New law focused on the requirements of a market economy, at least as it was perceived by legislators. Attempts were made to regulate minimum, basic issues only, leaving details to collective agreement and labour contracts. While former acts would only deal with collective labour relations in general or in a very narrow sense, the new ones had these for their main target.
  - The situation of organized labour became clearer. Stable frameworks, national confederations have come into being and camps of their supporters were also more visible. Forceful union action was on the increase, as well as the number of strikes.
  - The situation of collective bargaining did not change much, or it became more complex in certain respects. As a consequence of privatization, new companies, some of them foreign, appeared alongside the former socialist-type corporations. The number of small enterprises increased significantly. Foreign corporations had no business federations in common, they did not normally associate themselves with domestic employer organizations, and tried to avoid collective bargaining. The bulk of small- and medium-size entrepreneurs also avoided employer interest groups, and did not consider collective bargaining and agreement as being in their interest. Collective bargaining was concentrated in places where the state created tripartite bodies.
  - By this stage it had become evident that unemployment was permanent. Because of economic collapse, the dimensions of unemployment were much bigger than expected. Hence, almost all of the CEEC tried a comprehensive employment policy, usually by adopting special acts, and introducing special measures to tame unemployment.

c. The third period has been ticking since the middle or second half of 1993. Its main features are:
  - No particular alterations in labour regulation. Minor corrections and supplements are adopted in order to do away with the shortcomings of new regulation or to adapt old rules to new requirements;
  - The status of unions is further consolidated. Their internal proportions are by now more or less set, and – despite considerable ideological discrepancies between the various confederations – there are instances of joint action, such as strikes;
  - Progress is achieved in two aspects of collective bargaining. First, tripartite talks are held in more countries. These talks are normally initiated by governments in order to promote economic stability, to make tough economic measures acceptable or gain support for those. Second, collective bargaining begins, primarily at the corporate level, where collective agreements are also reached. More progress is still hampered by the lack of adequately backed employer organizations. The

national tripartite council continues to be the main forum of substantive collective bargaining;
  - Unemployment has stabilized – at a rather high level, and with certain fluctuations, – in most of the countries. Every country attempts to expand the range of measures aimed at forcing back unemployment. Young people, and those whose unemployment benefit schemes expired, are a particular problem.

III.   LABOUR LAW REGULATIONS AND RELATIONS

A.   Labour Law Regulation

Changes of the principles of labour regulation are summed up in what follows:

a. Formerly, labour law was predominantly state-regulated at levels ranging from acts to ministerial decrees. In countries where, parallel with economic reform, fully or partially normative collective agreements were introduced, legal limits significantly reduced the bargaining options and, consequently, the content of agreements. As of 1989 – as previously mentioned – all of the CEEC decided that the market economy requirements could only be met if basic rights and institutions were stipulated by law, with detailed regulation being left for collective agreements or employment contracts, in the absence of the former. This principle was respected as early as the amendments of 1989/1990, but in its full extent it was only implemented in the newly adopted labour codes of 1992/1994. This also meant acceptance of the option of limits of legal texts being stretched in favour of employees.
      At the time of codification, in the CEEC there were at best only germs of market economy. Hence, an imaginary ideal market economy was laid in the groundwork of codification. Consequently, there were several instances of contradiction between law and actual practice. This had a bidirectional effect. First, because of the disarray and weakness of the trade union movement, the law, which was too liberal for the given situation was not adequately balanced by organized protection. Second, the making of collective agreements – as was explained earlier – picked up very slowly and was limited to an area which remains too narrow even today. Regulation is waiting for collective agreements to be made. In the meantime, though, the limits of collective agreements and employment contracts are too broad. This deteriorates the positions of weak employees in the first place. Unemployment further aggravates disadvantaged situations.

b. As a consequence of the above regulatory concept, the scope of legal regulation changed too. Formerly the latter – including labour codes – dealt chiefly with individual labour relations, leaving little room for collective ones. The new labour codes and other acts regulate collective labour relations to the full extent.

c. Changes were made not only with respect to the system of regulation but also with respect to substantive principles. The CEEC ratified the most part of the major labour conventions before 1989. (Albeit, some of those were only implemented formally, e.g., conventions on freedom of association and on collective bargaining). Apart from international labour conventions, countries in transition wish to abide by international agreements on human rights and social rights of employees, in particular, the Council of Europe's European Charter of Human Rights and the European Social Charter. Most of the countries of the region ratified these in recent years. Constitutional amendments of the post-transition period embedded the principles of the above conventions in domestic law; thus, they became guidelines of labour law codification. In each country the right to work, bans on discrimination, the rights to association, collective bargaining, and strike were considered a priority in regulation, too.

d. The substance of regulation was equally affected by the principles and changes in labour policy. Formerly, it was an exclusively state prerogative, having three fundamental functions: definition and steering of legal regulation, wages, and employment policies. Following the transition, the role of the state is still dominant, but no longer exclusive. As was said earlier, this role is now limited to determination of basic guarantees and establishments. Domestic policies – the essence of which was centralized wage regulation, i.e., the determination of wage items and of the size of the funds earmarked for wages – were significantly relinquished in the period of 1989–1990s, in favour of decision making at the level of companies. Later in some countries, central wage regulation was only maintained in areas financed by the central budget, such as state administration, education, health care, etc. The role of the state significantly increased in employment policies. Formerly, there was a chronic labour shortage in the country. State employment policy focused on measures – at times administrative – aimed at promoting employment (e.g., compulsory jobs for those leaving vocational training schools). It also assisted in creating jobs for disadvantaged groups, such as handicapped persons, or mothers rearing small children. After 1989 the situation changed in two directions. First, as was mentioned earlier, the newly adopted constitutions declared the right to work. Accordingly, labour law provided for the principle of free employment, i.e., for entering into labour relations on free contractual agreements between parties. Employment policies could no longer limit free employment. Since unemployment appeared, the main task of state employment policy was to care for the jobless and to give assistance in job-seeking. At the outset unemployment was thought to be a temporary evil of market economies, which would stabilize at a low rate. Very soon it became clear that it was to be a lasting problem, much graver than expected. Some countries reacted quite promptly. In the course of 1991 almost everywhere in the CEEC acts on employment were passed, regulating not only the unemployment issue, but also created institutions to implement efficiently legal provisions.

As of 1989–1990, the state labour policies of most countries gradually incorporated a new element, namely, co-operation with employee and employer organizations. In some countries institutional frameworks were created (e.g., the National Interest Reconciliation Council in Hungary, Interest Reconciliation Council in Hungary, the Tripartite Secretariat for social dialogue in Romania, the Economic and Social Council in Slovakia).

e. In each country several principled disputes flared up concerning labour law modification. Two of these should be pointed out in connection with the decentralization of legal regulation and the broadened scope of collective agreements and employment contracts, it was repeatedly said that drastic liberalization would result in an equally drastic shrinking of labour law's traditional protection function and aggravate the dependence of employees. (Incidently, this dispute has been continuing with varying intensity also outside the CEEC for almost two decades). Partisans of liberalism argue, at the same time, that economic development, prompt adaptation to market terms, is only possible if the chance of swift adaptation is also there for labour

5

relations. One precondition for this, for both the social partners and parties, is that labour relations should be given much broader room for negotiated agreements than before. This should be more advantageous for the employee as well. In several studies, supporters of a protective labour law function agree with the need for a decentralized and more flexible regulation, but they disagree on its range and timing. No country can boast of an interest negotiating mechanism and social conduct mode that would provide required protection for employees. Hence, adequate transition also has to be ensured in the field of legal regulation. (*See* the study on Russia in this volume). The above dispute has been on and off in the various countries with various degrees of intensity and outcome. Typically, liberalization takes the upper hand, at least in legislation.

In most countries it is also disputed whether labour regulation should be based on a single, uniform notion of labour relations, or whether it should discriminate between state, corporate and private sectors and between work for the economy, public service, or co-operatives. Formerly, the scope of the labour code was identical for the employees of the various sectors in most countries. Agricultural co-operatives were an exception; there, labour relations were normally regulated by statutes related to co-operatives.

In Slovenia and Croatia the situation was different because the self-management system in the former Yugoslavia replaced 'traditional' labour relations with self-managed corporate membership relations.

New codification brought about alternative solutions and suggestions. In some countries work for economic entities and public service are treated distinctly. Alongside labour codes, special acts on public service have been adopted. Hungarian regulators make further distinction between state administration and state institutions (schools, health care, etc.). The prevailing view in labour law is that despite separate statutes, public service is also based on labour, rather than administrative, relations. Studies on Slovenia and Croatia also argue in favour of uniform labour relations and uniform regulation.

B.   Labour Administration

Prior to transformation, all of the CEEC had some sort of central state administration organ in order to deal with labour relations. The names and competencies of these differed. In some countries they were ministries of labour, or labour and social affairs, in others they were special offices supervised by ministerial cabinets or central planning authorities (like the State Wages and Labour Office in Hungary).

Following political transition, each country established labour ministries (e.g., in Hungary) or labour and social affairs ministries (e.g., in Poland, Croatia, Slovenia). These deal with employment policies. The newly established institutions are expected to comply with newly adopted employment statutes. The names of these employment institutions differ: Poland has national regional and local labour offices; Hungary has national, regional and local labour centres; Croatia has a national labour office; Slovakia has national, territorial, and local labour services; and Romania has regional and local social offices. Their assignment – with minor discrepancies – is identical, i.e. introduction and implementation of measures related to unemployment. Such measures include: employment mediation, registration of the unemployed and of job vacancies, management of vocational training, retraining and further training schemes, financial support for new job creation, promotion of individual entrepreneurialism, organization of public works, measures against the black market, and unemployment benefits.

In some countries (Poland, Hungary, and Romania), the above work is assisted by national territorial and local labour councils, comprised of representatives of trade unions, employer organizations, and state and local government bodies. In Hungary, councils of similar composition have been established in order to assist in the management of training activities.

The other institution is that of labour inspection. At an earlier stage such organs existed, either under the supervision of labour ministries or independently, and inspected the implementation of the labour law regulations or on-job health standards and job safety conditions. Due to privatization and expansion of private sectors, the role of these became more important everywhere. In view of this fact, the competence of such institutions was generally extended to include general monitoring of labour laws.

C.   Regulation of Individual Labour Relations

Mention should be made of 3 issues related to individual labour relations:
a. new rules for establishing and ceasing employment relations;
b. changes related to flexible branch and local regulation;
c. doing away with regulation which is out of tune with the objectives of transformation.

Apart from the above, alterations and amendments were also made with respect to other issues. Those were solicited not by transformation, but by other needs (to close legal gaps, to eliminate misleading rules, etc.).

a. The establishment of employment relations in every country is based on the principles of free agreement of the parties involved. A shift in principle only occurs in countries of corporate self-management (such as Slovenia and Croatia). The importance of agreement among the parties involved increased everywhere, because many former rules limiting the scope of the parties' agreement were deleted (such as central regulation of wages, or bans on provisions for conditions for employees more favourable than those stipulated by collective agreement).

As to cessation of employment relations, there were and still are two opposing concepts of regulation or drafting in almost all countries. One requires a complete liberalization of employer-initiated dismissals. The other refers to the overall weaker position of the employee and wishes to maintain the protective function of labour law. Formerly, employer-initiated lay-offs were limited by law in almost every country. In some of them, law determined the circumstances and cases in which the employer could unilaterally fire a worker. Similarly, in every country there were statutory definitions of personal and family circumstances that allowed for no, or only exceptional, unilateral dismissals. Debate on the above dichotomy ended, or may end, in compromise. Dismissal is normally made legal if it is related either to a change of the employer's economic activity or induced by an unacceptable job performance of the employee. The range of personal- or family-related circumstances protecting employment is much narrower in contemporary statutory documents or drafts, than before. (Such circumstances are normally now related to maternity or active military status of the employees). Court appeals are allowed in all cases of dismissal, if the employee disagrees with the employer's arguments, or the dismissal violates a prohibitive or limiting circumstance.

7

b. Flexible branch level or local regulation opportunities are chiefly related to working hours, leisure time, and remuneration. Legislation only regulates the main safeguarded issues (e.g., the minimal duration of paid leaves, maternity, or health protective working hours, or the limitation of extra hours). Apart from these, substantive regulation is left to collective agreements and employment contracts.

c. Amendments that are out of tune with the objectives of transformation concern several issues. For instance, rules which limited the freedom of trade union association, such as compulsory registration or uniformity of unions, were eliminated. Disciplinary measures at corporate level were abolished (in Hungary, for instance).

D.   Rules and Measures in Connection with Unemployment

At an earlier stage this introduction explained how, in all of the CEEC, employment policies – including those dealing with unemployment – have become a priority issue. Each country established a separate institution (*see* Section [B] on Labour Administration) and quite soon at the outset of transformation special acts were adopted in order to determine the tasks of employment policies. In view of the increase of unemployment and its lasting nature, a number of new problems emerged in the course of implementation. As a consequence, statutes on employment had to be repeatedly amended.

  Measures taken in order to decrease unemployment were similar with minor discrepancies in most countries. These can be divided into three groups:
a. Preventive rules, aimed at making unemployment avoidable. These include:
    – bans or limits on massive dismissals;
    – preliminary consultation with competent state organs, trade unions or works councils, or at least a preliminary notice addressed to these.
b. Measures aimed at assisting the jobless in reintegration into the labour market:
    – registration of job vacancies and jobless persons, advisory and information services;
    – improvement of the employment aptitude of those unfit for available jobs, and organization of training and retraining courses to this end.
    – creation of new job opportunities by either of the following two means:
        – financial support for unemployed, trained and fit to start their own businesses;
        – financial support for employers to create jobs for unemployed persons;
    – organization of communal work by local governments. (In Hungary the specific form of such activity is the so-called 'work for the public good'. It means that unemployed persons may be engaged and paid for work for the benefit of the local community without establishing employment relations).
c. The third group is made up of rules meant to help those who failed to get access to jobs or a living in accordance with the above. Here there are also several possibilities, of which the basic means is unemployment aid. Entitlement depends on the duration of preceding employment as well as on the mode of its cessation. The sum of the benefit depends on the earnings during employment. Benefits are paid for a limited period of time and their sizes gradually decrease. When unemployment was believed to be a temporary phenomenon, both entitlement and the sizes of benefits were determined rather liberally. The size could be as large as 80 to 90% of the last salary and paid for a duration of one and a half years. As unemployment grew, it became clear that the funds earmarked for the benefits were insufficient and could only be extended at the price of further burdens on employers, employees or the state budget.

Advanced retirement pensions are another form of material aid. If a person becomes unemployed within a certain time – normally 3 years – before retirement age, he or she may apply for an advanced pension, on condition that the employer or the state ('employment funds') agree to repay to social security the amount paid to the unemployed until he or she reaches retirement pension age.

As soon as the entitlement to unemployment benefit expires, material care for the unemployed is no longer an employment policy issue. In accordance with the given circumstances in each case, it becomes the problem of social aid organs (normally within the framework of local governments).

Statutory documents on employment policy stipulate the funding of unemployment benefits, from either of two sources. One is contributions paid by employers and employees. The other is the so-called Employment Fund which is drawn from the state budget. Employers normally contribute 3 to 5%, and employees 1 to 2.5% of their wages.

IV.   LABOUR RELATIONS

A.   Orientation of Changes of Collective Labour Relations

A significant consequence of transformation is the change of the substance and nature of collective labour relations. This was reflected already in the initial stage of transformation (1989-1990) when new legislation was adopted. While changes in labour policies, management, and individual labour relations were determined primarily by decisions at state level, the initiative of social partners played an equally important role in the field of collective relations. This is so, even if the basis for new relations was seemingly created by the measures taken by legislature (constitutional amendments, etc.). Actually, organized work – such as newly stated objectives by the existing unions, and the formation of new ones – had preceded statutory changes (also true for political parties). It is characteristic of labour relations that their legal regulation is anticipated by events in real life.

The essence of changes can be summed up in what follows:
–   obstacles of free union work and social partnership have been removed, statutory conditions for the above have been created;
–   unions have changed their structures and objectives;
–   collective bargaining has been launched;
–   employee participation in employers' decision making has been made possible;
–   issues such as strikes and lock-outs have been regulated.

B.   Creation of the Legal Foundations

In some countries, the most important step towards the elimination of obstacles to labour relations was the recognition of the freedom of association by the constitutions or Labour Codes. Poland is interesting, because there free unions and association rights had been declared in a 'round-table agreement' put together by the democratic opposition in April 1989. Since 1991, these have been guaranteed by the act on unions.

9

From the very beginning of transformation, some countries settled certain issues of labour relations by law. In Hungary the Labour Code was amended as early as 1989 in order to set the rules for collective agreements and a separate act was passed on strikes. In Slovakia, the Czech Republic, and Romania separate acts regulate collective agreements and stipulate relations between unions and employers. As was mentioned before, labour codes adopted in the subsequent years harmonized and pooled the rules of collective labour relations.

C. The Trade Unions

Two kinds of changes related to organized labour are obvious in the CEEC after transition. The uniform trade unions of the former period declared their main objective to be protection of the interests of employees and to proceed to a certain extent of restructuring. One or two major branch unions acquired a degree of autonomy, taking the form of independent union work, while maintaining membership in the uniform federations, or leading to new federations uniting workers of one or several branches. The shaping of brand new unions has also begun. These are far from uniform in their objectives and political orientation. Initially, the new unions have been small and dispersed. Gradually they have integrated into federations of identical orientations. Presently there exist several trade union federations and confederations in the various countries.

Two situations can be distinguished regarding legal regulation. In some countries special acts were adopted for unions (Poland 1991, Slovenia 1993). In others, labour codes or statutes on collective agreements deal with the issue of unions.

Legal regulation of all countries takes into account the principles and obligations of ILO Conventions 87 and 98. Essentially, the related statutory substance is similar in the various countries, but there are differences concerning details. Law on unions covers the following issues:

a. The notions of trade unions and their criteria. Statutory documents normally offer no definitions, but only determine the goals of union activity, i.e. protection of the workers' interests. The Hungarian Labour Code differs in as much as it contains a clear definition: namely, that a trade union is an organization of employees aimed at the protection of economic and social interests of workers, not necessary bearing the name of 'trade union'. Apart from the above, almost all statutes contain the conditions needed for union activity, such as:
– independence from the state, the employers and political parties (the latter are not mentioned in the case of some countries, e.g., in Slovenia);
– prohibition against any kind of discrimination (e.g., in the Polish law);
– commitment to democracy and acceptance of the principles of freedom of association (e.g., in Slovenia);
– an organizational framework to make the unions functional (in Poland), and deadlines for the start of activity (fixed at 6 months in Slovenia);
– a fixed minimal membership number (e.g., Slovenian law).

b. The following group of issues is related to establishment and safeguards of functioning. In this respect the essence of the contents of the 87th ILO Convention finds full reflection in each country: i.e., that trade unions may be established without any permission from the state, and that they determine their organization and internal rules without any supervision competence by any of the state organs whatsoever.

The right to establish a union at any company is another safeguard of organized functioning. The Polish law underlines, in this respect, that the various workshops of the same company may establish their own union organs, or unions independent of the company.

In all countries, law contains obligations related to provisions for trade union functioning (premises, office rooms, etc.). Provisions are also stipulated concerning the protection of trade union office holders' labour rights and concerning the time needed to attend to their duties, as well as training.

c. Union activities are covered to varying extents of detail by the laws of the different countries and can be grouped as follows:
– Free information and representation of employee interests before the employer, authorities, and courts of law. In the last-named case, the Hungarian law stipulates as a requirement an authorization from the employee concerned;
– The making of collective agreements;
– The soliciting of information from the employer concerning measures related to the economic and social situation of employees;
– The monitoring of implementation of labour relations provisions.
Apart from these generally stipulated rights, the union law of some countries provides for further rights and obligations on the part of the employer:
– In Poland, the employer is obliged to involve the union organs of workshops in determining the utilization of the so-called 'workshop funds', wage-scales, work order, and paid leaves arrangements.
– Again in Poland, the unions have the right to comment on draft laws concerning the situation of employees and have special appeal rights against unacceptable labour laws or social security provisions.
– Polish law stipulates the right for unions to hand in petitions pertaining to the implementation of rules concerning unions. In Hungary, a similar provision allows the unions to protest before the employer the implementation – and thereby delay the effect – of a decision adversely affecting the rights or interests of employees (no such protest is valid if the case requires, by law, a labour court hearing).
– In Slovakia the rules call for preliminary co-ordination with unions on issues stipulated by law, such as night shifts for women, or the shaping of corporate by-laws.

D. Employers' Organizations

Prior to the transformation, the task and activity of the employers' organizations were not similar to those in the market economy. Political transition changed the situation.

The difficulty is caused by the status quo, whereby the majority of employers' organizations can hardly be regarded as genuine business federations; i.e., they do not represent the bulk of employers of any branch. Consequently, at branch level employers are not really adequate partners of unions.

Presently there are three kinds of employers in the CEEC. The first group is the state-owned, or dominantly state-owned companies. Managers of these are appointed by supreme state authorities in most countries. They are dependant and therefore consider themselves employees, rather than employers. Their interest in representation is also limited, as is illustrated by the study on Poland. The second group is made up of subsidiaries of multinationals or foreign companies operating in CEEC. These do not form uniform business federations; their interests are primarily linked to the strategy and tactics of the mother firms. They have little in common with local employers. The third group consists of the private employers of any given country. Since the CEEC are extremely capital hungry nations, they have rather few big or medium-size companies. The overwhelming majority are small enterprises with very limited employee numbers. Small entrepreneurs are mainly concerned with keeping production costs down by avoiding any hindrance with unions through collective bargaining and agreements.

Legal regulation does not deal with the corporate systems of the employer, the other partner of labour relations. The employer is only mentioned in two connections. First, legal regulations acknowledge the notion of representation when reference is made to the right of the employer, or the employers' representative organization, to make collective agreements. Second, it establishes the notion of employer in the budgetary spheres. In countries such as Hungary that have statutory provisions of representativity, it is adapted to the scope of membership. As to budgetary spheres, collective labour relations are extremely limited. Collective bargaining and agreements are normally excluded in the field of state administration. In Hungary, again, collective local level state institutions, such as schools and hospitals, may act as partners in collective bargaining.

E.   The Role of the State

The state is forever interested in successful collective agreements. They affect economic stability, foreign trade balances, and social policies, while the peaceful or conflict-torn nature of bargaining also affects political order. International conventions, particularly the 98th ILO convention, oblige the states to promote collective bargaining. In the CEEC successful dialogue of social partners contributed to the peaceful nature of political transformation. The Hungarian government, as early as the year preceding the political shift, invited the old, the changing and the newly born unions, as well as the existing employer representatives to tripartite talks in the framework of the so-called National Interest Reconciliation Council. Initially, the body had no legal status, but in 1992 the newly adopted Labour Code proclaimed it a legal entity. The intention of the government was to discuss major issues with employee and employer organizations prior to parliamentary hearings. In actuality, the council acts as a consultative body of the government, however in certain cases determined by the Code the government has to request its agreement. The establishment of a similar body was proposed by the employees and employers' organizations in 1944. A similar body was established in 1994 in Slovenia. In Slovakia the obligation of the government to co-operate with the social partners has been prescribed by labour law. These arrangements are positive in as much as they promote social peace. On the other hand, they may be negative when the consultation of social partners prolongs the drafting of law, and, in some cases, may contribute to the obstruction of new statutes.

F.   Collective Bargaining

The collective bargaining system, which was similar to the Western one, ceased to exist in the CEEC. At the time the functions of unions differed from the present, and the main goal of agreements was to help fulfil production plans, rather than protect workers' interests. Collective bargaining – also serving to protect the interests of employees in some countries (for instance in Hungary in Poland) – started parallel with economic reform and was kept at a reduced spin until its full restoration parallel with the political transition.

In 1989 and immediately following – as was mentioned above – every country set up the rules for collective bargaining that were subsequently transformed into comprehensive and uniform systems in the newly adopted labour codes.

Statutory documents on collective bargaining contain quite a few provisions. These can be grouped as follows:

a. The first group is comprised of those which determine who can assume the role of negotiator on behalf of the employer. Locally, it should be the company, institutions, etc., represented by an individual in accordance with the respective statutes and by-laws. Polish rules are, in a way, an exception of the above. These stipulate that the various workshops, or units of a company, are independent bargaining parties if represented by their respective managers. At the level of industries or branches the respective business federations may assume the role of negotiators. If several business federations exist in the same industry, only the most representative – normally the federation with the largest membership – can become the negotiating party. Joint delegations are possible too. In Hungary, for instance, several independent employers may bargain and sign collective agreements in common, without being represented by their respective business federations. Actually, this solution amounts to several collective agreements in a single document, negotiated by *ad hoc* employer parties without ever forming a legal entity. In some countries collective bargaining is possible at national levels, above the individual industries. In such cases, collective bargaining must be with a national employer federation. Normally no collective bargaining is possible with state administration, and no organ of it can assume the role of a negotiator. Hungarian rules make it possible for state budgetary institutions – such as schools, hospitals, museums, etc. – to conduct collective bargaining on their own accord.

As to the employee side, the trade unions are responsible for the bargaining at local and all other levels. If any given branch has more than one trade union, the most representative union has the mandate. Slovak rules are an exception: the employer may bargain with any of the unions registered at the Ministry of Labour. The Hungarian provisions stipulate that non-representative unions shall be equally involved in bargaining, but with a consultative right only. In accordance with Hungarian rules, if none of the unions at a company are representative, then all of them should be engaged in collective bargaining, but an agreement can only be made on the condition that the majority of employees support it.

b. In some countries, the law stipulates mandatory bargaining. In Hungary and Slovakia the employer cannot reject a union's call for bargaining; moreover, in possession of annual data on wages, the employer is obliged to initiate bargaining. In Slovenia bargaining is mandatory at both branch and national levels, through the argument that since the law leaves a great deal for bargaining to settle, if it were not compulsory at both levels, gaps in regulation would inevitably appear. The author of the survey from that country believes that the above obligation is a breach of the freedom of bargaining. In Hungary this problem is solved by referring to employment contracts anything that is not regulated through free bargaining.

G. Collective Agreements

In the CEEC collective agreements are made at national branch and company levels. Apart from these, Hungary has collective agreements made by several employers in common. In Poland we know of agreements reached at the workshop level within a single company.

As far as the content of collective agreements is concerned, the situation is similar in the various countries. Collective agreements consist of two parts. One is normative and regulates labour relations between the employer and employee. The other part is the law of contract on the two parties' relations. The content of collective agreements is not restricted by law. Normally, any issue can be settled through a collective agreement with the exception of those excluded by law. In general a collective agreement should not contradict a statutory document or agreement of a superior level, except if the lower level provides for an employee advantage. Some countries differ in this respect. In Slovakia a collective agreement may not deviate from law, except for payroll provisions agreed upon with individual private employers. The wages provisions in a collective agreement at company level should not surpass the wage ceilings contained in national level agreements.

Regulation throughout the CEEC is also unanimous in as much as collective agreements are binding for all employees of the branch or company that they cover, regardless of whether or not they are members of the union that signed the agreement. Managers with employer rights are an exception.

Law normally allows for an extension of the high level agreements. This is the prerogative of ministers of labour, but in Hungary only so on the condition of a joint proposal by the employer and employee to that end.

No approval is required for collective agreements. Hungarian law stipulates that the branch level collective agreements have to be dispatched to the minister of labour in order to be officially proclaimed.

H. Participation Rights of Employees

Prior to political transition, there were three ways of providing such rights.
1. Employees took part in company decision making through their unions. The legal provisions therefore were contained in labour codes or laws on state enterprise. Trade unions had three forms of access. The first was that unions had to be informed by the employer on the company's state of business and production, and that the unions reserved the right to make comments and proposals. The second was in the field of social and cultural provisions: the unions had the right to decide alone, or in concert, with the employer. The third was the right to monitor the implementation of legal provisions related to labour relations. In Hungary unions were entitled to a veto right against measures contradicting law or hindering its implementation;
2. The second way of providing for the participation rights of employees was the self-management system of the former Yugoslavia, whereby employees were owners of their businesses and companies, through to a fusion of ownership and employee positions. The notion of employee participation was therefore irrelevant;
3. The third solution took shape in the '1970s and 1980s' in countries like Poland, Romania, Bulgaria and Hungary. Essentially, it attempted to amalgamate state management of the state-owned companies with the above-mentioned Yugoslav type of self-management. The details of such arrangements differed in the various countries: namely,

the scope of authority of bodies elected by employees, the relationship of state authorities, and the organizations of company management and of workers' organizations.

Essentially, these arrangements aimed at integrating elected employee organs into the texture of decision making to the extent where the former could exercise a degree of ownership rights. Thereby elected organs acquired a double function: on the one hand, they remained as representatives of worker interests and exercised the participation right, and on the other hand they became integral parts of their companies' management structures. In all countries, laws contained exceptions from the above, i.e., some companies remained fully managed by the state and maintained a limited employee participation through their unions, as described under point *a* above.

In some countries in the 1980s, laws were adopted on the newly emerging economic entities (shareholders' and limited liability companies, etc.). These laws provided for employee participation in the companies' supervisory bodies (in Hungary, for instance).

Following political transition, the self-management systems of Croatia and Slovenia fell apart. However in Croatia, according to the constitution, employees may participate in the company's decision making, in accordance with the law (similar are the joint management systems mentioned under C). Poland was the only country where worker participation rights caused heated – partly political – disputes. Views appeared to the effect that worker participation rights were only justified under communism, and are incompatible with the market economy. The prevailing opinion of labour law academics is that management participation rights for workers' elected bodies must be maintained.

Presently there are three kinds of participation opportunities in the CEEC: the right to a part in decision making is exercised by unions (*see* the Russian, Czech and Slovak studies); employees elect works' councils or representatives to exercise the above (in Hungary and Slovenia); and in Poland, law on collective agreements makes it possible for the parties to agree on ways of participation in decision making. Whatever the solution, statutory provisions of economic entities normally allow for a 1:3 proportion of employee participation in company supervisory bodies. In Slovenia, employees may also elect one of the managers.

In some countries (e.g., Hungary, or Poland), law allows or mandates the enabling of employees to acquire part of the business shares of their respective companies in the course of privatization. Certainly, when employee shareholders attend their meetings, they think of their own interests; hence, this is another form of participation in decision making.

As to the present scope of participation rights, in countries where those are exercised through unions, what has been said under A). is still valid. In countries with works' councils, their scope of authority is as follows:
– in economic matters, they usually have consultative rights, meaning that on whatever issues presented to them by the employer – obligatory or voluntary – works' councils can make their comments, proposals or express warnings;
– they share decision making with the employer on issues determined by law (primarily cultural and social allowances) or exercise their right of consent (mandatory for the employer to obtain on by-law drafts, personnel issues, etc.);
– they exercise the right to control and monitor (including the books and other data on business performance). Law obliges the employer to co-operate with the works' councils and present to them substantive draft decisions for comment.

I. Strike

Before political transition the right to strike was not legally recognized in any of the CEEC. When strikes occurred, they were dealt with by means of law enforcement. Yugoslavia was the sole exception; in 1981 a constitutional amendment made strikes legal under circumstances determined by law. After political transition, all of the CEEC introduced the right to strike, either into their constitutions or through special acts, many as early as 1989.

The situation is interesting in the Czech and in the Slovak Republics. Law on collective agreements provides for the right to strike as one means of settling disputes stemming from the process of making agreements.

Apparently, no law on strikes is emerging in other cases. In Croatia, strike procedure is determined by collective agreements. Regulation of strikes in all countries of the region is in harmony with international practice, namely:

a. In some countries not only recognition of strikes is regulated, but also who is entitled to strike:
   – the right to strike can only be exercised by trade unions (e.g., Czech Republic and Slovakia);
   – employees have an individual right to strike and they may exercise it collectively (e.g., in Poland);
   – a strike may be initiated by both unions and employee groups (e.g., Hungary, Slovenia).

b. Statutory limitations and bans are similar to those recognized internationally: political strikes, as well as strikes by armed forces are prohibited, basic services as well as life, property and physical integrity are protected by law. In some countries more limitations are stipulated. In Slovakia courts may rule against solidarity strikes, if the employer proves that his or her company or subsidiary maintains no such links and economic relations that could have an impact on the outcome of the strike. The Czech rules prohibit strikes in times of military mobilization or a threat to the state. In Slovenia the civil employees of the armed forces have the right to strike.

c. Any repression of the strikers by the employer is illegal. Strikes shall not affect the employment or social security status of participants, although they are not entitled to wages for the duration of the strike.

J. Lock-out

With the exception of the Czech and the Slovak legislation, the CEEC do not regulate lock-outs. Therefore, the Czech and Slovak Republics have detailed rules. Just as in the case of strikes, rules only apply to what happens in the process of collective agreement. In the countries where lock-outs are not regulated, they are not allowed; i.e. a lock-out by any employer would be illegal. Where they are regulated, they must be declared to unions three days in advance. The announcement must name those against whom the lock-out is aimed. The employer is obliged to pay 50% of the average wages to those involved for the duration of the lock-out.

K. Settlement of Collective Labour Disputes

1. Prior to political transformation, labour regulations contained no provisions for settlement of collective labour disputes. The only exception has been Poland, where a 1982 law regulates this issue. The habitual arrangement was that in a concrete case at the initiative of any of the parties, their superior bodies would jointly decide, without any prescribed procedural rule. Following the political transition, the emergence of collective agreements made a solution necessary for the settlement of collective labour disputes.

2. A collective labour dispute is termed such in cases in which a dispute arises between the social partners in connection with a collective labour relation (e.g., trade unions activity, collective bargaining and collective agreement, employees participation in the decisions of the employer, strike and lock-out). The rules of some countries determine the notion of the collective labour dispute in different ways. Collective labour disputes are considered only those that result from carrying out an existing collective agreement, referring to a general interest (e.g., rise of salaries, improvement of the working conditions). When the dispute is about the interpretation of the rule applicable only to one person (the calculation of his or her wage), the dispute is individual. In the Czech Republic only the dispute in connection with the collective agreement belongs to the sphere of the collective labour disputes. The Slovak opinion is similar. This rule tightens the sphere of the collective labour disputes. The uniform attitude of the above-mentioned definitions means that a dispute arising from the claim of an individual worker, which is capable of resolution through the courts, does not belong to the sphere of the collective labour dispute.

On the one hand, the parties to a collective labour dispute can be the trade union or a group representative of employees as determined by the law or a work council, and on the other hand, the employer. According to Polish rules, only trade unions, and according to the Romanian rules, trade unions or a group-representative, are granted the right to initiate or conduct collective labour disputes, as well as to conclude an agreement as a means of resolving disputes. In a workplace where more than one union organization legally functions, each has the right to initiate collective disputes.

The dominant point of view of labour law is that collective agreements are partly interest, and partly legal disputes. The rules governing the settlement of labour disputes are different in these two categories.

3. Typically, settlement of interest disputes happens outside of the courts. The principle is that the parties involved are to reconcile their interests and to end the dispute. Three possible solutions are contained in the rules:
(a) conciliation of the parties' representatives,
(b) mediation, and
(c) arbitration.

The Czech, Slovak, Polish, and Croatian rules determine two forms only: mediation and arbitration. In reality, conciliation is the true activity of these cases; but, according to the opinion of these countries, conciliation does not deal with collective labour disputes, but with the conditions out from which they arise. The situation is different in Romania. The Romanian rules prescribe direct and indirect reconciliation. The latter is organized by the co-operation of the State organizations.

In general, the parties jointly decide in which way they want to resolve the dispute. In most countries, the above solutions are ranked into order of priority. In Hungary, the Labour Code prescribes compulsory arbitration in a few specific cases (e.g., the employer is obligated to ensure conditions compatible to the activity of the trade union).

Settlement of disputes starts by the initiating party's submission of its written position to the other party. The first step is sought through voluntary reconciliation by the two parties' representatives, appointed in equal number – in general, two for each of them. In Poland, the employer is obliged to inform the labour supervisor; in Romania, the employer must inform the territorial department of the Ministry of Labour and Social Protection, regarding the ongoing collective dispute.

When the parties fail to agree, a mediator becomes involved. The parties have to agree on who will be the mediator. The mediator can be a person independent of the parties and not involved in the conflict. Czech rule stipulates that the mediator must be of the age of majority and legally capable. According to Czech rules, if the parties do not agree on a mediator, he or she will be appointed by the Ministry of Labour and Social Affairs. In some countries – Poland, Czech Republic – the ministries of labour maintain lists of eligible persons. The parties are free to agree on mediators not contained in the above list. Upon completion of the process, the mediator puts the parties' position and the results of the process into writing and delivers this to the parties. According to the Czech rule, proceedings before a mediator are deemed to have broken down if the dispute is not solved within 30 days after the day on which the mediator was made acquainted with the subject of the dispute, and if the parties to the agreement have not agreed on another deadline. The costs of proceedings before a mediator shall be covered by both parties, each party paying one half.

If the mediator fails, the parties may resort to an arbitrator or arbitration board, the latter normally comprised of three members. The Czech rule prescribes that the arbitrator must be a person who has reached the age of majority and who is capable of legal acts. In the Czech Republic there should be no alternative to the official list. The decision of the arbitrator is compulsory and enforceable, unless the parties agree on the opposite in advance. The rules of arbitration are regulated differently in Romania. If the labour dispute has not been resolved during the so called 'direct reconciliation' of the parties, the next stage is a reconciliation organized by the Ministry of Labour and Social Protection (indirect reconciliation). This procedure can be initiated by the trade union organ and, depending on the case, by the employees' representatives. Within 24 hours of its registration, the Ministry of Labour and Social Protection appoints its delegate. The delegate must summon the parties to the reconciliation procedure within seven days after the registration of the notification. In order to back up their interests at the reconciliation, the trade union, or, depending on the case, the employees choose a delegation formed of two to five persons entitled in writing to attend the reconciliation organized by the Ministry of Labour and Social Protection, at the pre-established place fixed by the parties. In the case that at the end of the arbitration procedure an agreement was reached, this agreement is compulsory throughout a fixed period and for all the parties that had been involved in the collective labour dispute.

4. Collective labour disputes of a legal character arise in the case of violation of a right, regarding an obligation determined in a statutory provision or in collective agreement, as well as if the fulfilment or non-fulfilment, or validity or non-validity, of an agreement is debated. In the case of legal disputes, the procedure and decision falls within the competence of the Labour Court, while in Croatia it falls within the

competence of the regular court. The procedure of the labour or regular court is prescribed by Civil Procedure law.

Most cases involving collective legal disputes can be taken to Labour or regular court. The rules normally stipulate that reconciliation by the parties representatives should be attempted before resorting to court procedures.

V. CONCLUSION

The situation described above shows that – during the transition period – the CEEC countries revised their former legislation and then established new laws in the field of labour legislation and labour relations within a relatively short period of time. This way, the essential legal framework necessary for the transition to a market economy has been already established. Presumably, such basic changes should not be made in the future. The task will be the further development of legislation on basis of the experiences gained during the emergence and operation of the market economy. Minor or major modification may be made according to the changes in the legislation of the European Union.

The new legal framework has set the ground for establishing and enhancing collective negotiations but the situation in this field is not satisfactory. One of the reasons is that the transformation of the former interest representation organizations and the development of new ones are rather time-consuming, especially the case with the employers' organizations. Hence, negotiations among the social partners take place at a slow pace and within a relatively narrow circle. For this reason, several countries try to make headway by promoting tripartite negotiations. However, the real advancement basically depends on the pace of privatization as it creates the economic basis for the negotiations among the social partners.

Finally, another important factor should be mentioned. It is essential to change the present concepts and attitude. Professor Mrachkov is correct when he points out in his study, published in this volume, that this change in the attitude should occur everywhere, from the employers and employees through to the interest representation bodies, and finally to the state itself. And the last-named should strive at promoting this change and at avoiding direct interference, which was the common practice in the past.

Recent Changes in the Labour Code and the Transition to a Market Economy: A Review of Bulgaria's Experience

Vassil Mrachkov

I. INTRODUCTION

1. The Bulgarian Labour Code of 1986 (Publ. *Official Gazette* 26/27 of 1986) was adopted in conditions of a centrally planned economy built on full state-ownership domination. Labour relations were regulated in a centralist and rigid manner, manifesting the administrative command system's approach to labour matters which used imperative legal provisions in order to regulate in detail the rights and obligations of the parties to the labour relations. The parties were not allowed to deviate from the norms that paralysed their initiative, limited the freedom of their will, and left them no legal space for any manifestations of their own. The parties simply looked up their established rights and obligations, observed them strictly, and could negotiate them only within narrow limits.

On the other hand, and despite all efforts made to improve the preceding legislation, the 1986 Labour Code provided for the adoption of some 50 sets of regulations, ordinances and instructions by the Ministerial Council and by individual ministers (most often jointly with the central leadership of the then existing Bulgarian trade unions). This in its turn burdened still further the legal regime of labour relations, making it complicated and awkward. Its centralist character was thereby reinforced. Actually as a whole, the legal regime in force until the end of 1989 acted as an obstacle to the dynamic development of labour relations, limiting the freedom of employment and reducing productivity. In the final analysis, it led to and has brought about the alienation of labour. These in fact were its direst social consequences.

2. Centralist and rigid regulation of labour relations was incompatible with the radical democratic changes which set in after 10 November 1989 in Bulgaria, and with the transition to a market economy. The amendments to the Labour Code were adopted by Parliament in this new situation. They became Law on 25 November 1992, and were published in the *Official Gazette* No. 100 of 10 December 1992, becoming effective from 1 January 1993. Its adoption came late in comparison with the overall course of the country's socio-economic development. Nevertheless, and however late, its adoption was an important step forward.

3. The amendments made in the Labour Code are *numerous in number* and *essential in substance*. They involve the repeal of some 130 articles and a change to almost 240 of the total of 416 articles found in the 1986 edition of the Labour Code. Taking a closer look into these quantitative data is of interest because no matter how expressive they appear, no clear idea can be obtained from them concerning the scale of changes which were effected.

a.   *The rescinded texts* compromised provisions that most openly expressed centralized regulation, totalitarian government, and the politicized and ideologist directionality of the regulation of labour relations by law. The most 'massively' repealed are the groups of texts for the self-management of labour collectives or workforces; certain grounds for the establishment of a labour relationship (such as appointment by order of the head of the local labour and social matters bureau, by court decision, the appointment of young graduate specialists, membership in a production co-operative) were also abolished. Certain trade union prerogatives that defined their functions of participation in enterprise management were annulled as well as the following items: the provisions that centrally and rigidly fixed wages and salaries; the system of settling labour disputes, this last-named because the new regime provides for labour relations to be settled, and disputes referred to the common courts, under the civil procedure, which meant an end to the labour dispute commissions.

b.   *The amended articles*, too, present an interesting picture. According to the degree of change made in them they could be divided into *three* groups. The *first* comprises texts of which only the numerical order has been preserved, while their *content* is *entirely new*: though designed as 'amendments' from the technical legal viewpoint, they actually contain entirely new legal provisions in place of rescinded former texts. Such are the provisions in place of rescinded former texts, and such are the provisions on tripartite co-operation (Article 3), the right of employers to associate (Article 5), the entire Chapter 4 on collective labour contracts (Articles 50-59), Article 333 concerning preliminary protection in the case of dismissal, and so on. The *second* group includes the provisions on the right to trade union association and trade union rights (Articles 4, 33, 37, 45), those concerning working hours, paid leave, wages, salaries, and indemnities, those which make of these fundamental labour law institutions a subject of collective and individual negotiation and agreement, etc. The *third* and largest group of amended texts comprises technical changes related to replacing the term of 'enterprise' with 'employer', the addition of the word 'employee' after 'worker', and the like.

As a result of this change the Labour Code has considerably shrunk in volume: 286 articles against 416 in its old version of 1986. This makes it comparatively easier to study and apply as law.

II.   CHANGES OF THE LABOUR CODE

From the viewpoint of subject, the changes in the Labour Code could be grouped under the following titles:

4.   'De-ideologization' of the legal regime of labour relations. Dropped were the texts that had a declarative or political, and not a specific legal, normative content.

5.   Changes were made also in the *Subject of Regulation* by the Labour Code. According to Article 1 paragraph 1 of the Labour Code: 'this Code settles labour relations between worker or employee and the employer, as well as other relations directly related to them'.

This provision determines the character of relations settled by the Labour Code: worker or employee on the one hand, and employer on the other. The *first* group are the relations of a labour character which arise from a physical (natural) person placing his or her labour force at the disposal of another person designated as employer. These are the true relations of labour. These relations comprise the appointment to a job (through a labour contract, election, or competitive examination), working hours, rest, paid leave, remuneration for the work, conditions of labour safety and hygiene, labour discipline and disciplinary responsibility, collective labour contract, termination of labour relations, and so on. These matters are treated in the fundamental part of the law on individual and collective labour relations, which makes up Chapters 4, 5, 6, 7, 8, 9, 10, 12, 15, 16, and 17 of the Labour Code.

The *second* group comprises 'the other relations directly linked with the labour ones'. They are oriented towards the protection and defence of the labour relations proper, and represent their continuation. Such are relations arising from the association of workers and employees, from the employers, from tripartite co-operation, from occupational and professional training, from social and everyday-life services for the workers and employees in an enterprise, from the specific elements of the procedure of hearing labour disputes in court, from supervision over the observance of labour legislation, and from administrative or penal responsibility for violating it (Chapters 3, 11, 14, 18, and 19 of the Labour Code). They certainly account for a smaller part of the Code of Labour's legal framework, but their presence is incontestable.

6.   Changes have been made also in the *scope* of the Labour Code. In most general terms, they are determined by its subject (*see* item 5 above). But more specifically, we have in mind here the range of questions of labour relations and those directly linked with them that the Labour Code, in its present form, regulates (i.e., its object range or scope), and the circle of persons to whom it is applicable (i.e., its scope of subjects). Changes were introduced in both directions.

7.   In conformity with Article 3, paragraph 1 of the Law on Normative Acts, The Labour Code, as law, regulates basic social relations that lend themselves to lasting regulation. On one hand, it drops certain former formulas that have proved inadequate to the current development of labour relations (*cf.* above item 3a), while on the other hand it has adopted certain new formulations which were unknown to its 1986 version such as: tripartite co-operation, employers' association, and so forth. Actually, relations regulated by the Labour Code, after its amendments of November 1992, show 'movement' changes along both lines: changes such as the shedding of certain kinds of social relations, and such as the inclusion of new relations in the realm of labour and other relations directly linked with them.

But the Labour Code does not regulate all basic issues that lend themselves to lasting regulation. For example, it fails to settle collective labour disputes and the right to strike, both of which are treated in a separate law – the Law on Settling Collective Labour Disputes (*Official Gazette* No. 21 of 1990, amended by No. 27 of 1991), which even after its latest amendment was, not incorporated into the Labour Code. The Labour Code also fails to rule on the issues of labour employment, which are still awaiting their legal regulation; incontestably these are issues of prime and basic importance; issues which lend themselves to lasting settlement and which are directly linked with labour relations. In this sense, the Labour Code regulates a large part of the basic issues of individual labour relations, and some issues of collective labour relations that lend themselves to a lasting regulation, but not all are encompassed. Hence, it is still not an exhaustively codified Law.

8. But while it settles a large share of the basic issues of labour relations and other relations linked with them that lend themselves to lasting settlement, the Labour Code contains legal delegation for the settlement of issues that are not basic ones, or even if they are, they do not lend themselves to lasting regulation, and for this reason the Code refers their regulation to by-laws (ordinances, regulations, etc. issued by the executive power and authorities). For the labour legislation which regulates such a socially sensitive and dynamic matter, this is unavoidable and it flows from the character of quickly changing labour relations. The whole issue boils down to finding the optimum in the distribution between legislative and sub-legislative regulation, and limiting the number of sub-legislative normative acts to the reasonably necessary minimum. In that sense the changes in the Labour Code of November 1992 mark a significant step forward over the Labour Code of 1986, and especially over that of 1951. Before the adoption the 1986 Labour Code, the sub-legislative normative acts in that sphere exceeded one thousand. The 1986 Code did its best to overcome this boundless issuing of sub-legislative norms by reducing them to fifty. At present, their number is down to about 30. The main reason for the substantial reduction of regulations and ordinances for the application of the Labour Code is that many of the questions previously settled by these acts have now been relegated to the sphere of collective and individual labour contracts (*see* item 15 below). This notwithstanding, even in the latest amendments of the Labour Code, recidivism from the past has surfaced in a number of excesses. Thus the useless legal delegation of powers to the Minister of Labour and Social Affairs in Article 139, paragraphs 4 and 5, which fixes workers' and employees' categories with unregulated hours of work and those obliged to be on duty or at the disposal of their employer during fixed hours, day and night. These categories of workers and employees could be much better and more accurately defined in the collective labour contracts, not through sub-legislative acts which threaten labour legislation with fresh clogging.

9. The second aspect of the issue concerning the scope of the Labour Code refers to the *circle of persons* to whom it applies. These are the parties to any individual labour relationship the employers and the workers (employees). The concept of 'employer' had been dropped from legal terminology as far back as 1951 owing to ideological prejudices; now that these have been overcome, the term has been restored in the Bulgarian legislation by the Law on the Settling Collective Labour Disputes of 1990 (Publ. *Official Gazette* No. 21 of 1990, amended in No. 27 of 1991), adopted in the Constitution of 1991 (Article 49, paragraph 2), and is widely used in the Labour Code especially in its latest amendments, and is just as universally applied as it is in other countries' legislation and judicial literature. The legal definition of the 'Employer' concept is contained in paragraph 1 item 1 of the Supplementary Provisions of the Labour Code. The definition is a broad one; it contains *two basic indications:*
a. the employer is a physical or a juridical person. When a physical person, he must have a civil legal capacity. It could also be a juridical person (corporate body), which has acquired this status in the legally established procedure (by law, by an act of permission, or with the founder's approval).[1] When the Employer is a corporate body, *the quality of Employer may be determined* by its subsidiary as well as any other

---

1.   V. Tadjer, 'Civil Law (in Bulgarian), General Part, Section 2,' published by Naouka i Izkoustvo Publ. House, Sofia 1973, pp. 82–84.

formation (enterprise, office, organization, or co-operative), regardless of whether that formation is itself an avowed body corporate or not. But in that case it must be *economically and organizationally independent*. This means that it must have its distinct subject of activity or a distinct part of it, its separate organization, and its separate finances (its own balance sheet and bank account). Hence, the status of juridical person is not obligatory, either for physical persons, or for collectives.

b. The next basic indication of the Employer is that he or she or it hires another's labour under a labour nexus, to be workers and employees in the performance of the Employer's activity. This means that he or she or it may independently hire and dismiss persons as workers and employees. The number of hired workers or employees makes no difference, nor does the kind of property on which the Employer's activity is performed. It may be public (state or municipal owned), private, or mixed.

The main consequence stemming from this broad definition of the Employer concept is that it *widens the possible circle* of persons who can be employers. This *new solution* is a legislator's expression and further development of the Constitution-proclaimed principle of free economic initiative (Article 19, paragraph 1) and its prescription saying that 'the Law creates and guarantees equal conditions for economic activity to all citizens and juridical persons ...' (Article 19, paragraph 2). These provisions of the Constitution, in fact, anchor some basic requirements of the market economy. The Labour Code, owing to its subject of regulation, is one of the key sets of laws called upon to give expression to the constitutional requirements for the development and approach to the market economy. So it is from this angle that one ought to evaluate both the juridical and the socio-economic significance of paragraph 1 item 1 of the Supplementary Provisions of the Labour Code for defining the Employer concept.

10. The notion of 'worker' or 'employee' has no legal definition. The changes in the Labour Code resulted in dropping its legal definition, which was given by paragraph 1, item 2 of the Supplementary Provisions of the 1986 Labour Code. But the Law still contains sufficient characteristics from which it is possible to reconstruct its definition. The worker or employee is primarily a physical person who has reached a minimum age decreed by the Law: in principle, the age of 16 (Articles 301 and 302 of the Labour Code). This person submits (places at disposal) his labour force for temporary use in the labour process, which means that he hires out his ability for mental or physical labour by concluding a labour nexus arising from a labour contract, selection, or contest, to another person who is the Employer, against payment, and submits to the employer's orders. As a party to the labour legal relationship, the worker hires out primarily physical labour, whereas the employee sells primarily mental labour.[2] The Law uses these as alternative concepts in order to underscore the predominant use of physical or mental labour, but not in order to contrast them; on the contrary, it places them on a par. Indeed, the labour relations deriving from them have the same, and not any different, legal consequences. This comes from the character of labour as a conscious and will-conditioned human activity that is a unity of mental and psycho-physical energy, since no physical job can be accomplished without a minimum expenditure of mental effort, and *vice versa*. Thus the terms 'worker' and 'employee' are employed as equivalent. Also, no difference is made between 'white-collar workers' and 'blue-collar workers'.

---

2.   L. Radoilski, 'Labour Law of the PR Bulgaria (in Bulgarian)' Naouka i Izkoustvo Publ. House, Sofia 1957, pp. 191–192.

The effects of the Labour Code on workers and employees call for some additional clarifications concerning the applicability of its provisions *to state employees and members of production co-operatives.*

11. Pending the adoption of a Law on Civil Servants as foreseen by the Constitution (Article 116, paragraph 2), the status of state employees (civil servants) is regulated on a general basis by the Labour Code, insofar as special acts do not explicitly provide for deviations from the Labour Code. Once the Civil Servants Law is passed, and depending on the solutions it will stipulate, one or another part of the Labour Code provisions will continue to apply also to civil servants. Generally speaking, the adoption of this new act will call for a fresh redistribution of the limits for the subjects (the circle of persons to whom it applies) of the Labour Code, and a new balance will be established between the scope of application of the two laws.

12. There is a difference in the status of *co-operative members* in production co-operatives (artisans' and invalids' production co-operatives). The 1986 Labour Code provided that its provisions applied on a general basis to members of production co-operatives, while it ruled specifically on certain peculiarities (Articles 105–106, and 341–343). This legislative solution for a unified legal treatment was an expression of the nationalization of co-operative property (including productive co-operatives), and was one of the most heavy-handed manifestations of the administrative command system. It also ran counter to the new law on Co-operatives (Publ. Off. Gazette No. 63 of 1991, amended No. 34 and 55 of 1992), and could be considered tacitly repealed by it, although it failed to state this explicitly, probably in expectation of the amendments to the Labour Code imminent at that time. Indeed, the amendments in the Labour Code of November 1992 did away with its Articles 105–106 and 341–343, and a rule was introduced by paragraph 2 of the Supplementary Provisions of the Labour Code. It says: 'The stipulations of this Code shall apply also to the labour relations of members of production co-operatives insofar as another law or statute does not provide otherwise.'

This fundamental observation calls for *two general remarks*. The *first* is that the Labour Code proceeds from the idea of legal labour relations of co-operative members in production co-operatives. They are part of the complex set of relationships of legal character between co-operative members and the production co-operative, which also encompass, besides labour relations, legal relations of organization, property and co-management.[3] The labour relations are limited to the performance of labour in the production co-operatives. These legal relations find a common legal support in Article 10 paragraph 1 of the Co-operative Law, which provides that 'a production co-operative's member is entitled to be given a job in the co-operative to suit his level of qualification (skills) and age.'

The *second* observation is that the Labour Code is applied only subsidiarily, i.e. only insofar as any law or statute does not provide 'otherwise'. The law which does provide 'otherwise' is the Law on Co-operatives of 1991. The 'otherwise' provided for here is the order and procedure of joining a co-operative, i.e., the incorporation and the winding up of co-operative relations, of which legal labour relations are a part. Applicable to them are the provisions contained in Articles 3 and 9 of the Law on

---

3.   V. Tadjer, 'Co-operative and Company Law of the PR Bulgaria (in Bulgarian)', Kl. Ohirdski Univeristy Publ. House, Sofia, 1985, pp. 47–51.

Co-operatives on the incorporation of co-operatives and the admission of new members, and Articles 14–15 of the same law on winding up membership and exclusion from a co-operative. (Authoritative and applicable to these matters are the indicated provisions of the Law on Co-operatives, not of the Labour Code, concerning the arising of a legal labour relation for workers and employees. As regards the functioning of legal labour relations of members of a production co-operative from the disciplinary authority aspect, the stipulations of Article 13 of the Law on Co-operatives apply.

The Statutes of individual production co-operatives also provide, on general grounds, some special rules for the admission of co-operative members and their rights and obligations (Article 3, paragraph 2, item 9 of the Law on Co-operatives), and the order and procedure of distributing the general income, the profits and losses, the funds, and the kinds of dividends (Article 3, paragraph 2, item 7 of the same law). The applicable provisions here shall be those of the Law on Co-operatives and the statutes of the respective production co-operative.

Remaining outside their scope, however, are a series of issues related to the functioning of legal labour relations of members of production co-operatives: working hours, rest, paid leave, safe and healthy labour conditions, material responsibility for property, and so on for which the Labour Code gives no direct stipulations. They can be settled directly in the Statutes of each co-operative under Article 3, paragraph 3 as 'Other Matters' not ruled upon by the Law on Co-operatives. This can be done applying the statutory provisions under paragraph 2 of the Labour Code. If not ruled upon in the statutes, they could be referred therein to the Labour Code and to the sub-legislative normative acts issued for its application. But even failing to do this, the provisions of the Labour Code shall apply on these matters under paragraph 2 of the Labour Code.

In this manner, in order to apply the Labour Code to labour legal relations of co-operative members of production co-operatives, one must first pass through the Law on Co-operatives, then through the statutes of the concrete production co-operative, and only then must one proceed to apply the Labour Code provisions.

13.   The numerous changes in the Labour Code have not impaired its structure, preserved as a whole. But its system and internal subdivisions were affected. The entire second chapter (Articles 12–30) was rescinded, and so were numerous internal subdivisions in the remaining chapters. In this manner the 19 chapters and 53 sections of the 1986 Labour Code were reduced to 18 chapters and 31 sections in its new version. Its internal system and structure are now simpler.

14.   Substantive changes were effected also in the *objectives of legal treatment* of labour relations (Article 1, paragraph 2 of the Labour Code). These types of provisions, as part of the general ones, remain in the 'shadow' of the concrete legislative solutions that have direct practical application. But in this case they deserve special mention and have an important bearing both on the interpretation of all Labour Code stipulations (Article 46, paragraph 2 of the Law on Normative Acts), and for the creation of new provisions in the future for settling labour relations, and directly linked with them, other relation, but primarily because they voice a new concept about the social role and function of labour legislation and a branch of the legal system.

The main function, which is also determinant, is the *social function* of the legal treatment of labour relations. Through that treatment labour is afforded protection and defence, which means that the workers and employees, which perform labour, are shielded and guaranteed favourable and equitable solutions for their problems. This has been, and ought to be, the main consideration of the lawgiver concerning the formulating and adopting of the legal regime of legal relations. It is a continuation and further development of the Constitution, which stipulates that 'labour is guaranteed and protected by the *law*'. Thus, the special law that protects and guarantees labour is above all the Labour Code. This is a basic function of labour legislation ever since it appeared on the historical scene: it is prompted by the necessity of life, and it is directed towards the protection of hired labour from the arbitrary power of employers; it also places limitations that the state must impose on itself. In that sense, Article 1, paragraph 2 of the Labour Code restores and vindicates that function of labour legislation. These objectives and goals, as formulated in Article 1, paragraph 2 of the Labour Code, could be formulated as follows:

a.   *Ensuring the freedom of labour.* This means the free (of the parties' free will) engagement in legal labour relationship and its free termination, at the will of the worker or employee and of the employer (in law-established cases). The freedom of labour under the labour legal nexus is a concrete and positive expression of the ban on performing forced labour established in Article 48, paragraph 4 of the Constitution, in conformity with the international standards (Articles 1 and 2 of ILO Convention No. 29 of 1930, Article 8, paragraph 2 of the United Nations Pact on Civil and Political Rights, 1966, ratified by Bulgaria).

b.   *Ensuring the protection of labour.* In essence this reflects, in the orientation of the Labour Code, provisions towards helping and protecting hired labour or employees, which are the economically and socially weaker side and dependent on the employer, party to the labour legal relationship, when starting work, in the course of the labour employment, and when it is terminated. Support and protection are provided for in the law, which decrees the minimum content of legal labour relationship and the possibility of establishing more favourable labour conditions in any collective or individual labour contract; sometimes this is achieved through the establishment of mandatory rules defining strictly certain fixed prerogatives of the worker or employee, and obligations of the employer, through the establishment of judicial protection of labour rights, etc. This is the *protective principle* in the legal treatment of labour relations. By proclaiming this to be its objective, labour legislation openly admits that the worker and employee, as the bearers of labour force, are the economically weaker and dependent-on-the-employer party. Also through this legislative regime, which is the content of the law, the aim is at least within certain limits, if not to do away with the employee's unequal status in comparison with the employer (this being a task that the law cannot cope with), to protect him or her from any encroachments on his or her rights and interests, which the employer might take the liberty of engaging in owing to his or her position of economic supremacy over the worker or employee. For this reason the law imposes legal obligations on the employer (Articles 127–129) of the Labour Code, while endowing the workers and employees with rights and creating legal guarantees for their implementation in life. This is a radical change in the basic course of legislation and a categorical rejection and negation of the dogma that the socialist state, being a state of the working people, dispenses with the need to have a protective attitude to the labour of workers and employees.

c.   *Ensuring equitable and dignified conditions of labour.* This concerns the conditions in which hired labour is performed. The conditions include not only labour safety and hygiene in the working environment, but all of the remaining labour conditions in the broad sense of this concept: pay, working hours, rest and recreation, leaves, professional and vocational training, and so on. We consider equitable those labour conditions in which workers and employees receive for their efforts, and the achieved results, a commensurate and equivalent counterpart of wealth. 'Dignified labour conditions' means taking into account and protecting the worker's and employee's personal sense of honour and human dignity, respect to him or her as a full-value human personality regardless of his or her subordinate position and economic dependence, owing to his or her legal contractual position as a hired worker or employee. Incompatible with this basic goal of the legal treatment of labour relations are stipulations or manifestations of their application that denigrate or humiliate the dignity, honour, or good name of the worker or employee, regardless of from where the maltreatment arises – the Law, the employer, or from state or public authorities.

15. Amendments in the Labour Code introduce particularly important changes also in *the method of regulating labour relations.* They are most immediately linked with the transition to a market economy and they help its manifestation in the domain of labour relations. The changes take *two different* but *interlinked and mutually complementing lines.*

a. On one hand, the changes consist in dropping the domination of centralized and rigidly fixed regulation of the legal relations to which the 1986 Labour Code adhered on the whole (in spite of certain toning-down modifications): the ambience of a centralized planned economy. This trend of change was expressed in a reduction of imperative provisions and norms, which fixed rigidly the volume and content of the rights and obligations of the parties to the individual labour legal relationship, and admitted no deviation from it as it was decreed by the law, and no freedom of agreement between the parties. These norms contained in the 1986 version of the Labour Code decreed the length of working hours (Article 136); the basic and additional days of paid annual leave (Articles 155 and 156); the amounts of the various indemnities paid under the labour legal nexus – such as in case of travel on missions (Article 215); compensations in the event of natural and social disasters (Article 218); payment for night-time and overtime work (Article 262); compensation on dismissal on certain grounds (Article 222); compensation for unemployment owing to unlawful dismissal (Article 225), and so on. The amendments of the Labour Code now adopt another essentially different legislative solution to these matters: they transform these imperative provisions into norms with a compulsory minimum and indefinite maximum. This means that a 'lower threshold' of kind is decreed, below which the parties may not descend, but above which they are free to agree on more favourable solutions. In this manner, a whole range of Labour Code provisions were transformed from being purely imperative into norms that fix only the minimum standards ('minimum floor') of legal labour protection and the protective principle in the regulation of labour relations. In another group of cases, the Labour Code establishes the broader limits of a framework for agreement between the parties; thus the maximum time-limit of the probation period of employment under Article 70 was increased from 3 to 6 months; and vocational training (Articles 229–236) was placed on a contractual basis, which thus abandoned the legal and imperative determination of workers' and employees' rights and obligations regarding vocational training as part of its administrative regulation, etc. In that way the regulation of labour relations was on the whole liberalized, and the contractual principle for deciding on labour conditions under legal labour relations was reinforced.

b. On the other hand, *new legal mechanisms* for regulating labour relations were introduced. For the first time, the amended Labour Code legalized and established by law *tripartite participation* for settling labour and insurance relations and for matters of living standard, with the participation of trade unions and employers' organizations (Article 3 of the Labour Code). Restored and legally established in its contemporary form was collective bargaining (Articles 50–59 of the Labour Code) between trade unions and the employer or groups of employers or their organization; the collective labour contract was promoted to the status of a normative agreement. It can now settle issues of labour and insurance relations not treated in the law or, although treated, not covered by imperative provisions of the law (Article 50, paragraph 1 of the Labour Code). Moreover, only more favourable conditions than the ones established by the law can be agreed upon in collective labour contracts – not less favourable (Article 50, paragraph 2). Individual labour contracts may stipulate labour conditions not settled by the law's imperative provisions, as well as conditions which are more favourable to the worker or employee than what the collective labour contract has to offer (Article 66, paragraph 2). In this manner, the vacuum left when the state backed away from excessive centralist and fixed regulation of labour relations was filled in by the indicated new legal mechanisms. The Labour Code thus establishes also a new hierarchy of sources forming the content of the individual labour legal relationship: the law with its minimum standard requirements for the protection of labour is primary, then comes the collective labour contract whose clauses become part of the content of the individual labour legal relations of the workers and employees to whom the contract applies (Article 57 of the Labour Code), and finally comes the individual labour contract (Article 66, paragraph 2). This gives an entirely *new appearance* to the method of legal regulation of labour relations during the transition to a market economy.

Evidently this does not in the least mean that the law loses its regulatory importance for labour relations, nor that their imperative regulation has been overcome and left behind once and for all, as incompatible with the new conditions now emerging in the country. The law has not lost its importance and this is corroborated by the very existence of the Labour Code and its provisions. By its latest amendments, the law has not left behind all imperative regulation and entirely switched over to free contractual regulation of labour relations. The arguments: *First*, even after the introduced changes in the Labour Code, imperative provisions remain, which regulate in a centralist and fixed manner entire institutions of labour law, such as: the procedure, form, and requirements for concluding labour contracts and the arising of legal labour relationships as the result of selection and contest (Articles 61–96); minimum age entitling to employment (Articles 301–303); workers' or employees disciplinary and material liability (Articles 186–212); special protection of certain categories of working individuals (minors, women and partly disabled - Articles 301–321); much of the provisions on winding up the employment legal relation (Articles 325–346), and so on. *Secondly*, in the cases when collective and individual negotiation of labour conditions is admissible, the law establishes the minimum standards 'upward' of which bargaining can take place. In fact, the law admits and regulates collective and individual bargaining. In general, the idea of establishing entirely imperative norms and/or norms with a mandatory minimum deeply inheres in the labour law whose function, as a social law, is basically to rule for the protection of labour. Nor can labour be protected without a definite minimum of imperative and fixed prescriptions of the law. Imperative and fixed-to-a-definite-limit regulation of labour relations derives from the very idea of protecting labour, which is and must become one of the basic and normative ideas of legal regulation of labour relations and this is particularly true during the transition to a market economy and its social 'cushioning'. Actually, the point is to mitigate it tangibly in areas where this is needed and its function could be 'taken over' by tripartite participation, collective and individual bargaining, and its co-ordination with free contractual regulation and with the new legal mechanisms. Or, in other words: in finding the correct measure of its inevitable presence in the regulation of labour relations. Under the Bulgarian legal system it is derived also from Article 16 of the Constitution, which prescribes *the protection and guaranteeing of labour by the law. Thirdly*, in cases when the settlement of certain issues is left to be ruled upon through the collective or individual labour contract and on the basis of the law (the Labour Code). In these cases, the law rules on the contractual freedom, the parties' contractual freedom and their limitations. In fact, the importance of the law for the regulation of labour relations is not diminished; the manner in which the law participates in regulating labour relations merely changes in accordance with the requirements for the parties' greater freedom of will when determining the content of labour relations (the parties' rights and duties under these relations), in the ambience of transition to a market of labour as a standard component of the market economy. In that sense the changes in the Labour Code, through alteration of the methods of regulating labour relations, do not reduce the role of the law, but rather express the ambition of the law-maker to enable the law to find the optimum and most adequate forms of interfering in labour relations in view of the new changes and changing conditions. This is an extremely difficult task, especially when considering that state ownership continues to be dominant in the economy and the process of the massive privatization unfortunately continues to progress very slowly, and, practically by end of 1993, is not yet started.

16.   The changes in the Labour Code as a whole have preserved its character of a social law whose main function it is to protect labour and defend it (*cf.* Section 14, above). At the same time, however, it also contains *some deviations* from that fundamental function of the Labour Code. They were made in the name of the transition to a market economy, and were substantiated by its objectives. But not all of them could be justified with these objectives. Some of them already conceal broken promises, other mask time-seeking political aims, and not 'market economic' considerations.

a.   Thus Articles 98–104 of the new Labour Code did away with the provisions for giving preference in finding employment through the labour offices to certain espe-cially socially vulnerable categories of citizens, namely pregnant women, mothers with children below the age of 3, soldiers' wives, partly disabled persons whose spouses are registered as unemployed, young graduate specialists, and so on. Obviously, this administrative procedure of posting jobs was incompatible with the requirements for a transition to a market economy and free economic initiative. But it is also clear that in the conditions of the present profound economic and social crisis, when the overwhelming majority of citizens are living through dire economic difficulties and runaway impoverishment, there are categories of persons who are in a particularly dire condition. In this state of affairs it would be necessary to select among the categories of persons under Article 98 of the Labour Code those who are in the most difficult position, and to provide for them special (Privileged) procedures of employment. When voting the amendments in the Labour Code in November 1992, the Parliament did not adopt this legislative approach under the pretext that a special Law on Employment was expected to pass soon and settle these issues along with the economic measures for retraining, opening new jobs and the like, which are of key importance if the galloping rise of unemployment is to be checked. At that time this consideration sounded convincing. Yet no such Bill of Employment, although tabled in the National Assembly as early as the beginning of 1992, has so far – more than two years after passage of the Labour Code amendments – been adopted, nor has its discussion even begun. That is why the categories of persons enumerated as examples above, and whom are in a dire social situation, remain without any elementary social protection whatever when taking a job, although the need for such protection could not be overemphasized.

b.   There are serious signs of retreat from social protection principles also in the new legal regime of dismissal from work established with the changes in the Labour Code. The need of changes in that field for a liberalization of the regime of dismissing from work was indisputable. The changes had to bring about great flexibility and give the employer freedom to get rid of workers and employees who do not fulfil their labour obligations or lack the qualifications for the respective job, and that would allow him or her to organize his production and service activities independently and efficiently. To meet these requirements, the amendments in the Labour Code included a broader and more general formula for the legal grounds for dismissal through the serving of a term of notice (Article 328, paragraph 1, items 3, 5, 11, 12 and paragraph 2 of the Labour Code), as well as the grounds for disciplinary discharge (Article 330, paragraph 2, item 5 in connection with Article 190 of the Labour Code). But by taking this line, correct in principle, the law has adopted also some extreme solutions through the newly drafted Articles 328a and 328b of the Labour Code, which provoke serious objections. Thus Article 328a of the Labour Code creates an unwarrantedly broad and indefinite justification (grounds) for dismissal from work through the serving of a term of notice to persons who occupy a leading post in an enterprise or office, under the formula '(sacked) in the interest of work'. It opens wide opportunities for arbitrary dismissal of workers and employees, which will deviate from the legality of grounds for dismissal. Article 328b goes even further, saying that it is possible unilaterally to cut short, through the serving of a term of notice, the labour contracts of workers or employees who are managers or members of artistic or art-creative staff and personnel in institutes of culture, of Bulgarian national TV, or of Bulgarian national Radio and Bulgarian Cinematography; an advance written notice of 2 months is sufficient. Leaving aside a series of unexplained concepts introduced by this legal provision (such as 'cultural institutions', 'artistic and art-creative staff and personnel' which need explanation in the law, and which are not explained), the basic content of Article 328b is that it provides as 'grounds' for dismissal the unilateral expression of will and decision of the employer, without any arguments to support these at all. This complete freedom of dismissal is applied in practice against workers and employees undesirable for temporary political considerations; it is therefore a grave breach of the requirement for elementary legal protection in the case of dismissal from work. It carries in itself a real danger of arbitrariness in the firing of these employees, and even the defence against unlawful dismissal cannot effectively counter it.

c.   Retreats from the principle are contained also in the preliminary protection in the case of dismissal under Article 333 of the Labour Code. It consists in the requirement for preliminary permission from the Labour Inspection Office for the dismissal of certain socially vulnerable categories of workers and employees (such as pregnant women, mother of children under 3 years of age, part-time disabled workers suffering from various ailments, and so on). The grounds for dismissal from work, to which this protection applies, do not include the gravest cases of subjectivism and bias with their attendant danger of genuine arbitrary treatment in dismissal under Articles 328a and

328b of the Labour Code. On the other hand, outside of the circle of protected persons by Article 333, some categories of workers and employees deserved greater care on the part of the legislator owing to the conditions of severe economic crisis and mounting unemployment; such as: the only wage earners in a family, and persons whose retirement is due in three years or less before they acquire the right to full pension rights. The circle of protected trade union activists is also seriously restricted. It has been limited down to only the president and the secretary of the trade union committee in an enterprise (Article 333, paragraph 3 in connection with paragraph 1 item 6 of the Supplementary Provisions of the Labour Code). Finally the protection of pregnant women workers and employees and of mothers with children under the age of 3 can also be by-passed with a permission of the Labour Inspection Office. This solution risks to find itself at variance with Article 4 of the Convention No. 3 of ILO treating of the work of women before and after childbirth of 1919 which has been ratified by Bulgaria, and other provisions.

d.   Workers' and employees' participation in the management of their enterprise has been tangibly and essentially curtailed (Articles 6 and 7 of the Labour Code). Here the law has swung to the other extreme of trying to react to the unwarrantedly large 'powers' of the labour collectives under the 1986 version of the Labour Code which are not applied in practice. Instead of seeking moderate and acceptable solutions to these problems by taking into account the social and democratic role that contemporary international development and the experience of a number of developed European democratic countries with a market economy (Germany, France, etc.) attach to workers' representatives and participation, the lawgiver has adopted the 'easiest' solution by considerably plying down the role of the workers' representatives.

III.   THE IMPACT OF THE CHANGES OF THE LABOUR CODE

17.   The purpose of the operated changes in the Labour Code of November 1992 is to make labour legislation capable to meet the new challenges that are posed before labour relations by the profound transformations continuing in the country as it makes a transition from an administrative command to a democratic social system and market economy. As a whole, these changes are an important step forward in the development of Bulgarian labour legislation. They correctly reflect the necessity of the transition that the country is experiencing and will certainly help its realization. Apart from that, the amendments contain some shortcomings as well. The need for social protection of working people in the conditions of severe economic crisis now experienced by the nation does not find any consistent reflection. The large limitations, to which workers' and employees' participation in management is subject, are also unjustified.

*18.   The last amendments to the Labour Code have substantially changed the overall aspect of the entire Bulgarian labour legislation and have introduced new concepts in it.
        In the past, the legal regulation of labour relations concentrated on individual labour relations and were contained in laws and sub-legislative normative acts. Its application required knowledge of these regulations. Now, the legal regulations cover not only individual but also *collective labour relations* (industrial relations). For the most part, legal regulation of individual labour relations establishes only the minimum standards; more favourable conditions can be agreed upon in collective and individual labour contracts.

19. This completely new approach demands profound insight and radical change in legal thinking and in the mentality of:

a. the employers and the wage earners in the practice of individual contracting;

b. the social partners (employers and trade unions) during the collective bargaining; and

c. the state's organs in order to refrain from, and to avoid, direct intervention in the labour relation and to have recourse, above all, to the dialogue with the social partners within the framework of tripartite participation.

A change in the mentality of state organs is also necessary in order to create all necessary prerequisites for an atmosphere propitious to collective negotiations between the social partners.

These changes in the conduct and mentality of all parties and participants in the regulation of labour relations, both individuals and collectives, and the application of these changes, which corresponds to the transition in the labour market economy situation, are the most difficult to be attained. But these very important changes are demanded by the latest amendments to the Labour Code. It includes not only a knowledge of the legal regulation itself, but much more common sense, good will, creativeness and imagination by its application – qualities which were not all cultivated by the former legislation. Only by responding to these changes will the new version of the Labour Code be able to play its role in accelerating the transition to a labour market economy, in adapting the new concepts and their practical application in the new social realities.

On the other hand, it is necessary to accelerate the process of the massive privatization and to foster the growth of the private sector, both of which shape the stable economic background for the transition to the market economy in general, and to the labour market economy, in particular. Without the creation of these absolutely necessary economic bases and prerequisites, the application and the functioning of the new version of the Labour Code will be considerably handicapped.

20. The changes made in the Labour Code of November 1992, and the resultant new version of the Labour Code of the Republic of Bulgaria, bear a transient character. Any lasting settlement of labour relations under the new socio-economic conditions now being treated in this country can be achieved through an entirely new Code of Labour or a system of new labour laws. When these are drafted, account will doubtless be taken of the experience by applying the amendments in the Labour Code adopted at the end of 1992.

Transformation of Labour Law in the Framework of Existing Economic and Social Situation in the Republic of Croatia

Anton Ravnic

I. INTRODUCTION

1. With the Constitution of 1990,[1] the Republic of Croatia was constitutionally established as a democratic and social state (Article 1). Some of its basic values, such as the respect for human rights, inviolability of ownership, a democratic multiparty system (Article 3), as well as some economic rights, for example, the security of plural ownership (Article 48) and of entrepreneurial and market freedom (Article 49), show that Croatia is organized according to the principles of capitalism of the Western type. Croatia has institutionally abolished the so-called self-management socialism of the communist orientation and has set the constitutional framework for the creation of a new social legal order. Within this framework, a transition from socialist traditions to new social, economic and legal relations is taking place, including the transformation of labour relations, or even broader, labour legislation.

When evaluating the achieved level of transition, in general, and of labour legislation, in particular, one must bear in mind the fact that Croatia is a young and small state[2] at war, fighting for its territorial integrity because one quarter of its territory is occupied.

2. It is our task to present the economic and social situation in which the transformation of certain laws is taking place and to present and explain what has been achieved so far, and where the transition is heading to.

II. ECONOMIC AND WELFARE SITUATION

A. Economic Situation and Unemployment

a. The present economic situation in Croatia is the result of earlier very unfavourable economic conditions (insufficient economic development and inefficiency, bad organization

---

1. 'Narodne Novine' (*Official Gazette*), No. 56/90.
2. The Republic of Croatia is a Central European country. According to the population census of 1991, it has 4,489,049 inhabitants. From that number, 2,039,833 persons are active work force, 748,424 have personal income and 1,710,692 are supported inhabitants (Statistical Annals of 1993, Zagreb, Bureau of Statistics, 1993, p. 67).

of production and labour foreign debts, a high rate of unemployment and so on) and of huge direct and indirect economic damage caused by the continuing war.

For a long time, industrial and other production in Croatia has been declining. According to the latest government-issued 'Social Policy Report of the Republic of Croatia',[3] the real gross domestic product has been decreasing since 1990. In comparison, in 1993 it was 28.3% less than 1990. In 1994 an increase of 0.8% was predicted.

According to the same report, a considerable portion of the industrial facilities have been destroyed by the war. The power generating capacities have lost 30% of their potential, 210,000 housing units, or 12% of the entire housing fund, have been damaged or destroyed. Railroad traffic has ceased to operate in 35% of the entire network; almost 25% of the agricultural land has been occupied. It has been estimated that direct and indirect material war damages amount to US$ 22,000,000.

At the same time, privatization is taking place in public (state-owned) enterprises, organizations, and in the public housing fund. The aim is to create the preconditions of successful market economy, to reduce the maintenance costs of the fund, and to acquire investment resources. However, many factors have had a contrary effect, particularly in the public sector, which is still much bigger and economically more powerful than the private one. It is very important to point out the negative side of privatization as it is practised here: a small section of society has become rich overnight, mostly from among its former 'socialistic' managers.

The economic situation is deteriorating due to the high expense for the army and the police. From the anticipated resources in the budget for 1995 (which was adopted in December 1994), almost 50% has been allocated for the army and the police.

All of this is causing a decline in the citizens' living standards and has led to deep economic and social divisions, creating tensions, causing strikes, and increasing poverty. It also increases the number of unemployed people, aggravates working conditions, and lowers salaries. According to the same report, the net salary per employee from January to August 1994 was an average 1,171.00 Kuna (hereinafter Kn), and the gross salary was 2,043.00 Kn.[4] However, a large number of employees received a smaller salary that was not sufficient for basic needs in light of the relatively high living expenses and retail prices.[5]

b. In such an economic situation, the level of employment is decreasing and there are more and more unemployed people.

The total average number of employed persons in 1993 was 1,198,200, which is 62,000 (or 5%) less than in 1992. From that number, 1,068,000 worked in the state sector of mixed and co-operative ownership (6.2% less than in 1992), and 130,200 in the private sector (5.8% more than in 1992).

The number of employed people in the state sector of mixed and co-operative ownership has constantly been decreasing in the last six years, and from 1987 to 1993, employment was reduced by 513,000 or 33%.[6]

---

3.   *Izvješæ o sociajalnoj politici Republike Hrvatske (Social Policy Report of the Republic of Croatia).* Government of the Republic of Croatia, Zagreb, 1 December 1994.
4.   The average monthly exchange rate for Kn with the National Bank of Croatia from January to August 1994 was: 1 DM = 3,7 Kn. (*Statistical Monthly Report, op.cit.*, pp. 20, 29 and 49).
5.   *Statistical Monthly Report, op.cit.*, pp. 49 and 52–55.
6.   Sources for employment and unemployment are: *The Employment Agency Yearbook*, Zagreb, Employment Agency, 1993, IX and similar; *Statistical Monthly Bulletin, Employment Agency*, 1994. No. 102, 1 and similar.

In 1993, on average 250,779 unemployed people were registered monthly in the employment agencies, which is 5.9% less than the average in 1992. By the end of October 1994, the employment agencies in Croatia registered 245,670 unemployed people, which is 0.9% more than in the previous month and 0.1% less than in October 1993.

In the course of 1991 and 1992, the unemployment rate was 17%. If we compare this figure with the 1993 employment level, it is a 20% higher rate.

B. Social Welfare and Pension and Disability Insurance

This very difficult and complex economic situation is having a negative impact on the social situation and on the system of social welfare and on the pension and disability benefit. More and more employed people are becoming social welfare users, and a great majority of people live with their pension and disability benefit rights.

Also, there is a large and ever increasing number of war invalids, civil war victims, widows, and children without one or both parents. The government reports that there are 383,115 displaced persons and refugees, mainly from the war stricken Bosnia and Herzegovina, largely taken care of by Croatia.[7]

What changes regarding the rights of these persons have taken place in these two systems of social security?

1. The Actual Situation and the Social Welfare System

1. A regular social welfare system[8] provides temporary financial assistance for sick, disabled, and other persons in need. This can include an allowance for assistance and care, lodging, and other similar benefits. Faced with the new circumstances, this system, according to the cited *Social Policy Report*, now ensures some new rights for employees and other persons: for instance, the right to a non-recurring financial assistance for public or municipal services (for the payment of rent, electricity, water, heating, urban sanitation, fuel, and so on). There is also some kind of natural assistance in the form of food (public kitchens), clothes, footwear, etc. Furthermore, the production of the basic groceries like bread and milk is subsidized.

According to the cited *Social Policy Report*, 16,706 persons benefited from the regular social welfare system in the period from June to October 1994; for about 10,392 beneficiaries, the costs were completely or partly covered by the budget.

2. One of the most significant new rights, resulting from the social policy measures in the new circumstances, is compensation in case of a social minimum, which is

---

7. During the war, 5,858 defenders were killed and 17,802 wounded. A total of 3,024 civilians have been killed and 8,646 of them were wounded. More than 2,000 persons disappeared or were forced to leave their homes. Government report given at Sabor (the Croatian Parliament) at the beginning of December 1994. According to the Ministry of Labour and Social Welfare (of 1 November 1993) up to November 1993 there were 19,122 war invalids.

8. *See:* 'Zakon o socijalnoj zaštiti' ('Law on Social Protection') (*Official Gazette*, No. 10/91 and 19/91); 'Pravilnik o ostvarivanju socijalne zaštite ('Regulations on Accomplishing Social Welfare') (*Official Gazette*, No. 10/91, 38/92, 5/93 and 113/93); and 'Odluka a socijalnom minimumu' ('Decision on the Social Minimum') (*Official Gazette* No. 71/91, 79/92, 29/93 and 113/93).

awarded on the basis of social identity cards. In 1994 there were, according to the *Social Policy Report*, 133,745 beneficiaries of this compensation, and among them there were:

1. 38,484 (28.8%) able-bodied unemployed citizens;
2. 32,906 (24.6%) pensioners; and
3. 22,714 (17.0%) employed citizens. The subsistence compensation for a one-member household in October 1994 amounted to 225 Kn (or 60.8 DM), and for a four-member household it was 675 Kn (or 182 DM). These amounts, calculated as a percentage of the minimum salary[9] for a particular household, cannot meet basic living needs.

2. Current Situation and System of Retirement and Disability Insurance

1. The system of retirement and disability insurance is regulated by a law which was enacted at the time of self-management socialism and belongs to the category of developed systems. Croatia modified the retirement and disability legislation but it did not modify the type of the corresponding rights or of its obligations several times.[10]

This system guarantees the following basic rights: retirement pension disability and family pension, protective allowance, pecuniary compensation for corporal damage, and an allowance for assisting and caring for another person.

2. In the last few years the number of retired persons suddenly increased, particularly beneficiaries of the retirement pension. In 1993 there were 60% more pensioners than in 1989.[11] Such an increase was the result of the fact that during a certain period there was a small difference between the full retirement pension and the salary for the same category of people. Also, many employed persons opted for the availability of a premature pension, fearing more stringent conditions for acquiring the right to a full retirement pension (e.g., longer length of service and higher age limit) and, of course, because of the insecurity of employment.

The possibility of purchasing the remaining years of service in order to acquire the right to retirement (*'outkup staza'*) was available to those who needed only five more years to achieve full retirement age, and it only contributed to the number of

---

9.   The minimum salary is determined by the Regulation on Salaries from 1994, and for the period from June to October 1994 it amounted to 225 Kn (*Official Gazette*, No. 42/94).

10.   The rights and obligations from the retirement and disability insurance are regulated by the following laws: 'Zakon o mirovinskom i invalidskom osiguranju' ('Law on retirement and Disability Insurance'), (*Official Gazette* No. 26/83, 5/86, 42/87, 34/89, 57/89, 49/90 and 9/91, 'Zakon o mirovinskom i invalidskom osiguranju individualnih poljoprivrednika ('Law on Retirement and Disability Insurance for Individual Farmers'), (*Official Gazette* No. 26/83, 57/83, 47/86, and 40/90); 'Zakon o preuzimanju saveznih zakona iz područja mirovinskog i invalidskog osiguranja koji se u Republici Hrvatskoj primjenjuju kao republièki zakoni' ('Law on Applying federal laws from the field of retirement and disability insurance applied in the Republic of Croatia as state laws'), (*Official Gazette* No. 53/91); and 'Zakon o preuzimanju saveznih zakona iz oblasti mirovinskog i invalidskog osiguranja i dopölatka za djecu vojnih osiguranika koji se u Republici Hrvatskoj primjenjuje kao republièki zakon', ('Law on Applying federal laws from the field of retirement and disability insurance and children's allowance for military contributors to pension funds applied in the Republic of Croatia as a state law'), *Official Gazette* No. 53/91.

11.   *See:* The Statistical Annals 1993, *op. cit.*, p. 43.

retired persons. During the period of 1990 to 1993, 45,032 persons purchased their remaining years of service and they became pensioners. Such an opportunity may have increased the number of retired people by more than 30%. During 1993, retirement was granted on that basis to men in the Workers' Fund on average 57 years of age and with 37 years of employment, and to women in the Workers' Fund at 53 years of age and with 32 years of employment.[12]

In such a way, persons still able to work and who had valuable experience became pensioners, which is bad for economic development in general and places a burden on the retirement and disability insurance funds. It also creates an imbalance between active contributors to the funds and pensioners.

According to the *Social Policy Report*, in September 1994 the situation in Croatia was the following:

a. 1,657,012 active contributors to pensions funds, out of which 1,369,738 used to be employees; and

b. 818,845 pension beneficiaries. To these we should add:

c. 61,441 disabled workers;

d. 22,433 beneficiaries who acquired the right to pensions in the republics of the former Socialist Federative Republic of Yugoslavia (hereinafter: SFRY). Thus, in September 1994, there were 841,278 pensioners.

The increase in the number of pensioners has resulted in an unfavourable ratio between active contributors and the retired persons. The Workers' Fund expected that by the end of 1994, the ratio between active contributors and the retired persons could be an average of 1.34 active contributors against 1 retired person. This ratio does not include the army and the police.[13]

This means that 1.34 active contributors, as a rule employed persons, have to provide the funds for the rights acquired by a single pensioner based on the retirement and disability insurance, health insurance, children's allowance, etc. Of course, an employed person also has to earn his own salary and cover the cost of these benefits. An employer's primary interest is to gain profit from the work of his employees. This, then enables other things, such as further development and improvement of production. It is very difficult to satisfy these needs with such a large number of retired people and with such a ratio between active contributors and pensioners. This unavoidably results in problems of financing the retirement and disability insurance.

3. The total income of the retirement and disability insurance funds (The Workers' Fund, The Farmers' Fund and The Self-Employed Businessmen's Fund) for the nine months of 1994 amounted to 5,817,974,887 Kn, with a total deficit of 159,667,769 Kn. The outstanding claims (mainly due to unsettled contributions to the Workers' Fund) amounted to 780,916,930 Kn.

In such a financial situation, which is the result of the overall economic situation, pensions cannot be generous. According to the Social Policy Report, an average retirement pension in September 1994 amounted to 725.55 Kn.[14] At the same

---

12. *See: Statistièki bilten mirovinskog i invalidskog osiguranja (Statistical Bulletin of the Retirement and Disability Insurance), The State Fund for Retirement and Disability Insurance of Workers of Croatia 1993*, Zagreb, 1994, No. 2, 7, and similar. *See also*: Zeljko Potoènjak, 'Povezanost preobrazbe radnih odnosa i mirovinsko-invalidskog osiguranja', ('The Connection Between the Transformation of Labour Relations and Retirement and Disability Insurance'), Zagreb, December 1993, p. 6.

13. *Social Policy Report, op.cit.*, pp. 21–22 and Table 6.

14. *Izvješæ o socijalnoj politici (Social Policy Report), op.cit.*, pp. 23–24.

time, 87,364 employees-beneficiaries had an average pension (retirement pension, disability pension and family pension), without the protective supplement, amount of 300,00 Kn. The largest number of these beneficiaries, 324,396 were entitled to pension ranging from 300.01 to 600.00 Kn.[15] These amounts are not sufficient to cover the basic living expenses.

III. LABOUR LAW TRANSFORMATION

A transformation of Labour Law is taking place in Croatia presently and it has so far consisted of changes and amendments (modifications) to the previously enacted laws and collective agreements. A few laws have been passed that regulate a particular type of labour relations.[16]

From the cited *Social Policy Report* we find that at the end of 1994 or at the beginning of 1995, a procedure for the adoption of the Law on Protection at Work and the Law on Employment is to be initiated. The Labour Act is in its second reading before Parliament.[17] The Law on Labour Inspection, which has to be passed, is not mentioned.

Some Labour Law issues have been explained in particular, work administration, labour relations and security of work, collective negotiations and collective agreement, strike, and settlement of individual and collective labour disputes.

There will be no word about lock-out because it is not known to the present labour law. As for the participation of employees in decision making, reference is made to the following constitutional provision: 'employees may participate in the decision making in companies in accordance with law' (Article 55). It is left for the legislator to decide on the existence or non-existence of such participation in the company or the economy in general, but not in the public service. The reluctance of the Constitution regarding employee participation is probably the result of bad experience with workers' self-management that was, together with the social ownership, the basis of the self-management socialism.

A. Labour Administration

Labour administration, the main topic of this paper, consists of the agency of labour inspection (hereinafter: labour inspection) and of the employment service.[18] The main bodies of this administration (The Labour Inspectorate and The Employment Agency)

---

15. *Monthly Statistical Report, op. cit.*, p. 30 and similar.
16. These are: 'Zakon o dravnim slubenicima i namjeŝtenicima i o plaæama nositelja pravosudnih dunosti' ('Law on Government Officials and Employees and on Salaries of Judicial Officials'), of 1994 and 'Zakon o placama slubenika i namjeŝtenika u javnim slubama' ('Law on Salaries of Officials and Employees in Public Services'), of 1994, *(Official Gazette* No. 74/94).
17. *Social Policy Report, op. cit.*, p. 56.
18. There will be no discussion here about the statistics of labour which also belongs to the labour administration. *See:* 'Zakon o evidencijama iz oblasti rada', (Law on Records in the Field of Labour'), *(Official Gazette* No. 34/91 and 26/93).

operate within the Ministry of Labour and Social Welfare. Being an agency of state administration, it deals, among other things, with administrative and professional activities in the field of labour relations, employment, and protection at work. It also carries out the acts of inspection in the same arena.[19]

1. Labour Inspection

1. Labour inspection is regulated by the Law on Labour Inspection of 1983, which has been amended several times.[20] Organizational changes were introduced with these modifications along with some insignificant changes regarding the competence, powers and duties of labour inspection.

2. Labour inspection supervises the application of regulations, contained originally in the Law on Safety at Work of 1983,[21] and labour relations in companies, banks, insurance companies, co-operatives, farming economies, and other entities. Apart from this general authority, there are activities that fall within the competence of the Labour Inspectorate and which are vested in the labour inspectors operating within the bodies of state administration centres and those seated in municipalities. The Labour Inspectorate, being the supreme organ of labour inspection, observes and analyzes the conditions related to on-the-job worker protection and to labour relations. It co-operates with other inspections, organizations, trade unions, employers' associations and similar groups.

3. Labour inspection is obliged to carry out, at least annually, the supervision of the application of regulations for workplace safety and labour relations. The supervision is to be carried out at the location of any event that caused death or severe injury to a worker, or an injury to two or more workers. The labour inspection is obliged to inform the Labour Inspectorate about any such event.

    If the labour inspector observes and establishes the violation of a law or of any other regulation that he is supposed to supervise, he has to issue a decision that will:
a. determine the deadline before which the regulation on workplace safety has to be applied; and
b. ban workers from performing jobs for which they do not fulfil the conditions established by the rules on workplace safety, if a direct danger to life exists.

2. The Employment Service

1. This Service is regulated by the Law on Employment of 1990. The Law has been amended several times;[22] however, the changes were not substantial but rather

---

19.   'Zakon o ostrojstvu republièke uprave iz 1990' ('Law on Organization of State Administration of 1990), *Official Gazette* No. 41/90, amended several times).
20.   *Official Gazette* No. 9/83, 17/88, 9/91 and 26/93.
21.   *Official Gazette* No. 19/83, 17/86, 46/92 and 26/93.
22.   The final draft of the Law was published in the *Official Gazette* No. 55/90. For its further amendments, *see*: *Official Gazette* No. 19/91, 26/93, 117/93 and 76/94.

organizational. At the top of this agency is the Employment Agency, which has its local bureaux. The service has the authority for:

1. employment, unemployment and employment procedure; and
2. financial assistance to workers while unemployed.

2. The activities regarding the employment, unemployment, and employment procedures are divided between the Employment Agency and its local bureaux.

A local employment bureau is responsible for the following jobs:

1. it follows and analyzes the trends of employment, unemployment and employment procedures and collaborates with municipalities, counties, trade unions, and other employers organizations;
2. it mediates employment procedures; and
3. it decides on the rights of unemployed workers and makes payments to them according to issued decisions.

The Employment Agency:

1. follows, analyzes and examines economic, social and other movements and their impact on employment, unemployment and employment procedures;
2. follows and proposes measures for improving the social security of unemployed workers;
3. develops proposals for the establishment of the contribution rate for the employment procedure; and
4. makes annual reports on the trends of employment, unemployment and employment procedures for the authorities of the Republic of Croatia, and so on.

3. In order to perform the above mentioned activities, the employment service keeps the necessary records and gives vocational guidance for choosing a profession, offers retraining, upgrading, and professional rehabilitation, and so on.

Compared with 1992, in 1993 the employment service records show an increase of activities regarding vocational guidance of more than 30% (taking into consideration the number of directly involved users of one type of vocational guidance). In the course of 1993, the measures of an active policy included a total number of 19,364 employed and unemployed persons and 213 service disabled patriotic war invalids (self-employment). From the total number of those included by the active measures and in the category of the unemployed, the following types of employment were achieved:

1. 4,053 people were trained for scarce skills;
2. 859 skilled workers with no working experience went through a job induction; and
3. 131 people were retrained.[23]

4. The employment service, as already stated, carries out the activities of financial assistance to unemployed workers. The most important rights to insurance according to the law on Employment are:

1. pecuniary compensation;
2. the right to health care and other rights belonging to health insurance, the right to retirement and disability insurance, and the right to child care support.

---

23.   The Employment Agency Annals, IX and similar; *Monthly Statistical Bulletin, op.cit.*, p. 1 and similar.

An unemployed worker has the right to a pecuniary compensation if at the time of the termination of employment, he or she has had at least nine months of uninterrupted service or twelve months of service with interruptions over a period of 18 months, and if he registered with the pertinent local service within a specific time period.

Such a right is not granted to a worker whose service was terminated voluntarily or on the basis of mutual agreement, or if, without good reason, the worker has failed to report for work for five working days in a row.

A pecuniary compensation is granted to an unemployed worker for a limited period of time, depending on the length of his service. It can be received for a duration of 3 to 30 months. However, a man who has worked for 30 years, or a woman for 25, has the right to a pecuniary compensation until employed again or until such a right ceases to exist (e.g. when employed, retired, fully and permanently disabled, and so on).

With regard to pecuniary compensation, it has to be mentioned that, because of the very strict requirements, only a small number of unemployed persons can acquire that right. In October 1994, the employment agencies registered 33,700 beneficiaries of pecuniary compensation (13.7% of the total number of unemployed), which is 77.7% more than the figure for the same period of the previous year. However, significantly larger is the number of unemployed people with health insurance. In the same month of 1994, there were 154,206 (or 62.8% of the unemployed) health insurance beneficiaries, which is 3.2% less than in October 1993.[24]

Employees, farmers, craftsmen *et al.*, whose workplace or facilities have been totally or partially damaged in the war, belong to a special category of the unemployed who are entitled to pecuniary compensation.[25] In September 1994, according to the mentioned *Social Policy Report*, there were 35,000 beneficiaries of that compensation.[26]

B. Employment and Job Security

1. Employment

1. It has to be mentioned again that employment and job security are determined by previous regulations, primarily by the Law on Basic Employment Rights of 1989[27] and the Law on Labour Relations of 1990.[28] Its final draft of 1992 is the subject of our consideration.

---

24.   *See*: Employment Annals *op. cit.*, IX–X, pp. 16 and 17; *Monthly Statistical Bulletin of the Employment Agency, op. cit.*, p. 1 and similar.
25.   It is regulated by the Act on ensuring funds and realizing the rights and ways of paying minimal salaries and compensation to natural and legal persons of 1993 ('Zakon o osiguranju sredstava, ostvarivanju prava i naèinu isplate minimalnih plaæa i naknada odredenim fizièkim i pravnim osobama'), *Official Gazette* No. 109/93.
26.   *Social Policy Report, op. cit.*, p. 33 and similar.
27.   The Law was published in the *Official Gazette* of the SFRY No. 60/89 and 42/90. It has been taken over by the Croatian legislation with the law on applying federal laws on employment and employment procedure which are, in the Republic of Croatia, applied as state laws (*Official Gazette* No. 34/91, 5/93 - final draft, and 26/93).
28.   The law was first published in the *Official Gazette* No. 19/90 and it was then amended and published in the final draft in the *Official Gazette* No. 25/92. Its latest amendments were published in the *Official Gazette* No. 26/93.

2. Employment, and not a work contract or, to be more precise, an employment agreement, is the central institute of both the previous and the present labour legislation. It is regulated by law, by collective agreement, and by a work contract in the private sector. In the social (now public) sector, it is regulated by law and by general acts, and, after the passage of the Constitution, by collective agreement.

In the private sector, according to labour legislation currently in effect, the parties in the labour relations or the work contract are the employer and the employee. According to the labour law, the employer is a natural person who does a craft, is engaged in a professional activity, owns a farm, or belongs to a narrow circle of private and legal persons, representatives of foreign companies or diplomatic or consular offices. The name 'employer' usually refers to a 'small' employer (Article 1). The work contract determines the work post, the starting day of work, the duration of employment, the trial period, the salary and compensations, the working hours, the breaks, the period of notice, and other rights and obligations of employees and of employers' organizations (Article 2).

In the social sector, according to the Law on Labour Relations, the employment is initiated by decision regarding the selection of a candidate who applied for the public competition. The decision is made by the management body of the company, institution, bank, insurance company, and so on, having a common name 'organization', which according to that law is not an employer but performs its role. With an organization, which used to be exclusively an organization of the public sector, there was a tendency to express employment as 'a relationship of co-operation among workers'. Workers appear at the same time in the capacity of workers and self-managers: a 'mutual relationship of workers in associated labour.

3. The Constitution of the Republic of Croatia extends the notion of an employer and of a collective agreement to the public sector as well (Articles 59 and 56). With the guarantee of plural ownership (Article 48), it abolishes the monopoly of social ownership. With the provision according to which the employed may have the legal rights to participation in decision making (Article 55), the workers' self-management was abolished. The Constitution has established the basis for a unified and contemporary employment in both the private and public sector and has thus directly broadened the application of the work contract. However, the Law on Employment still distinguishes an employer from an organization. It has been introduced, as we have seen, into other laws from the field of dependent work. The other party in the employment procedure is called a worker. However, the constitutional term 'employee' is used more and more (in Croatian language: *zaposleni* or even *zaposlenik*). Many different terms are used and there is a tendency to substitute the general term 'worker' (in Croatian: *radnik*).

4. As opposed to employment constituting a legal relationship, there is the so called 'black labour,' or illegal form of working for another person. Some trade unions estimate that more than 250,000 workers do such work and that such an 'illegal labour market' alleviates the problem of unemployment.[29]

On the other hand, black labour, which is generally found in the private sector, is becoming a real economic and social problem, as we can see from the *Social Policy Report*.[30] It is considered to be a consequence of the economic recession, restructuring

29.   Zeljko Potoènjak, *op. cit.,* p. 9.
30.   *Social Policy Report, op. cit.,* pp. 35–37.

of the economy, the social conditions, the struggle for an existential minimum, social policy, the inefficient system of work supervision, and so on. Corrective measures have included requiring a change in the system of social security financing, establishing actual working costs, and gathering data on all important factors contributing to the prevalence of black labour.

The main reasons for black labour on the part of employees are poverty and mass unemployment. In order to assure the basic means for living, the employee pushes out of his mind all the risks that may come about from such work (illness, injury at work) and forgets the fact that he can register with the Employment Service and realize, under certain conditions, the right to health insurance. There is obviously a lack of good organization and efficient control in that area.

Black labour is supported by the employer not simply because labour controls are insufficient, but also because legal labour has a very high price, due to heavy contributions for retirement and disability insurance. They are paid at the rate of 13.5% of the salary, (and 13,5% to the salary) and that is why, together with different taxes, surtaxes and other levies, the ratio between net and gross salary is 1 to 2.6.[31]

2. *Job Safety*

1. Job safety was in the previous Constitution of 1974[32] guaranteed by the following provision: 'A worker may lose his job against his will only under the conditions and procedures stipulated by law' (Article 159). The job safety was such that there was practically no way of giving the worker a notice of termination of employment. It was even expressly determined that it could not be done due to technological advancements that had resulted in surplus manpower. The Croatian Constitution does not contain such provisions, but rather stipulates what is reasonable and acceptable.

Later this solution was seen as inappropriate and according to the two laws mentioned above, it is possible to give a notice of termination of employment to one or more workers because of technological, organizational and economic reasons. However, there are very strict conditions for giving such a notice on the above grounds. A previous notification about the surplus manpower is necessary. It is also necessary for the employer to undertake measures attempting to avoid the termination of employment (transferring to another employer, retraining, upgrading). A special programme of workers' employment is required, and trade unions have to participate in it. If these measures cannot guarantee that workers will not be dismissed, a notice of the termination of employment is possible. It is not legally in effect until 4 months have elapsed from the adoption of the programme, and workers have the right, depending on their years of service and age, to a termination notice lasting from 4 to 6 months (Articles 20–26, and others, of the Law on Labour Relations).

In the period from 1987 to 1993, partly because of the application of these provisions, there was a termination of employment in the case of 390,000 workers (not including the army and the police), mostly in economic (361,000) and much less in social activities.[33]

2. Employment termination is expensive, unreliable and long-lasting. The economic transformation, together with the privatization of public enterprises, had a very

---

31.   Zeljko Potočnjak, *op. cit.*, p. 9.
32.   *Official Gazette* of SFRY, No. 9/74, 38/81, 70/88.
33.   *See*: Statistical Annals, *op. cit.*, p. 100; *Monthly Statistical Bulletin, op. cit.*, p. 64.

negative impact on job security. Legislation made this possible by introducing regulations on bankruptcy and liquidation. These regulations allow for termination of employment without notice. Later, the termination period of one month was introduced.[34]

During the period from 1990 to 1993, 250,000–300,000 workers lost their jobs due to bankruptcy or liquidation. According to the official data, that number is significantly smaller. At the end of October 1994, there were 33,326 people (or 13.6%) among the unemployed who ended up in that situation because their enterprise ceased to operate or because of their employers' bankruptcy. That number for 1994 was down 25% from the same month in 1993.[35]

A decrease in unemployment from bankruptcy and liquidation was the result of an awareness that such an economic stabilization and privatization create tensions and encourage strikes among workers. Also, with such massive termination of employment, or firing the surplus manpower, the burden of stabilization and privatization was passed to a large extent onto the state or, more precisely, on the Employment Service Funds.

C.   Collective Negotiation and Collective Agreements

1. The Constitution of the SFRY (1974) laid down the obligation of a collective agreement in the private sector. With such a contract, workers were guaranteed the right to the resources to satisfy their personal and common needs, as well as other rights established by law (Amendment XXI). The Law on Basic Rights Originating from Employment (*Zakon o ornovnim pravima iz radnih odnosa*) and the original (not amended) Law on Labour Relations (*Zakon o radnim odnosima*) also required the making of a collective agreement in both the private and the public sector. The content of such an agreement was also, for the most part, determined by the law. One party to the agreement was the Chamber of Economy. It used to be a compulsory association of the public, i.e., state, companies.

The other contractual party was the Trade Union, in which, according to the Constitution, 'workers were voluntarily organized as members'. According to the Constitution of 1974, it represented the 'largest organization of the working class fighting,' among other things, 'for the accomplishment of socialist self-management relations and for a self-management co-ordination of individual, common and general social interests,' (VIII/4). The Trade Union was a social and political organization whose leading ideological and political force was the League of Communists. The existence of a real collective negotiation was not possible between such contractual parties (especially not such a Trade Union), not only because of its compulsory character, but also because their possible diverse interests had to be reconciled.

---

34.   *See*: 'Zakon o izmjenama i dopunama zakona o prisilnoj nagodbi, steèaju, likvidaciji' ('Law on Amendments to the Law on Forced Settlement, Bankruptcy and Liquidation'), *(Official Gazette* No. 9/94).

35.   For the change in the number of unemployed persons because their enterprise ceased to operate, *see*: The Employment Agency Annals, *op. cit.*, pp. 16 and 17; *Monthly Statistical Bulletin, op. cit.*, p. 1.

2. The Constitution of the Republic of Croatia lays down that the right of the employees and their family members to social security and social insurance is regulated by law and by collective agreement (Article 45). Although 'social security' may mean different things, we can conclude from the provision that it encompasses some issues from the field of dependent labour: for example, the lowest salary.

This type of collective agreement is also used in both private and public sector. As for the parties to it, the Constitution lays down that all the employees and employers have the right, in order to protect their economic and social interests, to organize trade unions and freely join them or resign from them (Article 59). Each party has its interests and they can either be mutual, or entirely different. The parties are not obliged to reconcile them. We thus have a basis for the existence of real collective negotiation and collective agreements.

The Law on Labour Relations, in its final draft, defines the collective agreement in a very modern way (Articles 92–98). It also defines the concept of the agreement. With such an agreement, the draft states that employers and their associations on the one hand, and trade unions and the representatives of employees on the other hand, agree on their mutual rights and duties based on labour and labour relations (Article 92). The association of organizations or employers in the field of economy always used to be the Chamber of Economy (*Gospodarska komora*). The law explicitly states that throughout the Republic of Croatia, general collective agreements are made between the Croatian Chamber of Economy and Trade Unions or their units.[36]

The Chamber of Economy always used to be, and it still is, an organization (association) in which all public companies compulsorily become members. It is not independent but is rather a quasi-state organization. This problem is in the process of being solved. According to the proposal of the 'National Collective Agreement', there is a recommendation that instead of the present Chamber of Economy a collective agreement should be made, in the whole territory of Croatia, by the Croatian Association of Employers, which was established in 1993. It is an independent and voluntary organization of private employers. This problem does not exist in the public sector because the government, or some other state organ, signs the collective agreement in the name of the employer.

Today the trade union, being the other party to the collective agreement, is really a voluntary and independent association of employees. Its independence will be even stronger when it becomes economically strong and when it connects itself and joins the international trade unions. The fact that there are more trade unions in Croatia proves its voluntary character. The largest union is the *Savez samostalnih sindikata Hrvatske* (The League of Independent Trade Unions of Croatia) with more than 700,000 members and a few dozens of autonomous trade unions.

---

36.   In 1990, a 'General Collective Agreement' was made between these two parties and it ceased to be valid (*Official Gazette* No. 35/90).

It has to be mentioned here that there are a lot of experiences in making collective agreements in Croatia. Beside the already mentioned general collective agreement in the field of economy and the general collective agreement in the public sector[37] that ceased to be valid, there are many valid collective agreements for various fields and activities.[38] It is also very important to mention that the contents of these agreements are (*mutatis mutandis*) identical or very similar. They usually contain almost the same provisions on where to place workers, working hours, health care and job security, breaks and holidays, salaries and compensations, conditions for the work of trade unions, explanation and application of the collective agreement, settlement of disputes, amendments to the collective agreement, and so on.[39] This only proves that a real collective negotiation has not fully developed yet and neither has the labour market.

D. Strike

1. In the former SFRY and according to the Constitutional Amendment XXVII of 1981, workers had the right to strike under the conditions laid down by federal law. Much earlier, in the beginning of 1958 (in particular at the time of the break down of the former state) there were sporadic strikes.

At first, the employees and particularly the strike leaders were punished for disturbing the public peace. Later, court policy considered striking to be a violation of the working discipline or a failure to meet personal work duties which, under most conditions, led to the termination of the employment.

2. The Constitution of the Republic of Croatia guarantees the right to strike. In the armed forces, the police, the state administration and public services, the right to strike may be limited according to some laws (Article 60). However, strike is not yet regulated by law; only some provisions are contained in the collective agreements.

The collective agreement for the trade industry, as well as some other contracts, lay down that trade unions will refrain from a strike if all its contractual provisions are fulfilled in an orderly manner with respect to all the workers involved in the agreement. For all other issues, not regulated by the agreement or to be regulated by another collective agreement, the trade union will reserve the right to strike. The obligation for social peace is valid until the new collective agreements are made. However, a strike of solidarity is permitted. The trade union applies the union strike rules for the organization and the execution of a strike. When the obligations agreed upon in the collective agreement have not been fulfilled, a strike is organized and the costs of the strike will be borne by the company or the employer.

---

37. 'Opæi kolektivni ugovor za javne djelatnosti i javna poduæeca' ('General Collective Agreement for Public Activities and Public Companies') of 1992, *(Official Gazette* No. 66/92).
38. *See* 'Kolektivni ugovor za grafièko-preradivaèku i novinskonakladnièku djelatnost' ('Collective Agreement of Graphic and Newspaper Publishing Industry') of 1992, *(Official Gazette* No. 86/92); 'Kolektivni ugovor teksitlne i odjevne, koarsko-preradivaèke i gumarske industrije Hrvatske' ('Collective Agreement of Textile and Garment Industry and Rubber Industry of Croatia') of 1992, *(Official Gazette* No. 86/92).
39. *See* e.g. 'Kolektivni ugovor za djelatnost trgovine' ('Collective Agreement for Trade') of 1993, *(Official Gazette* No. 103/93).

3. Strikes, but not lock-outs, are very common in Croatia. However, they are much more common in commercial than in non-profit activities (such as schools and hospitals). At the beginning of the last school year (1994–1995), a strike occurred in primary and secondary schools to protect teachers' and professors' low salaries. The strike lasted for about ten days. Then, a compulsory work order was issued, and the teachers stopped the strike.

Not very long ago (16 December 1994), there was a general warning strike in the entire economy of Croatia. It lasted for two hours. The reason for the strike was the low salaries and the demand for a bonus of one month's salary for Christmas. The trade unions, with some differences in numbers, claimed that 70–85% of their members joined the strike.[40]

A further example is the strike of the railway workers, employed by the public enterprise '*Hrvatske zeljeznice*' (The Croatian Railways). It first included only the domestic trains but then it extended to the international ones travelling across the Croatian borders. Reasons for the walk out, according to the strikers, were their missing salary for November, low salaries and lack of safety of railroad traffic. According to the Government members, the strike caused a direct damage of 1.5 million Kn per day to the Croatian economy. After fifteen days on strike and a number of unsuccessful negotiations, a compulsory work order was issued (22 December 1994) with the explanation that the strike was jeopardizing the interests of the national economy and the defence of a country at war. However, the strike continued and on 27 December 1994, after compromise on both sides, an agreement about cessation of the strike was reached between the Management Board of the Croatian Railways and the Trade Union Federation of the Croatian Railways. The very next day, the compulsory work order was cancelled, so it had never been applied at all.[41] The strike showed that the Government respects the guaranteed right to strike, in spite of the fact that it had jeopardized the interests of the national economy in a time of war.

E.   Settlement of Individual and Collective Labour Disputes

1. In the former SFRY, individual labour disputes were settled within the work organization and before the court. There existed special labour courts, called courts of associated labour (*Sudovi udruzenog rada*).

The settlement of collective labour disputes was not institutionalized. Disputes were settled from case to case, usually by reconciliation, mediation or arbitration.

2. Today in Croatia, individual and collective disputes are solved outside and before the court. Individual disputes are settled before regular courts according to the rules of a civil procedure.

The Law on Labour Relations and collective agreement contain provisions on extra-judicial settlement of individual and collective disputes. The referenced Law lays down that the employee and the organization, or the employer, may agree on leaving the decision to an arbitrator or an arbitration tribunal when the dispute is over the right or duty resulting from employment. This decision is then final and has the power of an executive document. Pursuant to the collective agreement and according to the same

---

40.   The newspaper 'Veèernji list' of 17 December 1994.
41.   The newspaper 'Veèernji list' of 17, 22 and 28 December 1994.

law, a permanent arbitration can be established. Based on the agreement of the parties to the dispute, the arbitration makes awards regarding the individual rights and duties resulting from the employment.

3. According to all the valid collective agreements, collective labour disputes are settled in the same way. We shall give an example from the already mentioned Collective Agreement for the trade industry.

Pursuant to that agreement regarding the settlement of disputes between the contracting parties, which could not be settled by mutual negotiations, a process of reconciliation is to be initiated. It is done upon the written initiative of one of the contracting parties. The procedure cannot be carried out if one of the parties does not accept the proposal for reconciliation. The reconciliation commission, composed of the president and four members, will give a written proposal for the settlement. The reconciliation is successful if both parties have acceded to it. The settlement has the power of an extra-judicial settlement.

If neither the negotiation nor the reconciliation succeeds, the contractual parties submit their case to an arbitration tribunal of three arbitrators. The arbitration tribunal determines the violation of the collective agreement provisions and makes awards with regard to violations.

4. According to the same collective agreement, each contractual party has the right to propose a change or an amendment to the collective agreement. If the parties do not agree on these changes and amendments, or do not reach settlement through reconciliation, the decision is left with the arbitration tribunal. Either of the parties may terminate the collective agreement upon a previous written notice, at least three months before the date of termination. It also has the right to initiate a new collective agreement.

IV.   INSTEAD OF A CONCLUSION

1. Croatia belongs to the category of developing countries. It is undergoing a transition from a planned to a market economy. All this is accompanied by a complex and very difficult economic, social, political and war conditions. Very important is the fact that the largest part of the economy is in the public (state-) ownership and that the private sector is only about to be created through the process of privatization of public enterprises.

Economic transition is taking place in these conditions unfavourable to a market economy development. First of all, this course is pursued because of a faster economic development based on the market conditions. However, it is, as we have seen, accompanied by a significant decrease of the living standard and extensive unemployment.

It is understandable that the economy must rid itself of the vestiges of socialism or communism from the previous regime, particularly in connection with the surplus of employees. It should not, however, be done immediately and to their disadvantage, attacking the social welfare and social security funds. Actually, there is a transfer of social problems from the economy to the social services, instead of solving the problems in this transitional phase slowly and gradually in both the economic and social sphere (and separating them completely in the future). Conversely, there is a danger that citizens, when having to make political decisions (e.g., when voting) may choose in favour of a low level of material security rather than a broad democracy.

2. A large number of people in Croatia live on the edge of poverty; many of them are unemployed. Poverty and mass unemployment make it possible for the employer – because he is economically and socially more powerful – to impose unfavourable working conditions (low salaries, longer working hours, insufficient health protection, safety at work, and so on). In such unfavourable working conditions, it is the duty of the public authority to offer a greater protection for employees, while not harming or discouraging, at the same time, entrepreneurship and the market. Particularly in the form of mass lay-offs, neo-liberalism in the area of labour law may appear, because of an intemperate accumulation of wealth. Neo-liberalism agrees with the so-called free economy but not with a market and social oriented one that Croatia seems to be striving to achieve.

3. In every labour law norm, speaking philosophically, there is a condensed reality, not only of a single moment, but of the present time and the foreseeable future. The labour legislation of Croatia has to be adjusted to its reality. It is in principle unacceptable to simply adopt foreign labour legislation partially or totally from countries that are not at the same or similar level of economic development and that have different traditions and cultures. In a worst-case scenario, a disharmony between labour law and reality may occur and thus also make the application of the law impossible.

Labour Law and Industrial Relations in the Czech Republic

Miroslav Belina

I. INTRODUCTION

The political changes that took place in the former Czechoslovakia in late 1989, and the ensuing socio-economic changes, have required conceptual changes in the sphere of labour law. The decisive moments for these changes have been, above all the transformation of the command economy to a market economy, the transition to political and economic pluralism, the passage from a proclaimed democracy to a real democracy, and a new quality of international economic co-operation and integration. Labour law is closely bound to economic and social changes. It is, on the one hand, determined by economic development, while, on the other hand, it itself influences future developments. The socio-economic changes in the former Czechoslovakia (and, since 1993, in the Czech Republic) can therefore hardly be imagined without radical changes in labour law. The Czech Republic is one of the two successor states of the former Czech and Slovak Federal Republic, which is reflected in the fact that, on the basis of constitutional Act No. 4/1993 Coll., dealing with measures connected with the split of the Czech and Slovak Federal Republic, constitutional laws and other legal regulations of the Czech and Slovak Federal Republic, valid on the day of its split, remain in force on the territory of the Czech Republic.

II. FUNDAMENTAL LEGISLATIVE CHANGES IN THE SPHERE OF LABOUR LAW AND INDUSTRIAL RELATIONS

1. State of Labour Legislation before 1989

After February 1948, when the Communist regime seized power, the characteristic feature of labour legislation was that regulations were usually uniform for all employees. The process of unification in labour law regulations was considered a sign of the equal position of all members of society in relation to the means of production. The process of unification came to a head with the publication of the Labour Code in 1965. The typical features of the legal regulation were:
- uniformity;
- complexity and completeness;
- cogency;
- independence.

a. Uniformity of Legal Regulation

In 1965, the Labour Code introduced a uniform legal regulation between employees and all employers. Differentiation in legal regulation was allowed only where special conditions of labour required it (for example leading officials, domestic labour, and so on). The development was similar to that in all countries of the so-called socialist camp. In all of these countries the economic and social system, including the corresponding legal regulation of labour relations, led not only to unification and elimination of most preferences in labour law, but especially to levelling the working conditions and wages, leading to lack of stimulus to work, to loss of activity and initiative, and to lagging behind in the sphere of science and technology.

b. Complexity of Legal Regulation

The Labour Code regulated the sphere of labour law more or less comprehensively. Laws were created, consisting of many scattered, fractional, sometimes not easily accessible regulations, which conformed with the socio-economic context of that time.

c. Cogency of Legal Regulation

Labour law regulation contained for the most part compulsory norms allowing no exceptions for the benefit of, or to the disadvantage of, the parties to labour law. As a consequence, contractual freedom was suppressed, because a contract of employment had a very limited scope for contractual stipulations. The *de facto* liquidation of collective labour law and collective bargaining also took place, because the scope for possible regulation with collective agreements was minimized by labour legislation, and collective agreements lost their fundamental importance. Their role became formal to a considerable extent. Notwithstanding the original endeavour to unify and simplify legal regulation, this cogency led to a growing number and range of normative acts. Detailed directive forms of management led to the excessive augmentation and extension of regulations of lower legal power (orders and decrees of central bodies of state administration). The reason for augmentation of labour law regulations was above all the fact that the forms of management did not make it possible to use other means adequately when managing working processes. Thus there was an obvious endeavour to issue labour law regulations that were as detailed as possible, regardless of whether they concerned fundamental or secondary issues. Consequently, the scope for employees' initiative narrowed constantly and solutions according to local conditions were not possible. Observance of legal provisions was often only formal and thus the effectiveness of the law was weakened.

d. Independence of Legal Regulation

The Labour Code also deals with general issues of legal regulation: for example, legal subjectivity, legal acts, invalidity, transition of rights and obligations from labour law relations, and definition and limitations of time. Consequently, labour law was made completely independent of civil law, but at the same time further weakening of contractual freedom in labour law took place.

2. Changes in Labour Law Legislation since 1989

One of the first changes from the beginning of 1990 was the regulation of a plurality of trade union organizations, because until 1989 there existed only one official trade union in the former Czechoslovakia (which was dissolved after the November revolution in 1989). The new legal regulation enabled freedom of trade union association.

In 1991, quite new regulations in the sphere of employment (*cf.* Chapter II) and collective bargaining (*cf.* Chapter III) were adopted. These new regulations took into consideration the transition to a market economy. They were prepared in compliance with international norms in this sphere and with the awareness of making legal regulation compatible with the legal regulation of other European countries (especially those of the European Union).

On the other hand, in the sphere of individual labour law the existing Labour Code remains influenced by many amendments. The first fundamental amendment of the Labour Code after the November revolution was carried out in early 1991 with Act No. 3/1991 Coll., simultaneously with the adoption of new regulations in the sphere of employment and collective bargaining. The latest fundamental amendment of the Labour Code took place in the middle of 1994 (Act No. 74/1994 Coll.).

The most important material change in the sphere of individual labour law has been a gradual liberalization of the cogency of the Labour Code. Another fundamental change follows from the changes in the economic system. The legal order in the former Czechoslovakia before 1989 in fact excluded private enterprise through many nationalizing, planning, and other administrative acts; almost all businesses ceased to exist in the late 1950s. The general social climate was also against private enterprises. A fundamental change was introduced only by Act No. 105/1990 Coll., dealing with private enterprise by citizens, and legal regulation enabling the establishment of partnerships. Thus the preconditions were created for the entry of private entrepreneurs into economic life. However, certain differences have survived in the regulation of labour law, depending on whether an employer is a legal entity or an individual. The last differences concerning employers as individuals versus employers as legal entities were cancelled only by the latest amendment of the Labour Code in 1994.

3. Expected Tendencies in Legislative Development

A new conception of legal regulation of labour law relations is now being elaborated and discussed by the Government of the Czech Republic. In 1995, we can expect a start to be made on legislative work to prepare new labour law regulation, which will completely replace the Labour Code of 1966. The objective should be the creation of a modern labour law totally compatible with European Union legislation. The new law should extend the contractual freedom of parties of employment, and for that purpose it should further reduce the extent of compulsory provisions and so strengthen the importance both of contracts of employment and of collective agreements.

III.   PROVISION OF EMPLOYMENT

A.   Policy on Provision of Employment

Employment Act No. 1/1991 Coll. abolished the legal regulation of 1958, which proceeded from directive regulation of employment. The obligatory regulation of employment and the labour force secured full employment, but it failed to strengthen the national economy. In fact, there was no unemployment in the former socialist system. The present law proceeds from the focus of the state on an active employment policy and the creation of a labour market as part of the process of shaping the whole market economy. Administrative instruments of management of employment, from which the previous system of providing employment proceeded, are being replaced by economic instruments, especially by the tax and subsidy policy (above all, support for creation of new jobs).

The administrative instruments for providing employment are left to the state practically only in cases where provision of jobs for disabled citizens is concerned. Even with regard to the principles of the International Pact on Economic, Social and Cultural Rights of 16 December 1966, it was necessary to preserve the possibility of state intervention in labour law in the case of citizens who, due to their state of health, have difficulty in obtaining and keeping employment. For this category of citizens, the law envisages a combination of economic and administrative instruments for providing employment.

The creation of a market mechanism is conditioned by extensive structural changes requiring qualitatively new mobility of the labour force (between regions, between occupations, and so on) and also better qualified employees. On the other hand, this process also implies increased requirements for dealing with the social consequences resulting from the implementation of restructuring programmes and other structural changes, especially those resulting from temporary structural unemployment. In order to deal with these consequences, programmes have been implemented for the employment of redundant employees and for the creation of suitable jobs. Support has been given to the creation of a system of retraining, and to entrepreneurial activity.

The state's employment policy, aimed at reaching a balance between supply and demand for the work force, productive use of labour, and securing the right of citizens to work, is implemented by the Ministry of Labour and Social Affairs, and by the labour offices. When implementing the state's employment policy, the Ministry of Labour and Social Affairs puts forward measures aimed at influencing the demand for labour and creating a balance between the nation wide labour supply and the demand for labour. It also regulates the employment of foreign workers on the territory of the Czech Republic and Czech citizens working abroad. Labour offices play an important role in providing full productive employment in individual places. They act as employment mediators and keep records of vacancies, applicants for jobs and their financial support, and when appropriate, they also keep records of persons expressing interest in employment. They provide a stimulus for creating socially useful or socially beneficial employment, and participate in financing it. Labour offices can cover the costs of creating new employment for an applicant who wishes to set up in a gainful self-employed occupation. In order to reach harmony between the supply of qualified labour force and the demand for its services, labour offices provide retraining of applicants for employment within the framework of state retraining programmes. After all active means of employment provision have been exhausted, the labour offices deal with unemployment benefits for those seeking employment. It should be pointed out that the rate of unemployment in the Czech Republic is low, the nation wide average being about 3% in 1993–1994.

B.   The Citizen's Right to Work

Under the law as it stands in the Czech Republic, the right to work involves the right of citizens, who wish and are able to work and who really are applying for a job:
a. to mediation in finding suitable employment;
b. to retraining as is necessary for employment;
c. to unemployment benefits before entering a job, and in the case of the loss of a job.

A very important issue in the right of citizens to work is the interpretation of the expression 'suitable employment'. The Employment Act defines suitable employment as employment corresponding to the citizen's state of health with regard to his or her age, qualifications and abilities, duration of previous employment, and possibility of accommodation. As said above, labour offices mediate free of charge in finding suitable employment for citizens. In order to fulfil their function, labour offices deal with providing employment and ensuring that employers fulfil their obligations. An employer is above all obliged to notify the respective regional labour office of its vacancies and to submit job descriptions and further important data within five days of closing or opening up a job. Should an employer intend to implement structural changes, organizational or rationalization measures as a consequence of which employees will be made redundant, his duty is to notify the respective labour office and the respective trade union body in the enterprise within the prescribed time, usually three months before the implementation.

C.   Providing Employment for Special Categories of Citizens

The social position of some categories of citizens requires that the state provide them with more intensive guarantees of their right to work. As a rule, this concerns citizens who need to be assisted and protected by society in the interest of their engagement in labour activity. When mediating jobs, labour offices have an obligation to devote greater attention to those applicants who need it due to their state of health, age, maternity, or other serious reasons. To this effect, citizens with reduced working ability occupy a special status. Groups with a special position are:
a. juveniles who, after completing compulsory school attendance, do not continue with further preparation for employment;
b. secondary school leavers and university graduates on their first entry into the labour market;
c. pregnant women, citizens taking care of children up to the age of 15 years or providing special care for family members with long-term illnesses;
d. applicants for employment over 50 years of age and those made redundant as a consequence of structural changes, organizational or rationalization measures implemented on the basis of programmes implemented by the government and the central bodies;
e. applicants who have been unsuccessful in their search for employment for more than six months;

f. citizens requiring special care;
g. socially unadapted citizens.

If necessary, the labour office will require employers to select jobs that are suitable for applicants in the above-mentioned categories. The labour office will then recommend these citizens to the employers for the suitable jobs. However, it should be added that this is not a binding recommendation, and the labour office has no administrative instruments for providing employment for such citizens.

A special category consists of people with disabilities, i.e. persons having a considerably reduced possibility of employment or preparation for employment due to long-term ill-health; beneficiaries of pensions conditional on ill-health also belong to this category, if their remaining ability to work makes employment or preparation for employment possible. Employers have special obligations towards citizens with disabilities. For example, they have to reserve jobs especially suitable for citizens with disabilities, to carry out preparation for employment of citizens with reduced working ability, and to devote special care to upgrading their qualifications during their employment. The possibility of using administrative instruments to help to find employment for citizens with disabilities is preserved here for only one category of citizens. An employer is obliged to employ a worker with disabilities, if he or she has been recommended for employment in a vacant post by the labour office, up to an obligatory percentage of the company's total labour force. The employer is also obliged to employ only disabled workers for vacancies reserved for people with disabilities, if it is laid down by a regional labour office. Besides administrative instruments, employers are provided with tax incentives for employing citizens with disabilities.

D. Financial Support for Applicants for Employment

When the labour office is not able to provide a suitable job for a citizen, the citizen has the right to retraining as is necessary for his or her employment.

The labour office is obliged to register citizens as 'applicants for employment' who are not in employment or in a similar status, and who are not pursuing a gainful self-employment, and who apply for support in finding a suitable employment on the basis of a written application. Besides applicants for employment, the relevant paragraph (§ 4 Clause 2 of Act No. 9/1991 Coll.) distinguishes persons interested in employment, i.e. citizens who, unlike an applicant for employment, are in employment or in a similar status, or who have a gainful self-employment, but who are at the same time interested in other employment. Naturally, applicants for employment have a right to financial support, whereas employed persons interested in new employment do not.

Applicants for employment who were not offered a suitable job nor provided with the possibility of retraining for a new job suitable for them within seven calendar days after the day of submitting an application, will be provided with financial support. Financial support is provided from the date of the application, provided the set conditions have been fulfilled. An exception is when a citizen applies for support in finding employment within a maximum of three working days after the date of termination of employment. In such a case, financial support will be provided from the day following the day of the termination of the employment.

Naturally, an applicant for employment has not only rights, but also certain obligations. He or she is, above all, obliged to provide the labour office with the necessary co-operation in seeking for employment, when requested, and to follow the instructions. He or she is further obliged to provide the labour office with evidence of factual information required for granting financial support.

When granting financial support to applicants for employment, a waiting time requirement has been set down, which protects the allowance from misuse. This measure affects only applicants who meet the condition of having their preceding employment totalling at least 12 months in the last three years before the submission of the application for support. The law regulates compensatory periods to be considered as equivalent to employment for these purposes.

Some cases are set down where financial support is not granted to an applicant. In principle this concerns two types of situation. The first group are cases where the applicant is in receipt of other allowances (for example he or she fulfils conditions for entitlement to an old-age or disability pension, or is in receipt of money allowances for health insurance in compensation for lost wages) or if he is in military service, civilian service, or in prison. An applicant for employment who was granted severance pay (or compensation) is provided with financial support only after the elapse of time corresponding to the amount of granted severance pay (or compensation). The second group consists of cases where the applicant either refuses entry to employment (i.e. without serious personal or family reasons, he refuses to take a suitable job or to enter retraining for a suitable new job, or where a citizen deliberately thwarts co-operation with the labour office while seeking employment), or he himself terminated employment repeatedly in the last six months without due cause, or his employment was terminated repeatedly due to unsatisfactory work performance or an infringement of terms of employment.

E.   Financial Support is not paid Abroad

The time limit for the provision of the financial support is maximum six months, with the exception of cases where the labour office provides retraining for an applicant, and where financial support is provided only until the termination of the retraining. If no employment is secured for an applicant after the time limit for the provision of the financial support, he or she will be supported financially from the social welfare funds.

An applicant is entitled to financial support for the period of the first three months in the amount of 60% of the net monthly salary of his or her last employment. For a further period of three months financial support amounts to 50% of the above-mentioned salary. In the case of retraining, the applicant is entitled to financial support of 70% of the average monthly net wages until the termination of the retraining. This means that, with the exception of retraining, financial support is provided for a maximum of six months. For an applicant who has not been in employment yet, financial support is set at the above-mentioned percentage of the official salary rate set by the social security (at present, the minimum monthly salary for employees remunerated monthly). The maximum amount of financial support is an amount corresponding to 1.5 times the above-mentioned official set salary, and in the case of retraining 1.8 times the above-mentioned official set salary. If the applicant is a person with reduced working ability he or she will receive an increased sum for personal subsistence in addition to financial support under the conditions set down by the law.

IV. COLLECTIVE LABOUR LAW

As it was pointed out in the introduction, collective labour law was suppressed in the period of the so-called socialist system. Detailed regulation existed in the whole sphere of labour law, with legal norms giving minimal scope for individual or collective contractual stipulations. Thus little room existed for collective agreements to regulate conditions of labour and wage. Collective agreements were concluded, but these were little more than formalities. Collective agreements in the form known in market economies were in fact eliminated in the socialist system. On the other hand, the law acknowledged many rights and authorizations of trade unions, both joint decision making with the employer and the right to control the employer from the point of view of adherence to labour law regulations, including regulations concerning labour safety and protection of health at work. However we must bear in mind that there was only one official trade union, and it exercised its rights in many cases only formally.

A. Participation of Employees in Management

Shortly after the November revolution in 1989, right at the beginning of 1990, the only official trade union was abolished and a plurality of trade unions was introduced. The concept of the authority of the only official trade union was so broad in the preceding system that if this authority had passed fully to the newly established trade unions and had been exercised consistently, it would have restricted employers too much in the management of their firms. For this reason, the rights of trade unions were considerably reduced in Labour Code amendment No. 3/1991 Coll., especially regarding the authorization to co-decide some issues together with the employer. Most importantly, this amendment abolished the provision under which the previous agreement of the trade union was needed for the unilateral termination of the employment by the employer (i.e., notice and immediate termination of employment). Without the consent of the trade union the termination of employment was invalid. The requirement of trade union consent for the termination of employment was retained only in case of trade union officials at the workplace.

The present law in the Czech Republic in practice anchors a monopoly of trade unions (though it is a monopoly of democratic and pluralist trade unions today) in the participation in the management. Indeed, all authorizations are entrusted to trade unions by law. Here, the most important question from the point of view of future legal regulation concerns whether the powers of trade unions at the level of the workplace are to be left fully to trade unions, or whether they are to be at least partly transferred to a collective body of employees (works or enterprise boards, etc.). It is thinkable that in the future at least certain authorizations will be addressed directly to the collective body of employees and not to the trade unions at the workplace.

B. Collective Bargaining and Collective Agreements

A change in the social system has required a new regulation of collective bargaining, because in the socialist system, collective bargaining did not exist at all in the real sense of the expression. The formality of collective bargaining and collective agreements in the previous political system was reflected by the fact that the text of the normative contents of collective agreements was usually very brief, and was repeated in more or less the same form year after year. New legislation is included in Act No. 2/1991 Coll., on collective bargaining. In this act, the state as a legislator regulated the rules for collective bargaining and marked its boundaries. Act No. 2/1991 Coll. also regulates disputes arising during collective bargaining, including strikes and lock-outs. We will deal with disputes in the following chapter.

The Labour Code contains the material preconditions for collective bargaining between the trade union bodies and the employers (or their associations, as the case may be) with some influence from the state, and also provides the framework for collective agreements. The processes and technical issues of collective bargaining, and more detailed conditions for negotiating collective agreements (among other issues) are regulated by Act No. 2/1991 Coll., on collective bargaining. Regulation of the process of negotiating collective agreements is set down only to the extent that is necessary, leaving the greatest possible scope of contractual freedom between parties.

We distinguish two types of collective agreements in our country. These are, firstly, collective agreements of a higher degree, which are reached by trade union organizations with two or more employers, or by trade unions with an association or associations of employers. The second kind of collective agreements are collective agreements within a single workplace, negotiated between the respective trade union and employer on the level of the workplace or one of its organizational sections. Direct legal rights ensue for individual employees from the collective agreement of a higher instance. Consequently, it is not necessary to regulate such rights identically in workplace agreements. The relationship between obligations of a collective agreement of a higher instance and the obligations of a workplace collective agreement is regulated in the act on the principle of invalidity of the respective provisions of workplace collective agreements that are inconsistent with a collective agreement of a higher instance. The essential point is that if a workplace collective agreement regulates employees' rights in a less favourable way than it is regulated by a collective agreement of a higher instance, then the workplace collective agreement would be invalid in that part.

When setting down the contents of collective agreements, we must proceed not only from the act on collective bargaining, but from the Labour Code. The Labour Code still maintains the principle that wages and other labour law rights can be regulated in collective agreements only within the framework provided by the labour law. A valid act regulating wages (Act No. 1/1992 Coll.) proceeds from the fact that wages are regulated, above all, in the contract of employment or in the collective agreement, and it gives a maximum scope to collective bargaining on wage demands. While the scope for collective bargaining and collective agreements has been fundamentally extended in the past four years, we can expect this trend to continue in the years to come.

V.   LABOUR DISPUTES

A.   Individual Labour Disputes

Individual labour disputes (i.e., disputes between an employee and an employer concerning labour law requirements) were decided in the past by arbitration commissions, which were trade union bodies. Appeals against the decisions of the arbitration commissions were decided by general courts. Deciding labour disputes by trade union bodies, naturally became unacceptable after the change of social system and the abolition of these bodies. Arbitration commissions were abolished without being replaced, and individual labour disputes are now decided by general courts only. Such regulation cannot be considered very satisfactory, and experience, especially regarding the speed and economy of the solution of labour disputes, has been far from positive. In my opinion, it will be necessary to consider the introduction of special labour courts in the future, at least for hearing individual labour disputes in the first instance. These problems are at the agenda of expert discussion in the Czech Republic at present.

B.   Collective Labour Law Disputes

In the past system, collective labour law disputes were a rare occurrence. The respective law was very incomplete, and proceeded from the solution of disputes by conciliatory bodies consisting of representatives of employees and employers. Strikes and lock-outs were not legally regulated at all in the past. For these reasons, a new way of regulating such problems had to be prepared. This was done with Act No. 2/1991 Coll., on collective bargaining.

According to the present law in the Czech Republic, collective labour law disputes are disputes about the fulfilment of obligations of the collective agreement, from which no requirements of individual employees are derived. However, according to Act No. 2/1991 Coll., on individual bargaining, collective disputes are not only disputes on the fulfilment of the obligations of the collective agreement, from which no requirements of individual employees are derived, but also disputes about negotiating a collective agreement. Such a dispute involves no protection of a subjective right and no finding of a right. It is a matter of reaching agreement between parties as to the contents of the collective agreement.

Even though a dispute about negotiating a collective agreement is not a legal dispute from this point of view, due to its importance, it is regulated in detail by the act on collective bargaining. Solution of a dispute on negotiating a collective agreement is of fundamental importance for bringing about social conciliation between the employer (or the organization of employers), on the one hand, and employees, on the other.

1.   Disputes about the Collective Agreement

Disputes about the fulfilment of the obligations contained in the collective agreement from which no requirements of individual employees are derived are solved through mediators and arbitrators.

The parties can choose their mediator by themselves. If the parties do not agree on the mediator, he or she is appointed by the Ministry of Labour and Social Affairs. However, the ministry can appoint a mediator only on the recommendation of one of the parties from the list of mediators kept by the ministry. A mediator cannot decide a dispute; he only notifies the parties in writing of his suggestion for the solution of the dispute. It is then for the parties to the agreement to accept or not to accept the mediator's suggested solution.

The proceedings before a mediator are regarded to have broken down if the dispute is not solved within 30 days after the mediator was made acquainted with the subject of the dispute, and if the parties to the agreement did not agree on another deadline. The costs of bringing the proceedings before a mediator shall be covered by both parties, each party paying 50% of the costs.

If the proceedings before a mediator have broken down, new proceedings can take place before an arbitrator. Unlike proceedings before a mediator, the arbitrator does not suggest a solution to the parties, but has direct authority to decide the matter. Proceedings before an arbitrator are initiated by the acceptance of an application by the parties to the collective agreement for the dispute to be decided by an arbitrator. A mediator can be any person who has reached the age of majority and who is capable of legal acts (or a legal person) even if he or she is not registered in the ministry's list (naturally only if the parties to the collective agreement have agreed to this mediator and he or she agrees to execute the post). On the other hand, not only must an arbitrator be a person who has reached the age of majority and who is capable of legal acts, but he or she must also be registered in the list of arbitrators kept by the Ministry of Labour and Social Affairs.

Should the parties not agree on an arbitrator, the Ministry of Labour and Social Affairs appoints an arbitrator on the suggestion of any party to the contract. In this case the proceedings before the arbitrator are initiated by the delivery of a decision of the Ministry of Labour and Social Affairs to the arbitrator.

The arbitrator notifies the parties to the agreement in writing of his or her decision within 15 days after the initiation of the proceedings. Any party to the agreement can submit an application to annul the decision within 15 days after the delivery of the decision by the arbitrator. An application to annul the decision of an arbitrator is decided by the regional court in proceedings to review the decision of other bodies. The court will annul the arbitrator's decision on fulfilment of the obligations of the collective agreement if it is inconsistent with the legal regulations or the collective agreements. With any new decision, the arbitrator is bound by the legal opinion of the court. A binding decision of an arbitrator on the fulfilment of the obligations of the collective agreement is legally enforceable.

2. *Disputes about Negotiating a Collective Agreement*

Disputes about negotiating a collective agreement are solved through a mediator or an arbitrator, similarly as in the case of disputes about a collective agreement. However, unlike disputes about collective agreements, in disputes about reaching a collective agreement, a strike or a lock-out may be used as an extreme measure under conditions set down by the act on collective bargaining.

It is understandable that neither trade unions nor employers have a legal obligation to conclude a collective agreement, but on the other hand the state is interested in a conciliatory solution of social conflicts between employers and employees, and negotiation of a collective agreement is a sign of the achievement of social peace to this effect. For this reason the act on collective bargaining imposes upon the parties to the agreement the obligation to initiate negotiations for a new collective agreement not less than 60 days before the expiration of the existing collective agreement.

a. Proceedings before a Mediator

Should the parties themselves not have agreed on a collective agreement, the dispute on negotiating a collective agreement shall be resolved before a mediator. The parties can choose their own mediator. If the parties do not agree on a mediator, he or she shall be appointed by the Ministry of Labour and Social Affairs. However, the ministry can appoint a mediator in a dispute about negotiating a collective agreement only at the suggestion of one of the parties to the agreement, and from a list of mediators kept by the ministry. If the parties agree on a mediator, they can do so at any time. Nevertheless, a petition to the ministry to determine a mediator, in cases where no agreement has taken place between the parties to this effect, may be submitted not less than 60 days following the date of presentation of a written suggestion for negotiating such an agreement. For proceedings before a mediator in disputes on negotiating a collective agreement, the above-mentioned holds good as regard failure and costs of a proceeding, as mentioned in connection with disputes about a collective agreement.

b. Proceedings before an Arbitrator

In disputes on negotiating a collective agreement in the case of a breakdown in proceedings before a mediator, the parties to the agreement may also, after mutual consent, ask an arbitrator in writing for a decision in a dispute. However, unlike in the case of proceedings before a mediator and disputes about the collective agreement, here the proceedings cannot be initiated if the two parties do not agree on an arbitrator. So it is in principle impossible – with the exception of disputes on negotiating a collective agreement arising at a workplace where it is forbidden to strike – that the Ministry should appoint an arbitrator at the suggestion of any party in disputes on negotiating a collective agreement.

Similarly as in disputes about a concluded collective agreement, the arbitrator shall notify the parties to the agreement in writing of his or her decision within 15 days after the initiation of the proceedings. However, in disputes on negotiating the collective agreement, the arbitrator's decision replaces the wishes of the parties to the agreement, and the collective agreement is concluded on the delivery of the arbitrator's decision.

c. Strike in a Dispute on Negotiating the Collective Agreement

The act on collective bargaining proceeds from the principle that, in the case of the emergence of a dispute on the collective agreement, the dispute should be resolved through proceedings before a mediator. However, should no solution to a collective dispute on negotiating a collective agreement be reached through proceedings before a mediator, and should the parties to an agreement not apply for a solution of the dispute by an arbitrator, a strike or a lock-out may be announced as an extreme measure in the dispute.

It follows from the above that a strike may not be announced without previous proceedings before a mediator; such a strike would be unlawful (with the exception of a solidarity strike, to be mentioned below). Previous proceedings before a mediator are thus obligatory for the announcement of a strike. This is not, however, the case concerning proceedings before an arbitrator. Previous proceedings before an arbitrator are not obligatory for the announcement of a strike. However, should the parties to the agreement decide in favour of proceedings before an arbitrator, they – in principle – exclude the possibility of a strike or a lock-out. A strike initiated or continuing after the initiation of the proceedings before the arbitrator would be unlawful. As soon as the arbitrator decides in the dispute on negotiating the collective agreement, it is not permissible to strike, because this agreement has been reached by the decision of an arbitrator.

A strike refers to a partial or complete interruption of work by employees. The act on collective bargaining also regulates a solidarity strike, under which we understand a strike in support of the claims of employees striking in a dispute on negotiation of another collective agreement. A solidarity strike is considered by law acceptable only if the employer of the participants in such a strike is able to, especially through economic links, influence the course or result of the strike of employees in support of which the solidarity strike was announced.

In the case of a strike in a dispute after the negotiation of a collective workplace agreement, the strike will be announced and its initiation will be decided by the respective trade union body in the workplace, if the majority of the employees involved in the collective agreement agree to it. In disputes after the negotiation of a higher-level collective agreement, the strike shall be announced by the respective higher-level trade union body. The announcement of a strike by a higher-level trade union body is a condition for initiation of a strike at individual workplaces. On the other hand, employees of individual workplaces can, but of course also need not, initiate a strike in such a case. The respective trade union body in a workplace also decides to initiate a strike in disputes after the negotiation of a higher-level collective agreement, if a majority of the employees involved in the collective agreement agree to it. The respective trade union body in a workplace must notify the employer in writing not later than three working days before the date of the initiation of the strike, stating when the strike is to begin, the reasons for and objectives of the strike, and a list of names of representatives of the respective trade union body authorized to represent participants in the strike.

Every employee has the right to decide freely whether or not he or she will join the strike, and an employer is not allowed to recruit new citizens in the course of the strike as replacements workers for the jobs of the participants in the strike.

The act on collective bargaining lists those cases where a strike is unlawful. Besides the above-mentioned cases, it further applies especially to strikes at a time of military preparedness of the state, and during a state of emergency. A strike by a selected circle of employees is also deemed unlawful where life, health or property would be put in danger by the strike (for example, a strike of health service employees, or fire fighters).

We must point out that the act on collective bargaining does not regulate the unlawfulness of strikes generally, but only in relation to this act. Should a strike be announced or initiated for reasons other than for solution of a collective dispute after negotiating the collective agreement (or strikes arising from a concluded collective agreement), it will not be a strike pursuant to this act. Strikes other than strikes after negotiating a collective agreement (or from a concluded collective agreement, which are always deemed unlawful) are not regulated legally, nor are they prohibited.

Whether or not the strike is lawful, it has significant impacts on the position of the participants in a dispute, and also on the individual employees. For this reason, the determination of the unlawfulness of a strike comes under the competence of the district court.

Participants in a strike have no right to payment or compensation for loss of payment at the time of their participation in the strike (but trade unions can provide them with certain financial contributions from trade union funds). Employees taking part in a strike will usually be persuaded of the lawfulness of the strike. They must be protected from the negative consequences of the participation in the strike from the point of view of their labour law position, if the court later declares the strike to have been unlawful. For this reason, participation in a strike prior to the legal force of the decision of the court on the unlawfulness of the strike shall be treated as absence with leave from the workplace. However, if an employee takes part in the strike even after a court decision comes into legal force declaring that the strike is unlawful, for this subsequent time the employee's actions will be regarded as absence without leave from the workplace, with all the negative labour law consequences following therefrom. If the court has decided that the strike is unlawful, the trade union that announced the strike is liable to the employer for the damage caused to it by the strike.

Termination of the strike shall be decided by the trade union body that announced the strike or decided to initiate the strike. It has to notify the employer in writing of the termination of the strike without undue delay.

d. Lock-out in a Dispute after Negotiating a Collective Agreement

In order to keep a balance in collective bargaining, the employer or employers have the right to use a lock-out as an extreme measure for resolving a dispute after negotiating a collective agreement. In this concept, a lock-out is a counterbalance to strike, which can be used by trade unions. Lock-out is defined as a partial or full stoppage of work by the employer. Similarly, as in the case of a strike, employers can announce a lock-out only if no collective agreement was concluded, even after proceedings before a mediator, and if the parties to the agreement have not applied for a solution of the dispute by an arbitrator. Initiation of a lock-out, its extent, reasons, objectives, and a list of names of employees towards whom the lock-out is directed must be announced by the employer in writing to the respective trade union body and to the employees toward whom it is directed, not less than three days in advance. Cases of unlawful lock-outs are regulated similarly as cases of unlawful strikes.

Unlike a strike, a lock-out is an impediment to work imposed by the employer's side. Employers are obliged to pay wages amounting to fifty % of average wages for the duration of the lock-out. In case of an unlawful lock-out (the regional court also decides whether or not a lock-out is lawful) an employee is entitled to compensation for lost wages amounting to average wages.

C.   Experiences of Collective Labour Law Disputes

The present regulation of collective labour law disputes has been in force for about four years. Experience of its implementation in practice is not very extensive yet, because it has been valid for only a limited period of time, and also because social conciliation between employees and employers in the Czech Republic has remained to a considerable extent satisfactory during this period. However, until now the experience of the application of the present law, including negotiations of collective labour law disputes by mediators and or arbitrators and legal regulation of strikes and lock-outs, has been relatively satisfactory.

Transformation of Labour Law and Industrial Relations in Hungary

László Nagy

I. SOCIAL AND ECONOMIC BACKGROUND

Starting from 1949 and the early 1950s, instead of the former democratic regime and market economy, Hungary was characterized by the omnipotent direction of the Party, a planned economy and a corresponding centralized legal regulation and administration. The economic reform that started in 1968 contributed to a certain relinquishing of the economic centralization. This also manifested itself in the field of labour law. According to the Labour Code of 1968, regulation had to be based on two pillars: the law and collective agreements concluded at the enterprise level. Unfortunately, these were made valid only in a very limited extent. In the mid 1980s, steps were taken for enlarging the scope of authority of collective agreements. During this period, experiments were introduced concerning the employees' participation in the decision making of the enterprise. The transformation of a state enterprise into a share holding company became possible. However, due to the given political and state structure, all of these factors could have only a limited effect, but they matured the conceptions that facilitated the formation of the legal regulation that conformed to the market economy. The fact that Hungary – especially from the second half of the 1960s – made efforts to ratify and implement as many international labour conventions as possible had a similar effect.

The collapse of the socialist block at the turn of 1989–1990 meant that Hungary had the new task of establishing the new democratic state and market economy mechanisms. There were three indications of how difficult this task would prove to be: a dictatorial system had to be replaced by a democratic one, where freedom of association and speech, as well as equal chances for citizens, are norms. This includes the rule of law and the creation of its institutions. It also means a transformation of the economy in order to obtain a predominantly private ownership and to have the market mechanism institutions in place. The difficulty and complexity of the transformation stems from the fact that the above requirements are not separable from each other; life produces them in their interrelationship. Another indication is that a well-orchestrated transformation takes vision, experience and time. The West took centuries of gradual development and occasional conflicts to arrive at the present-day political, administrative, and economic standards. These allow for a concert of state institutions, legal regulation and of the social and economic background. By contrast, Hungary only has had the extremely short period of time of a few years. As well, the past decades allowed for no theoretical foundations to be laid, or even less, for practical experiences to be accumulated by well-established organizations (parties) that would now steer the transformation and equip it with foresight and resources.

The failure of the economy of the country rendered the course of transformation much more difficult and in some cases loaded it with conflicts. The economy of Hungary was based fundamentally on the trade with the socialist countries. As, however, the socialist economy everywhere collapsed at the same time, the economy of each country – among them Hungary – became essentially inoperative. In addition, Hungary was burdened by a large national debt.

Finally, the functioning of democracy requires new conduct, attitude, and habits of the citizens, including also those working in the state apparatus. For the citizens who have grown up in the last decades – and they make the majority of the population – all this is totally new. Similarly, a different attitude, and in many cases new skills, are required by the functioning of the market economy itself and by the participation in it. This field, too, has many deficiencies. The change of the situation requires a different activity of school, family, and social education. If this education is not efficient enough, it can delay the transformation. In several cases it may create a gap between the realization of the legal regulation and the conduct and knowledge of the citizens.

II.   THE PRINCIPLES OF THE TRANSFORMATION OF LABOUR LAW

a. The Impact of the Transformation on Labour Law and Industrial Relations

The transformation has had a strong impact on labour law and industrial relations. In this field the transformation required the realization of three principles:
- change of the state and of the conception of the legal regulation;
- enlargement of the role of the social partners;
- enforcement of the employees' instruments to defend their rights.

b. The First Steps were made in 1989 and 1990

- The legal regulation was limited to amendments considered to be most urgent for transformation; e.g., regulations related to collective agreements, and the establishment and cessation of labour relations were amended.
- Significant changes started in the trade union movement. The traditional trade unions shifted the focus of their activity onto representing workers' interests.

The organizational framework had altered. The homogeneity of unions had ended, and thus trade union pluralism appeared in socialist countries. The situation brought about a fierce, mostly politically charged in-fighting among the various trade unions.
- Although the legal conditions of collective bargaining had been in place, in practice collective bargaining was rather rare, partly due to the unclear situation of unions and partly owing to the lack of adequate partners on the employers' side, either at branch or at corporate level. New employers' organizations had appeared but their background and support base remained uncertain. State company managers lacked interest and, primarily, decision making powers in conducting substantive bargaining. The government had tried to promote collective bargaining and had initiated the establishment

of a tripartite interest reconciliation council which would comprise representatives of the trade unions, employers' organizations and the state representatives.
- The right to strike was acknowledged in a separate act. The employees made use of this right during the following years.

c. The New Regulations

During the following years new regulations were made to replace earlier amendments e.g. the new Labour Code, the Act on Employment Policy, the Act on Labour Safety and Health Protection. These focused on the requirements of the market economy, at least as it was perceived by the legislators. Attempts were made to introduce a minimum of regulation, which addressed the basic issues only, leaving details to collective agreement and labour contracts. While former acts would only deal with collective labour relations in general or in a very narrow sense, the new acts had these for their main target.

By now, it has become evident that unemployment is here to stay. Because of the economic collapse, the dimensions of unemployment are much more extensive than expected. Hence, the Act on the Employment Policy determines the condition of a comprehensive employment policy, and introduces special measures to tame unemployment.

III. LABOUR POLICY, CODIFICATION LABOUR ADMINISTRATION

A. The Role of the State

Market economy countries experienced an essential change in the concept related to the role of the state and to the method and extent of legal regulation. According to this concept, the state diminishes its intervention in the economic life, and it entrusts its tasks to the participants of market. This change also had an effect in the field of labour law. This concept was decisive in the period of the transition; it manifested itself in the concept of labour policy, in the determination of the legal system, and in the arrangement of the labour administration. This concept lead to discussions in the sphere of labour law.

B. Labour Policy

The direction of labour policy was exclusively a state prerogative. It had three fundamental functions: the definition and observance of legal regulation, wages, and employment policy. Following the transition, the role of the state is still dominant but no longer exclusive. As was said earlier, this role is now limited to the determination of the basic guarantees and establishments. The Hungarian practice – the essence of which was centralized wage regulation, i.e. the determination of wages and the size of the funds earmarked for wages – was significantly relinquished in the period of 1989–1990, in favour of decision making at the company level. Later, central wage regulation was only maintained in areas financed by the central budget, such as state administration, education, health care, and so on. The role of the state significantly increased in the field of employment policy. Formerly, there was a chronic labour shortage in the country. State employment policy focused on measures – at times administrative ones – aimed at promoting employment (e.g., compulsory jobs for vocational training school graduates). The state also assisted in creating jobs for disadvantaged groups, such as disabled persons or mothers rearing small children. After 1989, the situation changed in two directions. The role of the state to limit free employment could no longer prevail. The main task of state employment policy was to care for the jobless and to assist job-seeking. In the course of 1991 – as was mentioned before – the Act on Employment came into effect. The act not only regulated the unemployment issue, but also created institutions to efficiently implement legal provisions.

As of 1989-1990, state labour policies gradually incorporated a new element, namely, co-operation with workers' and employers' organizations. An institutional framework was created: the National Interest Reconciliation Council.

C. Labour Law Codification

Formerly, labour law was predominantly state-regulated at levels ranging from acts to ministerial decrees. In the case of normative collective agreements which were introduced parallel to the economic reform (as mentioned before), the bargaining options and, consequently, the content of the agreements were significantly reduced by legal limits. As of 1989, the concept became dominant according to which market economy requirements could only be met if basic rights and institutions were stipulated by law while detailed regulation was left for collective agreements, or employment contracts, in the absence of the former. This principle was respected as early as the amendments of 1989–1990, but was only implemented in the newly adopted Labour Code of 1992. There was a full consent concerning the necessity of liquidating the detailed, central regulation of labour law connected with the planned economy and state direction. It was, however, disputed up to what measure the legal regulation should be extended. In the sphere of the study of labour law, and among the trade unions, there were opposite views in a relatively wide circle. These were motivated by two factors.

On the one hand, due to the recent situation of the trade union movement, the law, which was too liberal for the given situation, was not adequately balanced by organized protection. On the other hand, the process of concluding collective agreements started very slowly and was limited to an area that is too narrow even today. Consequently, the rights and duties that ought to have been regulated by collective agreements were determined by employment contracts. Therefore, the content of the contracts is too broad. This deteriorates the position of weak employees in the first place. Unemployment further aggravates the disadvantageous situation.

As a consequence of the above regulatory concept, there was a twofold change in the scope of legal regulation. Formerly, the Labour Code mainly dealt with individual labour relations, leaving little room for collective relations. The new Labour Code regulates collective labour relations to the full extent.

The former Labour Code covered all layers of the labour relations, in a unified manner, including the state administration. It was justified by the fact that the content of the legal relation (i.e. work performed in a subordinated position for the interest of others), the position of the employer (the state directly of indirectly), and the source of the remuneration (i.e. the unified national plan) were identical. In the course of the codification it was also disputed whether labour regulation should be based on a single,

uniform notion of labour relations, or whether it should discriminate between the state and the private sector. The latter concept was accepted and codified. Consequently, the Parliament passed three acts instead of one unified act:
- the Labour Code (Act XXII of 1992), which is of general character, relevant to all labour relations unless another act otherwise provides;
- Act XXXIII of 1992 on the legal status of the employees of civil service, which covers the employees of the network of institutions financed by the state budget (public health, education, culture, research, etc.);
- Act XXIII of 1992 on the legal status of public employees, covering the employees of the central and regional bodies of state administration.

D. Labour Administration

1. The fundamental tendencies of labour policy are determined by the framework of acts passed by Parliament concerning the social and economic development of the country. The special tasks of realizing labour policy fall within the domain of labour administration. The central organ of labour administration is the Ministry of Labour. The ministry deals with the legal regulation of issues concerning the employment policy and the labour force, wage policy and labour safety. In addition, it supervises and controls special training schemes, as well as the training of workers, and medium-level specialists and supervisors outside the school system. The Ministry of Labour governs the Labour Market Organization and the National Labour and Labour Safety Inspectorate.

Act IV of 1991 lays down the principles of the employment policy system and other labour market institutions. According to Articles 3, and 4 of the Act, the achievement of the goals as defined in the Act shall be promoted by a state organization providing labour market service nation wide. The organization carries out its task through its central and local bodies. Employers, employees and – with regard to local bodies – local municipalities participate in the control of the labour market organization. The labour market organization carries out its activity as a service having consideration for the psychological and social aspects of unemployment.

2. The labour market organization system established by Act IV of 1991 on employment policy operates as follows:
- the Ministry of Labour shall direct the National Labour Centre and the activities of the regional labour centres;
- The National Labour Centre is the central body of the labour market organization. It directs the labour centres, creates and operates on-line information systems of the labour market, provides information on professional and public request about issues concerning the field of labour, has set up an information network, and provides professional training for the labour centre and branch office staff;
- On local level, the labour market organization shall be represented by labour centres operating in the capital and in the counties. They are specialized administrative authorities that are organizationally independent from the local municipalities. Within its own jurisdiction, the labour centre fulfils the tasks arising from the allocation, payment, and control of unemployment benefits, assist in preventing unemployment, promotes employment opportunities, carries out labour exchange and counselling activities, and renders advisory service;
- A labour centre can set up branch offices in various regions to deal with local employment tasks.

3. In order to ensure co-operation and conciliation concerning the realization of the employment policy aims, Chapter II of the Act provides for the establishment of the Labour Market Commission, the National Training Council, and the County Labour Councils.

The Labour Market Commission, consisting of representatives of the government and representative bodies of employers and employees, shall decide on the allocation of financial assets of the Unemployment Solidarity fund. It shall be consulted on draft rules directly affecting employment proposed by the Government or members of the Government.

The National Training Council, consisting of representatives of the government and representative bodies of employers and employees, shall decide on projects, and so on, relating to vocational training.

In the counties (and the capital), conciliation of interests concerning employment shall be carried out by the county (metropolitan) labour council, which consists of representatives of interested employers' and employees' organizations as well as representatives of the local government.

IV.   REGULATION OF INDIVIDUAL LABOUR RELATIONS

a. Mention should be made of 3 issues related to individual labour relations:
– changing of the rules of law of establishing and ceasing employment relations;
– changes related to flexible local determination of working hours and wages;
– changes of the employers disciplinary authority.

It should be noted that over and above these changes amendments were made with respect to other issues, too. Those were solicited not by transformation, but by other needs (to close legal gaps, eliminate misleading rules, and so on). The latter issues go beyond the scope of the present paper.

b. The establishment of employment relations is based – as earlier – on the principles of free agreement of the parties involved. In the contract of employment, the employer undertakes to employ a person for defined duties and for a determined payment, while the employee undertakes to be employed in the enterprise. The employee shall only be requested to make a statement, fill out an information sheet, or take an aptitude test if it does not violate the employee's personal rights, and if it may provide substantive information from the viewpoint of the establishment of employment. The importance of employment contract has increased significantly due to two factors. The first factor is that many former rules limiting the scope of the parties' agreement were deleted, e.g. central regulation of wages or working hours. The second factor is that the agreement may determine more favourable conditions for the employee than those stipulated by collective agreement. Contracts of employment shall be constituted in writing with the exception of employment for two days or less. If this contract does not take place, the employee can terminate the labour relationship with immediate effect, but can do so only within 30 days.

c. Regarding the termination of the employment relation:

1. The employment relation may be terminated by bilateral agreements of the parties, or by the unilateral declaration of one party. In relation to the unilateral declaration the Labour Code provides essential changes.

2. The employment relation of indefinite duration may be terminated by ordinary or by extraordinary notice, by either the worker or the employer. (The latter is a new form introduced instead of the dismissal by disciplinary decision).
3. The employer may give ordinary notice in writing when justified and when no prohibitions or restriction to prevent notice are present. The justification shall clearly indicate the cause of the notice. The reason for the notice shall only be a cause connected with the employee's ability or his conduct in relation to the employment, or the employer's operation. In the case of a notice on the grounds of the employee's work or conduct, the employee shall be given an opportunity to defend himself or herself against the objection raised against him or her, unless this cannot be expected of the employer in view of all the circumstances of the case.

Labour Law establishes absolute prohibition on notice by the employer if it may cause disproportionate hardship to the worker in the case of illness or other personal or familial reasons. The range of personal or family related circumstances protecting employment is much narrower in the new Labour Code than the earlier one. (Such circumstances are normally related to maternity, to active military status, to employees within five years of becoming eligible for an old-age pension). The period of notice varies from 30 days to one year, determined by the collective agreement or the parties agreement.

According to the new Labour Code an employee shall be entitled to severance pay if his employment ceases in consequence of ordinary notice by the employer, or his dismissal without legal successor. Exceptions: if the employee has become eligible for an old-age pension or has been granted a pension prior to reaching pensionable age, or upon expiry of a secondary occupation. Severance pay is due to an employee after at least three years with the same employer. Severance pay amounts to one month average earning in the case of at least three years service, and increases according to the extent of the employment relation up to six months pay in the case of at least 25 years.

The employer, or the employee, may terminate employment by extraordinary notice if the other violates any substantive obligations arising from the employment relationship, either intentionally or by being seriously negligent, or otherwise either party demonstrates conduct which renders the retention of the employment relationship impossible. A collective agreement, or the employment contract, may determine those cases in which there is scope for extraordinary notice. The right to give extraordinary notice shall be exercised within three days of learning the reason that serves as its basis, within six months of the occurrence of the cause, and within a maximum of one year in the case of a collective agreement provision.

An unlawful termination of employment by the employer is invalid and must be considered as though it had not occurred. To this end, the original situation must be restored. According to the new Labour Code, upon the employer's request, the court shall waive reinstatement of the employee provided the employer pays to the employee twice the sum of severance pay due to him in the case of ordinary notice. This provision shall not apply if the employer's ordinary or extraordinary notice violates the requirements of proper execution of the law, the prohibition against detrimental discrimination, or the prohibition against notice. The employee, if he does not request continuation of employment in his original position, shall, in addition to his wages and compensation, be entitled to twice the sum of severance pay. If the employee terminates the employment relationship by extraordinary notice he is entitled to his average earnings for the notice period and severance pay due to him in the event of ordinary notice.

4. Flexible local regulation opportunities are chiefly related to working hours, leisure time and remuneration. Law only regulates the main safeguarded issues: e.g. minimal duration working hours, maternity or health protective working hours, limitation of extra working hours, and the wage system. Apart from these, substantive regulation is left to collective agreements and employment contracts.

d. Rules and measures in connection with unemployment

At an earlier stage it was mentioned that employment policies – including those dealing with unemployment – have become a priority issue. A separate institution, and quite soon after the outset of transformation, a special act was adopted in order to determine the tasks of employment policies. In view of the increase of unemployment and its lasting nature, a number of new problems emerged in the course of implementation. As a consequence, rules on employment had to be repeatedly amended.

Measures taken in order to decrease unemployment were similar with minor discrepancies in most counties. These can be divided into three groups:

1. Preventive rules, aimed at making unemployment avoidable.
– An employer who employs at least 30 persons and intends to reduce his staff either by at least 25%, or 50 persons, within six months, must notify the labour centre and the local employees' organization three months prior to the cessation employment;
– The employer shall notify within 30 days the employees concerned, as well as the competent labour centre, of all his decisions concerning any reduction in personnel affecting at least 10 persons. In this case a committee shall be established with the participation of the employees' representatives. The duty of the committee is to determine the principles and schedule to be followed and to decide on extra benefits, which are to be guaranteed over and above the benefits payable according to the provisions of the law to employees affected by the reduction.

2. Measures aimed at assisting the jobless in reintegration into the labour market: registration of job vacancies and jobless persons, advisory and information services, improvement of the employment aptitude of those unfit for available jobs, and organization of training and retraining courses to this end.

3. Creation of new job opportunities by either of the following two means:
– Promoting training, and promotion of the unemployed setting up new business;
–- Support for creating new jobs, support for part-time employment, and assumption of the costs of retirement with the exemption of age. The granting of these forms of support shall be within the authority of the labour centre. Support is financed by that part of the Employment Fund allocated to a given county.

4. Rules meant to help those who failed to get access to jobs or a living in accordance with the above. Here there are several possibilities, too.
– The basic means is the unemployment benefit. Entitlement depends on the duration of the preceding employment as well as on the mode of its cessation. The sum of the benefit depends on the earnings during employment. Benefits are paid for a limited period of time and their sizes gradually decrease. The size could be as large as 60% to 75% of the last average salary and is paid for a duration of 270 days;
– Advanced retirement pensions are another form of material aid. If a person becomes unemployed within a certain time – normally 3 years – before retirement age, he or she may apply for an advanced pension, on condition that the employer or the state ('Employment Funds') agree to repay to social security the amount paid to the unemployed until he reaches retirement pension age;

– As soon as entitlement to unemployment benefit expires, material care for the unemployed is no longer an employment policy issue. In accordance with the given circumstances in each case, it becomes the problem of social aid organs (normally within the framework of local governments).

Statutory documents on employment policy stipulate the funding of unemployment benefits, from either of two sources. One is contributions paid by employers and employees. The other is the so-called Employment Fund, drawing from the state budget in the first place.

V.   COLLECTIVE LABOUR RELATIONS

A.   Introduction

In Hungary, the development of collective labour relations was previously of little interest due to the existing planned economy. However, in 1989, it was an essential task of the codification of the legal arrangement of the collective industrial relations. In the course of codification, especially the following had to be regulated:
– national interest reconciliation;
– the rights of the trade unions;
– the system of collective negotiation and collective agreements;
– the participation of the employees in the decisions of the enterprise;
– the right to the strike.

B.   Interest Reconciliation Council

According to Article 16 of the Labour Code on matters of national significance involving labour relations and employment, the government shall co-operate with the organizations representing employees' and the employers' interests in the Interest Reconciliation Council.
        The Minister of Labour, on the suggestion of the council, shall promulgate the agreements made by the Interest Reconciliation Council as a provision of law. The government shall initiate national wage negotiations in the Interest Reconciliation Council. The government must agree with the council's decision concerning determination of the regulations that depart from the code in relation to the termination of employment on economic grounds, its decisions regarding the minimum wage, the supervision of labour relations, the determination of the maximum duration of a working day, and the number of non-working days.

C.   The Trade Union

1. Freedom of Trade Union Organization

Articles 4 and 65 of the Constitution guarantee all citizens the right to establish trade unions and guarantee the freedom of association and organization. It follows from this that no kind of state approval, permission, or registration is needed for the creation and functioning of trade unions. The organs of the state administration are not entitled to exercise any kind of supervision of association over trade unions.

Because the state provides for the complete autonomy of trade unions, it follows that the state cannot intervene in the internal life of the unions and in relations between the union and its members; the law cannot contain any provisions in this respect. This is a field beyond the domain of legislation. Trade unions establish in their statutes the rules and regulations governing their own functions. The Supreme Court of the Hungarian Republic has held that 'the courts must recognize the validity of trade union statutes.' In drawing up these statutes, the unions are entitled to regulate their activities, organization, management, and the rights and obligations of their members. The only limitation in this respect is that the statutes cannot contravene the provisions of the Constitution.

Trade union autonomy includes the right of a union to possess property in order to perform their functions, to conclude legal transitions, and to assume rights and obligations under the laws of property for this explicit purpose. Section 68 of the Civil Code vests corporate rights in trade unions as legal persons. In consequence, the position of trade unions from the point of view of property rights and obligations is the same as that of other legal entities under civil law.

2. Concept of Trade Union

According to Article 19 of the Labour Code, each employees' organization whose primary function is the development and protection of employees' interests concerning employment shall be considered a trade union. This means that it is not necessary to use in the name of the organization the term 'trade union' (e.g., the name of one of the Hungarian trade unions is the National Confederation of Workers' Councils).

Membership in a trade union is completely voluntary both as regards admission and withdrawal. No social or economic pressure is exerted to compel citizens to become members of trade unions or to resign from them.

The Hungarian trade union movement has a pluralistic character: there are about six trade union organizations on the national level.

3. Regulation of the Trade Union Rights

According to the Constitution, the Labour Code provides the fundamental possibility of protection for interests necessary in connection with labour matters, as well as for the free organization and intervention of the trade unions within the organization of the employer.

The following rights flow from the trade unions' autonomy:
- to establish organizations inside a company and to involve their members in their operation;
- to inform their members of their rights and obligations concerning their material, social, cultural as well as living and working conditions, to represent them in actions against the employer on matters concerning labour relations and employment, and to represent them before state authorities;
- to represent its members, on the basis of authorization, before a court or any other authority or office on matters concerning their living and working conditions;

- to conclude a collective agreement in accordance with the regulations determined under the Code;
- to request information from the employer on all issues related to the employees employment-related economic and social welfare interests. The employer shall not refuse to provide such information or a justification of his actions;
- to verify compliance with the regulations pertaining to working conditions. Before an inspection takes place, it must inform the competent authority (e.g. labour safety inspector);
- to declare an objection to an unlawful action or decision by the employer that directly affects the employees or the organizations representing their interests. (There is no possibility of objection if the employee is entitled to initiate a legal dispute against the measure).

The objection shall be delivered to the employer or his or her executive officer within five days of learning about the measure to which there is an objection. No objection shall be delivered more than one month after the commencement of the measure. If the employer disagrees with the objection, there is scope for reconciliation. If the reconciliation does not produce any results within seven days, the trade union may turn to the Labour Court within five days of the establishment of the failure of reconciliation.

4. The Employer's Duties

According to the Labour Code the employer's obligation are the following:
- to ensure trade unions the opportunity to publicize information and appeals regarded as necessary, as well as data related to its activities, in a manner customary with the employer or in another appropriate way;
- to ensure to trade union officials reduced working hours with pay (one or two hours per month for every three trade union members employed by the employer; and for every ten trade union members, one day a year of extraordinary paid leave for the purpose of training organized by the trade union);
- in the case of an employer wishing to transfer an elected trade union official to another place of work, or wishing to terminate his employment by notice, the employer must request the appropriate higher ranking trade union organization's consent in advance. In the case of an extraordinary notice, or applying legal consequences provided for in collective agreement, or transfer (in the case of varying working sites) to another post, the employer must inform the appropriate trade union official in advance. The official is entitled to this protection for the duration of his commission and for a year upon its termination, provided that he or she has held his position for at least six months.

5. Obligation of State Organs

The Labour Code provides that state authorities are obliged to co-operate with the trade unions to promote activities that reflect their interest by ensuring the information required thereto, and to make known to them the viewpoints and reasons pertaining to their comments and proposals.

D. Collective Negotiations and Collective Agreements

1. Negotiations

According to the Labour Code, neither party can reject a proposal for negotiations aimed at concluding a collective agreement where the proposal was made by a party entitled to conclude a collective agreement. Such conditions also apply to negotiations directed towards an amendment of a collective agreement. The employer, in addition to providing the necessary data, proposes the collective agreement annually to the trade unions that are entitled to conclude the settlement on the regulations pertaining to remuneration for work.

All of the trade unions represented in the employer's employment, irrespective of their representativity, may attend the talks aimed at concluding the collective agreement.

2. The Concept and Content of the Collective Agreement

According to the Labour Code, the collective agreement is an agreement concluded on the basis of the collective negotiations between a trade union and an employer, or an employers' organization.

The parties may determine two kinds of rules in the collective agreement: on the one hand, the rights and obligations arising from employment, the mode of exercising and fulfilling these, and the order of the procedure related thereto; and on the other hand, the relations between the parties concluding the collective agreement. The collective agreement cannot stipulate rules contrary to the rules of law, except where these are more favourable for the employee. However, in any given case, the law may prohibit such a departure from the rules.

3. Types of Collective Agreements

The Labour Code distinguishes between three types of collective agreements: by the branch level, by several employers together, by one employer.

A collective agreement concluded at a lower level shall only depart from one with a broader validity insofar as it specifies regulations more favourable to employees.

4. The Parties to a Branch Collective Agreement

The parties to the collective agreement at branch level are the trade union and the employers' organization. They shall be independent of each other in representing their respective interests. The organization representing the employer's interests requires authorization by its members in order to act. If there is more than one trade union or employers' organization at branch level, the representatives are entitled to conclude the collective agreement.

5. Parties to a Collective Agreement at Employer's Level

At the employer's level only one collective agreement may be concluded. The representative trade union is entitled to conclude the collective agreement. If there is no representative trade union, the draft must be discussed by the employees. The employees shall vote thereon. The vote is valid if over half of the employees entitled to vote in the Works Council election participate.

6. Validity of the Collective Agreement

The collective agreement, in the absence of an agreement departing thereof, enters into effect upon publication. The validity of a collective agreement extends to the employer and his employees irrespective of whether or not they are a member of the trade union that concluded the collective agreement.

Upon the joint request of the contracting parties, the effect of the agreement may be extended to the entire sector by the Minister of Labour.

7. Termination of the Collective Agreement

Collective agreements concluded for a definite period cease upon the expiration of such a term. If the employer or the trade union ceases to exist without a legal successor, the collective agreement loses its validity.

The collective agreement may be repealed by any of the contracting parties with three months' notice. No party shall exercise the right of repeal within six months of the conclusion of the collective agreement. In the event of a collective agreement concluded jointly by several employers or several employers' organizations being repealed, the collective agreement loses its validity only with respect to the employees of the employer who exercised their right of repeal.

E. Workers' Participation

1. The Right of Participation

The Labour Code introduces, as a new form, the direct participation right of the employees in decision making. This right is exercised in the name of the workforce by the Works Council, or a representative elected by the employees.

2. Composition and Election of the Council

The Works Council shall be elected if an employer or his independent branch or subsidiary employs more than 50 employees. If the number of employees is less than 51 but more than 15, a representative shall be elected. The Works Council or the works representative are elected for three years.

The number of works council members is three if the number of employees does not exceed 100, seven if it does not exceed 200, nine if it does not exceed 500, 11 if it does not exceed 1,000, 13 if it exceeds 1,000. A central Works Council must be elected if several Works Councils or works representatives operate at the same employer.

All employees in the employer's employment shall be entitled to participate in the election of a Works Council. The election committee shall establish and make public the list of employees entitled to elect or to be elected.

Any employee who has been in the employer's employment for at least for six months may be elected as a Works Council members. A person who is an employer, who exercise employers' rights, who is a close relative of the employer, the employer's executive officer or a member of the election committee cannot be elected as a member of the Works Council.

3. Termination of the Activities of the Works Council

The Works Council shall cease to exist:
- if the employer ceases without a legal successor;
- if the term of its appointment expires;
- if it is recalled;
- if its membership, for whatever reason, decreases by at least one third.

A vote shall take place for a recall if this is proposed by at least 30 % of the employees. The recall requires over two thirds of the valid votes cast. The vote is valid if over half the employees eligible to vote participated; a proposal to recall shall not be repeated within one year.

4. Termination of Works Council Membership

Membership as a Works Council member ceases:
- by resignation;
- by recall;
- through loss of ability;
- if the member becomes entitled to exercise employer's rights for a period exceeding six months;
- if the member becomes a close relative of the employer or the employer's executive officer;
- if the Works Council ceases to exist;
- upon the termination of the member's employment.

If a member of the Works Council becomes eligible to exercise employer's rights for a period of no more than six months, his or her membership shall be suspended during this period.

5. Competence of the Works Council

The rights of the Works Council are the following:
- the Works Council has the right to jointly decide with regard to the utilization of the welfare fund specified in the collective agreement and with regard to the utilization of institutions and property of this nature;
- the employer requires the agreement of the Works Council for the issuing of the labour safety regulation;
- the employer requires the Works Council's opinion prior to decision making in the following cases: draft measures affecting a large group of employees, especially in relation to plans regarding the employer's reorganization, transformation, conversion of an organizational unit into an independent organization, privatization, and modernization; the organization of a personnel records system; plans connected with employee training; utilization of assistance in order to promote employment and plans pertaining to retirement prior to reaching pensionable age; plans for measures pertaining to the rehabilitation of workers with altered working capacity; a plan for allocation of annual leave; the introduction of new methods regarding the organization of work and performance requirements; plans for internal regulations affecting employees' essential interests; tenders announced by the employer accompanied by financial or honourary rewards;
- the employer is obliged to inform the Works Council, at least every six months, about basic issues affecting the employer's business position; about plans for major decisions pertaining to a significant modification of the employer's activities or investments; and about changes in wages and earnings, in solvency related to the payment of wages, in the characteristic features of employment, in the utilization of working time, and in the nature of working conditions.

6. The Promotion of the Activity of the Council

The employer is obliged to:
- meet the justified and necessary costs for election and operation of the Works Council;
- provide the Council with the opportunity to publish information, appeals, as well as data related to its activities, in a manner customary to the employer, or in another suitable way;
- to ensure to a Works Council member an allowance of 10% of his weekly working time, and the president to 15% of his weekly working time (paid in average wages). In a factory with more than 1,000 employees, the president has the right to a remuneration ensured by the employer, determined by the Works Council in agreement with the employer.

7. Legal Protection

Works Council members are entitled to the same protection determined by Labour Law pertaining to elected trade union officials, with the exception that the right accredited to the trade union shall be exercised by the Works Council.

F. Strikes

The Constitution of the Hungarian Republic lays down the right of any citizen to strike. Act VII of 1989 provides for the conditions for exercising the basic right.

1. The Aim of a Strike

The strike can be instituted in the interest of the protection of the economic and social interest of employees. The political strike is prohibited. Every worker has the right to strike. This is not attached to trade union membership. However, it is the legal duty of trade unions to initiate a solidarity strike.

Participation in a strike is voluntary; nobody can be forced to participate in it or to stay away from a strike. No coercive measures aimed at stopping a strike shall be used against workers participating in a lawful strike.

2. Precondition of a Strike

A strike can be initiated if: reconciliation procedures on the debated issue did not bring about any results within seven days; or, reconciliation procedures did not take place for reasons the initiator of the strike cannot be blamed for. In the case of a solidarity strike a previous conciliation can be omitted. A strike can be organized once, even during the period of conciliation procedures taking place, but it cannot be for longer than two hours.

3. Prohibition and Limitations of a Strike

A strike is illegal if:
- it is not initiated to defend the workers' social and economic interests;
- it has omitted the reconciliation procedures;
- the aim of the strike is anti-constitutional;
- it is organized in opposition to any individual measure or default of the employer whereas the decision on changing it comes within the jurisdiction of the courts;
- it is organized during the effective period of the collective agreement in order to change the arrangement fixed in the collective agreement;
- it would directly and seriously threaten human life, health, security, and the environment or hinder the prevention of elementary damage.

No strike can be organized at institutions of the judiciary, military forces, and the police organizations. The right to strike can be exercised in the organs of state administration according to specific rules laid down in an agreement between the Council of Ministers and the trade unions concerned.

If working for an employer whose products or services meet society's basic requirements, e.g. especially in the field of public transport and telecommunication, the supply of electricity, water, gas and other forms of energy, the right to strike can only be exercised if it does not restrain the performance of yet satisfactory services. This condition must be determined prior to the strike.

An interested party can request the Labour Court to decide on the question of legality or illegality of a strike.

4. The Legal Position of the Worker

Initiating a strike and participation in a strike cannot be considered as disregarding the obligation arising from employment; no measures can be applied against an employee as a consequence of him striking.

VI. SETTLEMENT OF LABOUR DISPUTES

A. The Concept of a Labour Dispute

Hungarian Labour Law distinguishes between individual and collective labour disputes. The first may arise from a labour contract made between an employee and an employer and/or from the labour relationship established on the basis thereof. The second may arise between the trade union representing the employees' interests, or some elected employees body, and the employer. A collective labour dispute may also come into being because the existence or the lawfulness of an action of an individual labour dispute has come into dispute. In the sphere of collective labour disputes one can distinguish – as regards the subject-matter of the dispute – between legal disputes and extra-legal disputes, the so-called interest disputes. Within the scope of the first belong those cases in which the existence or non-existence of a right of one of the parties is disputed, or in which violation, non-performance, or non-satisfactory performance has given rise to the dispute.

The latter are comprised of cases where the dispute arises in the interest of protection or enforcement of the interest of one or the other party, which is not secured by law. The Labour Code that came into force in 1992 means progress from two points of view in comparison with the former situation. On the one hand, it makes it possible, with general character, to bring to court both the individual and the collective legal disputes. On the other hand, it regulates in a uniform manner the system of conciliation preceding the court procedure, with respect to the case of non-legal disputes.

B. Collective Labour Disputes

1. The Concept of Collective Labour Disputes

Disputes qualify as collective labour disputes if they arise in connection with collective labour relations between the employer and trade union or Works Council or employers' organization, (or between trade union and employers' organization); between two or more trade unions (or between two or more employers' organizations). One can distinguish – as mentioned above – between two categories of the collective labour disputes. On the one hand there are disputes arising as a result of a conflict of interest (non-legal disputes); on the other hand there are disputes arising from the violation or non-performance of rights or obligations, or disputes on the existence or non-existence of certain rights or obligations.

2. Solving Non-legal Disputes

The Labour Code determines three kinds of conciliation procedures for solving collective labour disputes: conciliation, mediation, and, finally, arbitration. In agreement with the parties, experts or witness may be consulted during conciliation or arbitration. Justifiable and necessary expenses arising in connection with the conciliation and arbitration process shall be borne by the employer in the absence of agreement departing therefrom. The arbitrator's procedure shall be obligatory in regard to disputes determined by the Labour Code.

3. Collective Legal Labour Disputes

Labour disputes of a collective nature can be classified into several groups:
– a legal dispute can arise concerning the activities of trade unions;
– a legal dispute can arise in connection with collective negotiations and/or a collective agreement in question;
– a legal dispute can arise concerning the right of an employee to participate in the decisions of the employer;
– a legal dispute can arise in connection with exercising the right to strike.

C.   Individual Labour Disputes

1. The Concept of Individual Labour Disputes

According to Article 199 of the Labour Code, an employee, the trade union, and the Works Council may initiate a legal dispute under the provisions of the code against an action of the employer that is in violation of the regulations pertaining to employment. Unless otherwise stipulated in the code, the employer may initiate a legal labour dispute towards the assertion of his claim related to employment.

2. The Procedure

In the case of individual labour disputes, competence lies with the Labour Court.
     The parties shall seek conciliation prior to going to court. In the course of conciliation, any accord reached by the parties qualifies as an agreement; this has to be put in writing. In the case of an injurious measure taken by the employer, conciliation shall be initiated in writing within 15 days after notification or implementation of the measure. Failure to comply with the time limits mentioned above, may, if the other party does not accept it, be justified before the Labour Court within a maximum of six months.
     If conciliation does not yield any results within eight days of its initiation, it is then possible to turn to a Labour Court within the remaining period. However, the term of initiating a claim within 15 days only applies in the cases determined by the Labour Code (e.g., if modifications have been implemented unilaterally by the employer, or cases of cessation of employment including termination, which must be based on mutual consent).

Changes in Polish Labour Law and Industrial Relations during the Period of Post-Communist Transformation

Michal Sewerynski

I. THE ADMINISTRATION OF EMPLOYMENT POLICY

A. Employment Policy

Despite the fundamental political and economic changes in the direction of free market liberalism that have taken, and are taking, place in Poland, the government remains the principal actor of employment policy. It has retained the fundamental principle of guaranteeing to its citizens full and appropriate employment and actively fighting unemployment and its effects. This principle has been affirmatively voiced in the statutes of 1989 and 1991 regarding work and unemployment, as well as in the Law of 14 December 1994 concerning work and measures against unemployment.

The government's active role in employment policy is related to the retention, in the amended constitution of the Republic of Poland, of the provisions guaranteeing Polish citizens the right to work, encompassing as well the right to a fair wage according to the quality and quantity of work performed. Another factor which impels the government's active involvement in employment policy derives from the very process of building a free market economy, which necessarily involves the elimination of unprofitable state enterprises, and streamlining of employment in those retained, according to the dictates of the new economic rules. As a consequence of these changes, the number of persons employed in state enterprises significantly decreased and a sharp rise in unemployment was experienced.[1] The successive governments during the transformation period have all tried to ameliorate the effects of these changes, primarily because of the danger presented by the social discontent that they have created, but also because each successive government has promised to combine implementation of a free market economy with an active social policy.

---

1. Rapid increase of unemployment, decline in living conditions and worsening of the social climate are typical phenomena in all European post-communist countries during economic transformation. *See:* B. Biagi, 'Human resources Management as Strategic Element in the Process of Social and Economic Development of Central and Eastern Europe,' *The Changing Face of Labour Law and Industrial Relations. Liber Amicorum for Clyde Summers*, R. Blanpain, M. Weiss (eds.), Nomos Verlagsgesellschaft, Baden-Baden 1993, p. 12ff; and M. Sewerynski, 'Trade Unions in the Post-Communist Countries: Regulation, Problems and Prospects,' *Comparative Labour Journal*, Vol. 16, No. 2, 1995.

Implementation of the twin policies of full and appropriate employment and active countermeasures against unemployment is left to the regulations that provide workers with protection against unfounded or illegal dismissal in individual cases, that set forth specific procedures which must be complied with in the case of group or mass employment termination, and that establish a system of administrative organs equipped with appropriate powers, and measures in the area of employment policy.

Employment policy in Poland since 1989 has met with frequent criticism. Initially the criticism was directed toward the excessively liberal provisions of the existing employment law which allowed for manipulation of the employment statistics so as to create artificially high unemployment figures, which in turn mandated excessive government expenditures to counteract the high unemployment.[2] Subsequent modification of the regulations were designed in large part to correct government policy in this regard. Nevertheless, the fundamental postulate of integrating unemployment benefits with the existing social security system remains not implemented.

B. Labour Administration

The statutes relating to employment policy that have been passed during the transformation period have implemented essential changes in the system of labour administration organs as well as in their functions and activities. Worthy of special mention is the National Labour Office, placed at the apex of the system of provincial (*wojewodzki*) and local labor offices. While the National Labour Office is nominally subject to the supervision of the Minister of Labour and Social Policy, its authorizing statute gives it the status of a central government administrative agency, which carries with it a high rank and guarantees it significant autonomy in carrying out its activities.

The tasks carried out by the labour administration organs include: labour exchange (registration of the unemployed as well as of job vacancies announced by employers); organization of job and skills training and retraining programs as well as vocational counselling; distribution of financial benefits to the unemployed; rendering financial assistance to qualified employers; creating new workplaces; the organization of public works and emergency work projects; and analysis and evaluation of trends and phenomena relating to employment patterns. The costs involved in carrying out these tasks are covered by a specially-created Labour Fund, made up of both employer contributions and government subsidies.

The role of inspiring and formulating opinions of labour administration organs is carried out by employment councils (the National Employment Council as well as provincial and local councils) established by the 1991 Act concerning labour and unemployment. These employment councils consist of equal numbers of representatives of trade unions, employers, government, and local self-government organs. This structure gives all interested groups the opportunity to exert influence on employment policy and labour administration.

---

2.   *See*: W. Szubert, 'Orientations générales du droit du travail à l'époque contemporaine.' Perspective polono-espagnole, '*Changements politiques et droit du travail: perspective polono-espagnole*,' sous la rédaction de M. Sewerynski et A. Marzal, Wydawnictwo Uniwersytetu Lódzkiego 1992, p. 20.

Two tendencies may be observed in the legislation regarding employment policy and labour administration. The first is of an expansive nature and consists of finding ever new and varied forms of counteracting unemployment and of easing the requirements for rendering financial assistance to those involved in creating new jobs. The second is of a restrictive nature and involves narrowing the definition of unemployment and sharpening the criteria for granting unemployment benefits. The latter tendency is partly justified by the fact that the earlier existing regulations regarding unemployment were excessively liberal in their definitions. However, the 1994 act seems to exceed the bounds of rationality in its attempt to reduce the statistical measure of the unemployment problem and thus also to reduce government expenditures mandated by unemployment.

II.   LABOUR CODE AMENDMENT AND ITS PRINCIPAL DIRECTIONS

A.   Adjusting the Code to the Principles of a Democratic Political System

The centrepiece of Polish labour law remains the Labour Code of 1974, which is comprised of provisions regulating employment relations and collective bargaining agreements. The Labour Code has been frequently amended since 1989, but the changes implemented to date have been mostly of a cosmetic nature. In order to adjust existing Polish labour law to the economic and governmental changes demanded by the transformation process, fundamental reform of the Labour Code is necessary. Having this purpose in mind, in 1990 the government created a special commission to direct labour law reform, whose tasks were to prepare, in the short-term, necessary revisions and amendments to the Labour Code; and in the long-term, to develop a project for the total recodification of Polish labour law. The suggested revisions and amendments of the Labour Code involve significant modification of its principles and provisions while at the same time retain in force a number of its original provisions and solutions. The concept underlying the suggested changes corresponds to the presumption that building a free market economy will not be accomplished overnight by one sweeping set of changes, but rather will take place in stages over a period of time, during which time newly created institutions and mechanisms will exist simultaneously alongside some remaining institutions and practices of the old economic system. Thus, based on the project of suggested changes and revisions, submitted by the government to the parliament in mid 1994, one may characterize the likely shape of the changes in Polish labour law in the near future.

In the first instance the Polish Labour Code had to be adapted to the principles of a democratic system of government, since the political transformation to democracy was the first change to take hold in Poland, and it took place quickly, fundamentally, and irreversibly. Implementation of a free democratic system requires a clean break from principles typical of communist and totalitarian systems, i.e. that the creation of legal norms is the exclusive domain of the state and that the state has the right to regulate all spheres of its citizens' life and activities. It becomes necessary to recognize that citizens also have their own autonomous power to establish norms regulating their own activities, linked to fundamental human and civil rights. The role of the state should be reduced to the function of establishing the minimum of public order, leaving to its citizens the freedom to flesh it out by themselves creating the norms and conditions that they deem necessary in order to carry out social and economic activities. In the area of labour relations, this fundamental change in approach brought with it recognition of the principle that, in addition to legislative acts and governmental regulations, collective bargaining agreements equally constitute a primary source of labour law. The role of legislation in labour relations should be to provide workers with protection of their fundamental rights and to guarantee a necessary legal order in labour relations. All other matters should be regulated by negotiations authorized between employers and trade unions, i.e., by collective bargaining.

Certain provisions in the Labour Code, which are a direct product of the former socialist system, cannot be reconciled with the principles of free democratic government. Therefore, the commission's proposed revision completely eliminates some provisions from the existing Labour Code:

a. those that refer directly to the previous order (i.e., the provision requiring that the Code be interpreted in accordance with the governing principles of socialism and the goals of the People's Republic of Poland);
b. ideologically tinged phraseology (i.e., references to 'socialist work discipline');
c. provisions granting the directors and managers of government enterprises privileged status as well as special obligations (i.e., special rights and obligations regarding the attainment of state production quotas, observation of the principle of community life, support of socialist work competition, and provisions creating a special duty of care for state property).

B.   Adjusting the Code to the Principles of a Free Market Economy

The economic transformation in Poland, undertaken immediately following the political transformation in 1989, has the fixed aim of establishing a free-market economic system. Such a system requires, above all, equal treatment of all enterprises under labour law, without regard to the sector of the economy in which they carry out their activity or the nature of their property ownership.[3] In the newly proposed Labour Code, such equality of treatment is to be attained, in part, by establishing a uniform concept of 'employer.' Employers are no longer to be classified according their status in the public and private sectors, as was previously the case ('work establishment' was the common appellation designating public sector employers, while private sector employers were limited to 'natural persons employing workers', and different provisions with different consequences were applied to the two classes). In the same vein, sanctions for labour discipline violations are now equally applicable to public and private sector employees, and no longer is special protection granted to public property.

In the prevailing new conditions, it is not enough that collective bargaining agreements be recognized as a source of law, but in addition conditions must be legally assured that grant to the parties to such agreements wide negotiating freedom. Only then can the flexibility necessary to adapt to changing conditions be assured to both employees and the enterprises employing them. The only limitation on negotiating freedom is that the fundamental rights of workers guaranteed in the law cannot be abridged. In order to implement the principle of negotiating freedom, those excessively regulative provisions of the Labour Code that restrict the realization of flexible employment policies and work conditions must be eliminated. As an example, one might cite those provisions regulating work hours in excessive detail.

---

3.   *See* L. Florek, 'Zasadnicze kierunki kodeksu pracy', ('The main directions of labour code amending'), *Panstwo i Prawo* 9, 1994, pp. 19–20.

The new proposed Labour Code incorporates the increased role of contracts of employment and collective bargaining agreements and clears the path for expanded negotiating freedom of its parties. This principle, suspect in the previous system, assumes ever-increasing importance in a market economy. It is discussed in Chapter III hereinafter.

The effect of market economy principles on employment policy forced the authors of the proposed Labour Code to revise the previously existing principle that the government will provide work for all its citizens. The new, significantly weakened, version of that principle underlying the proposed code was the subject of considerable controversy, and finally was given expression in formulations somewhere between the dictates of a completely liberalized market economy, on the one hand, and a welfare state model, on the other. The final outcome of the controversy on this issue, that is, the final expression of right-to-work provisions in Polish labour law, will be ultimately resolved in the context of preparation and ratification of a new Polish constitution, which is currently being drafted.

In a free market economy, those provisions of labour law which touch upon workers' rights in the context of change of employer, bankruptcies, liquidations, and mergers are of special significance. In the context of a centrally administered, government-owned economy such events rarely, if ever, occurred, and therefore they remained outside the regulatory scope of the original Labour Code. After 1989, such provisions began to be developed and attached, and in the proposed code revision, considerable space is devoted to them. Similarly, such concepts as protecting employers against competition from their own workers and provisions forbidding workers to divulge trade secrets and practices that would cause harm to their employers are new issues in Polish labour law, and provisions regulating such practices have been worked out in the proposed code in a whole separate chapter.

The expected dominance of private enterprise in the new economic system also explains and justifies the proposed changes whereby workers' rights and benefits arise from length of employment in a given firm or enterprise, and not from cumulative employment history as was the case in the previous system. While the latter principle may have been appropriate in the old system, where the government was the sole employer and all firms were nationalized, in the private sector each enterprise has its own discrete owner(s), and there seems no justification for saddling a subsequent employer with respecting the privileges and benefits an employee earned through his or her tenure at a previous place of employment. The only exception proposed to this principle is in the area of vacation leave, the entitlement to and length of which remains subject to determination based on cumulative length of employment.

C. Adjusting the Code to International Standards. Improving Workers' Status

International norms, especially the standards developed by the International Organization of Labour (ILO), constituted a primary point of reference, especially with regard to reforming those provisions concerning collective bargaining and collective labour law. 'Solidarity' based its earliest appeals on ILO norms regarding trade union freedoms,[4]

---

4.   *See:* L. Florek, 'International Labour Law and Polish Legislation,' *The Changing Face...*, *supra* note 1, p. 160.

and international norms in the entire field of labour law permeated work on the proposed revision of the Labour Code. This process was aided, on one hand, by the desire on the part of 'new' Poland to show that it respected international obligations, and on the other by its genuine desire to improve the situation of its workers by adopting internationally recognized standards.

The intention of the revision committee to conform the revised Labour Code to international standards is most evident in the changes suggested in the chapter that sets forth the underlying principles of labour law. The principles enumerated therein are expanded to include the following: the requirement that employers respect the worker's right to be treated with dignity and not violate his or her personal rights; the right of workers to a fair wage for work performed; and a prohibition on discrimination based on sex, age, race, nationality, religious or political convictions, or membership in a trade union. Two fundamental principles of collective labour law are also added: the right of both workers and employers to organize for the purpose of protecting their legitimate rights and interests; and the right of workers to participate in management of the enterprises in which they are employed. Other principles of collective labour law, however, were omitted. In part this is due to an assumption on the part of the commission that a separate industrial relations statute should and will be created in addition to the Labour Code, and in part results from the still unresolved dispute over the range and content of basic citizens' rights involved in the presently ongoing work on the new constitution.

The proposed new provisions regarding workers' vacation leaves also reflect the intention of the committee to adapt the new norms to international labour law. In particular, one may cite the proposed increase in the minimal annual vacation leave to 18 days (in accordance with convention No. 132 of the ILO), the addition of provisions strengthening the workers' rights to regular annual leave, and the provisions prohibiting curtailment of workers' vacation leave as a form of disciplinary action (for example, workers dismissed without notice by reason of their conduct may not be stripped of their right to vacation leave).

The attempt to adapt the norms and standards of the proposed Labour Code to the ILO conventions is especially evident in the new regulations regarding workplace safety and hygiene. Title X of the Labour Code, primarily devoted to such issues, was fundamentally reconstructed with the aim of harmonizing its provisions with ILO conventions Nos. 136, 139, 148, 155, 161, 162, 167, and 170. As a consequence, employers are held to a much higher standard as regards their duty to guarantee safe working conditions, and workers are granted much greater authority to demand the same. Worthy of note are the provisions guaranteeing workers free medical checkups and authorizing them to refuse to work in conditions that are hazardous to their life or health. Provisions regarding women's protection from dismissal during pregnancy and maternity leave, in case of temporary contract, are also proposed in accordance with international standards.

The proposed revisions to the Labour Code also include a number of provisions that improve the relative position of workers, even though they may not be deemed to directly arise from international labour law. Worthy of mention are the following: establishment of a fixed financial allowance for workers going on pension or disability; the right to compensation in the event of the death of an employer who is a natural person; the automatic transformation of a third consecutive definite period employment contract into an ongoing, indefinite employment contract; provisions granting courts jurisdiction over penalties for breaches of labour discipline; the establishment of maximum allowable overtime hours in the course of a 24-hour period; shortening of the minimum period of employment as a condition to obtaining first vacation leave; and a prohibition on deducting the first three days of sick leave from vacation time. Another manifestation of strengthening workers' rights is the expansion of the liability for infringements of workers rights.

The above-enumerated provisions strengthening workers' rights, included in the proposed revisions of the Labour Code, are offered only as examples of the nature of the changes proposed. They will be more fully amplified in Chapter III, wherein workers' protection against dismissal is discussed.

D.   Modifying the Legislative Technique Encompassed in the Code

The currently existing Labour Code may be subject to a number of criticisms arising from the legislative technique it prescribes in fulfilment of its aims. Among them one must first mention the excessive authority granted therein to issue binding executive regulations. As a result, many important matters and issues which involve either essential civil rights or are ordinarily within the sphere of the legislative process and thus should be established via parliamentary legislation, are in fact issued at a lower hierarchical level of authority as binding executive regulations stemming from the government and/or specific ministries, who, in addition, acted as *de facto* employer in the previous system. Particularly noteworthy in this regard are the regulations concerning work conditions and hours. In these areas executive regulations play a greater role than the code's provisions. While the proposed revision of the code changes the proportion of provisions to regulations, it nevertheless still grants too wide an authority for executive organs to issue binding regulations. The author recognizes, of course, that such regulations are a necessary part of legislative technique and essential to allow basic legislation to be adapted to changing conditions and specific circumstances. Nevertheless, if too wide a range and scope of activity is subject to executive regulation, the basic legislative function of the underlying statute may be undermined or abrogated.

In addition to the above, it should be noted that based on ordinary and rational principles of legislative technique, the proposed revisions to the Labour Code fill up a number of loopholes and imprecise concepts and loose terminology that raise doubts as to their proper and intended interpretation.

III.   CONTRACT OF EMPLOYMENT, PROTECTION OF EMPLOYMENT, AND MEASURES AGAINST UNEMPLOYMENT

A.   Contract of Employment

Under the previous conditions of far-reaching regulation and control of labour relations, when government enterprises were under the management of directors severely hampered and hemmed in by the directives of their superiors, the role of employment contracts was limited. While it is true that they constituted the most common and fundamental evidence of the employment relationship, nevertheless the parties thereto had very little negotiating freedom when it came to establishing their stipulations. On the basis of the new Labour Code this situation has been fundamentally revised inasmuch as the parties to an employment contract may negotiate all its terms and conditions, with the only proviso being that the same may not be less advantageous to the worker than the existing provisions of the Labour Code. The parties also have greater freedom to choose the type of employment relationship they choose to conclude, and in addition the role of employment contracts is further strengthened by the limitations placed on appointments as a basis of employment.

By strengthening of the role of employment contracts, the natural obligation character of an employment relationship is enhanced. The majority of labour law scholars, already in the past, defended that character of the employment relationship, seeing such recognition as a way of strengthening the legal status of individual workers. The significance of the mutual obligation relationship mechanisms grows in importance under the provisions of the new Labour Code. As evidence, one may cite the restoration of the principle of equality, applied to both employers and employees, as regards immediate termination of the employment relationship; the increase of the indemnification of damages in cases where the provisions of either a contract or the Labour Code are violated; or, the harmonization of the statutes of limitations applicable to employment contracts with those applicable according to civil law.

B. Employment Protection

As regards protection of the employment relationship, Polish labour law underwent fundamental revision already in 1989. Two laws were passed at the time. The first facilitated termination of individual employment contracts for economic reasons;[5] and the second regulated mass terminations.[6] Both acts were necessary for economic reform that involves the privatization and transformation of state-owned enterprises and rationalistic employment.

As regards mass terminations of employment, the 1989 law provides a wide assortment of legal justifications therefore. They are permissible for economic, organizational, and technological reasons, as well as to streamline productivity, or correct environmental or workplace hazards. In addition, the law establishes the procedure to be followed in mass terminations, which makes rigorous their implementation.

A special protective function, however, is assigned to trade unions, which are equipped with special authority in cases of mass termination. Employers are required to inform the appropriate plant trade union organization of their intention to terminate their employment relationship with a group of workers at least 45 days prior to the date of termination, giving the justifications therefore, and the number and group of workers subject thereto. Upon receiving such an announcement, the authorized plant trade union has the right to demand from the employer information regarding the economic plight and financial condition of the enterprise as well as the level and structure of employment envisioned for the future. Subsequently, the union may propose a plan to the company seeking to limit the nature of the mass termination. The final act of this dialogue is intended to be an agreement between the employer and all trade unions operating within the enterprise or company which sets forth the manner and method of

---

5.   *Dziennik Ustaw* No. 20, 1989, item 107.
6.   *Dziennik Ustaw* No. 4, 1990, item 19, with following changes. *See:* M. Matey, 'Labour Law and Unemployment in Poland,' *Polish Contemporary Law*, No. 2, 1990, pp. 42–50; and L. Florek, 'Job and unemployment security in Poland,' *The American University Journal of International Law and Policy*, Vol. 7, No. 3, Spring 1992, pp. 533–538.

the mass termination. In those cases where no agreement can be reached, ultimately the employer can carry out the mass termination according to regulations issued by itself. If there are no registered trade unions operating in the company or enterprise, the employer can issue the above regulations after obtaining the opinion of the entire personnel.

In order to ease the effects of a mass termination, the law requires employers to pay employees a dismissal allowance ranging from one to three months salary, depending on length of previous employment. In the same vein, employers are required to reinstate the dismissed employees in the event they rehire any additional employees from the same trade, craft, or professional group. In such cases, the dismissed employee can declare his intention to return to work within one year from the date of dismissal.

As presented above in its general outlines, one cannot doubt that the 1989 law is designed to protect workers from, and in, the event of mass termination. In practice, however, its protective provisions often turn out to be largely illusory, especially because the courts are not inclined to be sharp in questioning the justifications offered for mass terminations so long as they fall within one of the above-mentioned general categories.[7]

Protection against dismissal accorded to individual workers on indeterminate contracts was well-developed under socialist law. It was based on the twin concepts of causality and legality. Prior to termination, protection of the relationship was the domain of the relevant trade union, and in the event of a termination, protection was offered by the courts if the terminated employee chose to contest the same. A further necessary element in the chain of protection was the right of the courts to issue a decision of reinstatement of the employee to his or her previous workplace in the event a dismissal was found to be unjustified or illegal. Damages were of a secondary and supplementary nature.[8]

In fact, while the foundation underlying socialist labour regulations was the malfunctioning system of a socialist economy (i.e., massive, full-scale engagement of the workforce in inefficient production in exchange for extremely low salaries and wages), nevertheless the system undoubtedly offered the worker a high degree of protection against illegal or unjustified dismissal. This positive attribute of the old law suddenly became highly valued by employees during the period of economic transformation. Therefore, the existing provisions regarding individual employment protection have been retained in the proposed revision of the Labour Code, and even strengthened. This can be seen in the requirement that employers must give employees the full reasons for their dismissal, both at the first level of control whereby the intention to dismiss must be directed to the appropriate trade union, as well as in writing to the employee himself or herself at the time of dismissal.

C.   Means of Combatting Unemployment

During the transformation period, combatting unemployment has been one of the key elements of existing employment policy. This is evidenced by the three successive

---

7.   *See* A. Swiatkowski, 'Labour Law in Post-Socialist Poland,' *Yearbook of Polish Labour Law and Social Policy*, A. Swiatkowski (ed.), Vol. 5, 1994, pp. 190–200.
8.   *See* M. Matey, *Labour Law and Industrial Relations in Poland*, Kluwer 1988, pp. 74ff; and Florek, *supra* note 5, pp. 530–533.

statutes that have been introduced and ratified concerning this problem since 1989, as was earlier mentioned in Chapter I herein. Because unemployment in Poland grew at a dizzying pace and continues to exist at a high level, the aforementioned legislation has successively introduced various solutions thereto in an attempt to combat its effects on the national standard of living and on public morale.

The most recent 1994 statute[9] continues the earlier practices of registering unemployment and providing government employment agency services and vocational counselling as means of combatting unemployment. It devotes considerably more attention, however, to active means of countering unemployment, means which encompass job training and retraining programs as well as which authorize administrative employment offices to undertake initiatives to create new jobs. Job training services are designed to provide programs allowing the unemployed to increase their qualifications or to add new skills so that their chances of obtaining employment will correspondingly increase. During their (re)training period, which may last from six to twelve months, the participants receive financial allowances.

Special attention is given to promoting activities designed to create new jobs. The 1994 act authorizes government employment offices to grant financial assistance to employers who create new jobs for the unemployed as well as to organizers of public works and temporary work projects. The unemployed themselves may also receive a one-time loan for the purpose of carrying out their own business activities, 50% of which is forgiven if they carry on the activity undertaken for more than two years.

Traditional unemployment benefits replacing lost income from the previous job were established already by the 1989 law concerning employment and unemployment. Subsequent revisions of this law have more carefully defined the criteria for entitlement and increased the prerequisites, in addition to lowering the initial rate of calculation. Presently it stands at 36% of the previous average salary or wage and is payable for up to 12 months. Upon extinguishment of the right to unemployment benefits, the recipient is thrown onto existing social welfare programs.

All the costs of the above programs and benefits paid come from the National Labour Fund, which is a specifically directed government appropriation fund consisting of employer contributions and government subsidies.

IV.   TRADE UNIONS AND EMPLOYER ORGANIZATIONS

A.   Trade Unions

On 5 April 1989, the democratic opposition in Poland, headed by 'Solidarity,' signed the 'Round-table Agreement' with the then existing political union establishment.[10] In addition to the provisions of a political nature, which initiated the process of building a new democratic system, a measure of trade union freedom was also agreed upon. The latter was implemented by agreed upon amendments to the Trade Union Act of 1982,[11] which had prohibited the existence of more than one trade union in a given factory as well as the creation of regional and national trade union structures.

---

9.   *Dzennik Ustaw* No. 1, 1995, item 1.
10. *See:* M. Sewerynski, 'Les accords de la Table Ronde et les rapports de travail en Pologne,' *Revue Internationale de Droit Comparé*, année 1989, No. 4 pp. 1005–1015.
11. *Dziennik Ustaw* No. 20, 1989, item 105.

Fundamental change in Polish trade union law, however, appeared only after ratification of the new law concerning trade unions of 1991.[12] This act represents a complete break from the communist trade union model, completely eliminating production goals and ideological functions from trade union activities.[13] Instead, the law recognizes the traditional function of workers' protection as constituting the major function of trade unions; in other words, the major function of trade unions is representing and vindicating the rights and interests – both social and professional – of workers. In the context of collective representation of workers' rights, trade unions represent all workers, including both those registered therewith as well as those unregistered therein. In the case of individual representation of a worker, trade unions may only represent a worker not registered therewith on his or her own application.

The International Labour Organization Convention regarding trade union freedom is a fundamental construct underlying the 1991 law.[14] This means recognition of the worker's unfettered right to belong to the trade union of his or her choice, both national and international. This 'freedom of association' also encompasses the so-called 'negative union freedom,' which is the prohibition against discrimination based on nonmembership in a particular union. This prohibition extends to hiring, continuing employment, as well as to professional and career advancement. The law also recognizes the principle that trade unions are entitled to be independent of employers, governmental and local self-government organs, and other organizations. The latter clause certainly encompasses political parties, which is a clear abnegation of the Leninist concept that trade unions exist as a conveyor belt transmitting communist ideology to the masses. The third pillar of trade union freedom – freedom of self-government, manifested by free choice of organizational structure, membership qualifications, competencies of various organs, as well as decision making procedures – is also specifically recognized in the 1991 law.

The 1991 law grants trade unions the powers necessary to carry out their basic protective functions outlined above. In terms of collective representation, in the first instance obviously unions are granted the right to collectively bargain and to conclude binding collective agreements and contracts. The specific provisions governing collective bargaining, however, are contained in a separate statute, which is hereinafter discussed in the next chapter. In addition, the union's right to exercise supervisory control and review is worthy of special emphasis. Unions are granted supervisory rights to see that the provisions and regulations regarding workers, pensioners (both retired and disabled persons), and the unemployed, as well as their families, are enforced; the right to officially comment on legislative projects and executive acts concerning activities within the scope of trade union functions; the right to petition for the issuance of legal acts and directives deemed necessary in order to carry out trade union functions; and the right to extraordinary appeal against a final sentence in the matters involving labour law and social insurance.

The 1991 law grants explicit rights to union organizations at the plant level, which usually represent the lowest organizational unit in a union's hierarchy, but in some particular instances themselves constitute an independent union registering only the workers of a particular plant. They have the right to jointly determine with

12.   *Dziennik Ustaw* No. 55, 1991, item 234. 'Documents de Droit Social,' 1991 Pol.1, Bit.
13.   *See:* M. Sewerynski, 'Les particularités du syndicalisme de pays de l'est et les tendences recentes dans ce domaine,' *Revue Internationale de Droit Comparé*, année 1990, No. 1, pp. 115–117.
14.   *See:* L. Florek, 'Problems and dilemmas of labour relations in Poland,' *Comparative Labour Law Journal*, Vol. 13, No. 2, Winter 1992, pp. 113–114; and Swiatkowski, *supra* note 6, pp. 194–195.

employers the principles governing distribution of plant benefit funds, the establishment of wage and salary scales, work rules, time schedules, and vacation leaves. Plant-level union organs are also authorized to postulate an official position in cases involving individual workers. Of particular importance in this regard is their right to supervise the justification and legality of workers' employment terminations.

The 1991 law goes beyond simple verbal recognition of trade union freedom. It includes provisions designed to guarantee that the principles established and the rights assigned to trade unions are made into reality. Among such provisions are the aforementioned prohibition against discrimination based on membership, *vel non*, in a particular union; provisions to protect union activists against retaliatory dismissal or reductions in work status; the requirement that employers guarantee to unions the physical and material conditions necessary to carry out their activities; and protection of unions' property and funds. Union officials have the right to paid leave for training and conduct of official union business, and certain members of the union's governing board at the plant level are entitled to complete exemption from plant work during the term of their duties while retaining their full salary. The provisions requiring employers to make available to unions all financial information necessary to properly carry out their functions, and especially that information necessary to carry out fair collective bargaining, are also in the nature of guarantees, as are the provisions providing sanctions for violation of trade union rights.

Nevertheless, however much the 1991 act conforms in its basic outline to the principles of trade union freedom, some of its provisions raise questions. In addition the present stage of trade union development in Poland, characterized by ideological divisions and conflicting organizational interests,[15] necessitates supplementation and further precision of many of the existing provisions. In this context, answers need to be supplied to the following questions: How broad is the scope of the right to organize? Does it apply only to employees (with some exceptions), or may it be exercised as well by anyone performing work activities, including those outside traditional labour relations? When and how does a union obtain permission to operate? Does it have to register itself, subject to judicial approval of its charter as being in accordance with the statute, or is only notification required, which would entail later both supervision and control of its activities? Are unions limited to the function of protecting the professional interests of their members and their rights to receive benefits, or may they engage in such political activity as they wish as well? What criteria should be required of unions to be representative? This issue is of special importance in Poland bearing in mind the present trend toward ever more numerous and smaller-based unions together with the demand made by each of them for equal treatment, regardless of their size. Also, how can union representation be assured for workers in small businesses, where their numbers are not sufficient to constitute a union unit?

B.   Employer's Organizations

Prior to 1989 there were no true employer organizations in Poland, nor was legislation existent with regard thereto. The nature of the economic system – state-owned and centrally administered – precluded the necessity of their existence. The only real

---

15.   *See:* W. Szubert, 'Problems of the Transformation of Labour Relations in the Light of the Polish Experience,' *The Changing Face...*, *supra* note 1, p. 143.

employer was the government itself, and in practice it was the true partner to collective agreements.[16]

As a result of economic transformation, based on the creation and development of a private sector and privatization of the state-owned enterprises, employers in the traditional sense of the word have appeared. When they first began to organize, they did so based on an existing law regarding voluntary associations. In 1991 a separate law regarding employer organizations was enacted.[17] As was the case with the law regarding trade unions, this statute is also based on the principle of freedom to associate and fundamentally emerged from the conventions of the International Labour Organization. The provisions of the 1991 law, however, do not grant equal treatment to both unions and employer organizations as envisioned by convention No. 87 of the ILO. In particular, they specifically limit the representative function of employer organizations those employers have registered with. Therefore, while unions may claim to represent all workers in a particular trade, craft, or branch, employer organizations may not make the same claim unless all such employers are specifically registered therewith. In addition, some of the specific grants of power and authorization in the statute distinguish between unions and employer organizations, although there is no justification for them being disadvantageous to employer organizations. It is also worthy of note that the statute limits, by definition, 'employers' to those entities engaged in a business activity, thus excluding actual employers whose activity is not of business character.

The above-mentioned inadequacies in the law on employer's organizations hamper their ability to fulfil the role expected of them in collective negotiations. An even greater hindrance, however, is the continued widespread existence of state-owned and operated enterprises. Here no employer in the traditional sense may be found to exist. The governmental enterprise directors are hemmed in by their position and dependence on the government, and even worse, often do not identify themselves with the profit-making interests of the particular enterprises of which they are directors. This is evidenced by those instances when directors join trade unions in pressing the government to grant wage and salary increases to workers which may not be economically justified. Such a gesture facilitates the director in carrying out his management duties, while the negative economic consequences of paying unjustifiably high wages have no direct influence on him or his position.

Against this background, simply improving the provisions of the law on employer's organizations will not bring about their desired role in the field of industrial relations. To achieve that end, privatization of the state-owned enterprises must be carried out to its conclusion. Only then can labour relations be framed in terms of equal partners in the entire labour enterprise, and will government be able to play its appropriate role as mediator, arbitrator, and guardian of the public order.

---

16.   Szubert, *supra* note 14, pp. 144–146.
17.   *Dziennik Ustaw* No. 55, 1991, item 235. 'Documents de Droit Social,' 1991 Pol. 2, Bit.

V. COLLECTIVE BARGAINING AGREEMENTS, GENERAL AGREEMENTS, AND COLLECTIVE NEGOTIATIONS

A. Collective Bargaining Agreements

While it is true that collective bargaining agreements were formally recognized as a primary source of labour law during the communist period in Poland, nevertheless, with the exception of a short period of time of relative political relief and in a small number of privileged enterprise branches of particular economic significance, they played a limited role. This was primarily due to the lack of independent negotiating partners: trade unions were subservient to the communist party, while enterprise directors were subservient to the centralized administration of a nationalized economy. Enterprises, saddled with economic plans and far-reaching regulation of labour relations via government-established norms, were offered little negotiating freedom. In addition, constant and continuing difficulties of a crisis nature plagued the economy and were continually used as justifications for a restrictive wage policy and rejection of most workers' demands.[18] Under such conditions, collective agreements were primarily designed as a means of binding trade unions to participate in the implementation of the principles and goals of a politicized economy, and in no way resembled a source of legally binding norms and conditions collectively bargained by free trade unions in the interests of their worker-constituents.[19]

The reforms undertaken by Poland since 1989 provided much different – and better – conditions for negotiating collective bargaining agreements in that free trade unions and a private sector economy both arose therefrom. Nevertheless the role of collective bargaining agreements continued to be minor. There were several primary reasons for this. In the nationalized sector of the economy, a government administrative organ appeared in the role of employer, and negotiating freedom for wages continued to be limited by regulations controlling wage funds. In the private sector, on the other hand, the spurt in the growth of real, independent employers not subject to any wage controls was not accompanied by trade union penetration into such businesses. In addition, the development of collective bargaining agreements was hampered by the old existing legislative provisions with regard thereto, contained in Title XI of the Labour Code. Despite their having been revised in 1986, they were still fundamentally a product of the old communist system. In such conditions, the most critical regulatory role assigned to collective agreements was found not in all-inclusive collective bargaining agreements, but rather in the more narrow plant wage agreements, negotiated by the director of the governmental enterprise with the trade union organ at a plant level, according to the 1984 law regarding such agreements.[20] These agreements, however, failed to fill in many blank spaces ordinarily assigned to collective bargaining agreements, especially as regards the supra-plant level.

Fundamental change in the regulations regarding collective agreements occurred only recently, when the Title XI of the Labour Code was fundamentally revised by the

---

18.   *See:* H. Lewandowski, 'Évolution de la négociation collective de travail dans le droit polonais - periode communiste et postcommuniste,' *Changements politiques.., supra* note 2, pp. 95–106; and Florek, *supra* note 4, pp. 118–121.

19.   *See*: M. Sewerynski, 'Development of the Collective Bargaining System in Poland after the Second World War,' *Comparative Labour Law Journal*, Vol. 14, No. 4, Summer 1993, p. 452.

20.   *Dziennik Ustaw* No. 69, 1990, item 407. *See:* Sewerynski, *supra* note 18, pp. 458–462.

1994 act.[21] Collective bargaining agreements may now be concluded at either the plant or supra-plant level, with no limitations placed on the range of the latter. Such agreements may be concluded in all branches of the economy, with the exception of government functionaries and plant agreements in those plants that are government-financed.

Collective bargaining agreements must be concluded, on behalf of workers, by trade unions. On the other side, they are concluded by employers themselves or employer organizations. Taking into consideration the considerable pluralism in the trade union movement in Poland, the 1994 act allows for the creation of a common union negotiating representation, authorized to negotiate and sign collective bargaining agreements on behalf of all the various trade unions that may be involved. In the event no such representation body is or can be formed, only representative union organizations are authorized to participate in the collective bargaining process. Thus, for the first time in Polish labour law history, the law requires a representative union, both at the plant and supra-plant levels. The formula set forth, however, cannot be deemed satisfactory inasmuch as its application allows for an impasse to arise during the negotiations. Specifically, collective bargaining negotiations are not authorized if no trade union registers at least 50% of the workers subject thereto, or if no common union negotiating representation representing at least 50% of the workers involved, can be agreed upon. Even the creation of such a common union representation does not eliminate all barriers. The law further requires that both plant and supra-plant collective bargaining agreements must be signed by all unions who negotiated the same. For a single union involved in the negotiations to reject the agreement reached is enough to prohibit conclusion of the same.

The 1994 law significantly increases the negotiating freedom of the parties to collective bargaining agreements. The permissible content of such agreements includes all areas of labour relations and other matters that are not otherwise subject to unconditionally binding provisions of Polish law. In addition, the parties thereto may agree to binding dispute resolution mechanisms designed to resolve disputes concerning the application and/or interpretation of the agreements reached. This negotiating freedom as regards content is not fully unrestricted, however. The 1994 law itself eliminates from the bargaining process certain aspects regarding employee termination, workplace regulation, maternity and childrearing leaves, and wage protection for certain types of work.

This means, in effect, that the existing legislation with regard thereto is unconditionally binding. Negotiating freedom is also restricted by the principle of 'workers' privilege', which has long existed in Polish labour law. This principle forbids the inclusion, in collective bargaining agreements, of conditions that are less advantageous to workers than similar conditions already guaranteed by law; or in the case of plant agreements, of conditions less advantageous than the existing provisions of an applicable supra-plant agreement.

A matter related to negotiating freedom is the required registration of collective bargaining agreements. Such agreements must be registered with the Ministry of Labour and Social Policy (in the case of supra-plant agreements) or the regional work inspector (in the case of plant agreements) in order to acquire legal effect. A prerequisite to registration is that they be deemed to comply with all existing applicable legal provisions. In the event registration is refused, however, any party thereto may apply for judicial review of such refusal.

21.　*Dziennik Ustaw* No. 113, item 547. *See:* L. Florek, 'Rokowania i uklady zbiorowe pracy', ('Negotiations and collective bargaining agreements'), *Panstwo i Prawo* No. 12, 1994, pp. 3–17.

The new provisions regarding collective bargaining must be acknowledged as significant and fundamental reform. Nevertheless, they retain too many unnecessary restrictions on the scope of negotiating freedom in the collective bargaining process. The restrictions all concern special legal protection afforded workers in particular instances. One may thus conclude that the restrictions on the collective bargaining process in the law are designed to ensure that workers' conditions are not worsened by collective bargaining regulation. From that point of view, however, it seems that the 'workers' privilege' principle explicitly encoded in the act is sufficient to avoid a worsening of workers' situations. In addition, trade unions in Poland are sufficiently strong and independent to avoid pressures to conclude an agreement worsening the interests of the workers they represent.

The provisions of the 1994 law formulating requirements for a representative union also need some improvements. They should be formulated in such a way that the multiplicity of union organizations does not act as a barrier to collective bargaining negotiations. In particular, at least one union should always be authorized to negotiate on behalf of the workers regardless of the number of unions that may exist in a particular plant. In the event that the unions are unable to agree on a common representation and none fulfil the requirements to otherwise represent the workers, the only solution would appear to be designation of a representative union in an all-workers' referendum. Finally, in the event that more than one union meets the law's representation requirements and no common union negotiating board can be agreed upon, the negotiation and conclusion of a collective bargaining agreement by at least one of such unions should be allowed.

The reason for these legislative deficiencies in the 1994 act may be inferred from the attitudes of the interested parties regarding its subject matter. Trade unions anticipated a wide-ranging grant of authority, the lack of which they so keenly felt in the past. As a result, the specific grants of authority are too widely extended and scattered.[22] In addition, as a result of ideological divisions and the multiplicity of current union organizations, the unions themselves feared strict representation requirements, especially the numerous smaller unions who feared loss of their accreditation to negotiate. Finally, the government, continuing to be heavily engaged in the public sector economy, may be regarded as generally suspicious of too broad a grant of negotiating freedom. Only the employers (of both sectors) have nothing to fear thereby. The combination of the trends and tendencies outlined above exercised a significant influence on the content of the collective bargaining law, which was negotiated by the government, unions, and employers as part of the 'Pact on the Transformation of State-owned Enterprises.'

B. General Agreements

General agreements played an essential role in the construction of democratic Poland. They include both the Gdansk Agreements, concluded in August 1981 between the government and the workers' strike committees (which constituted the embryo of 'Solidarity'), as well as the 'Round-table Agreements,' concluded in 1989 between the communist government and 'Solidarity.' While it is true that the agreements cited were primarily politico-social in nature, one can see in them the original pattern of general agreements as applied to industrial relations.

---

22.   See: Florek, supra note 20, p. 4.

Another prototypical general agreement is the above-cited 'Pact on the Trans-formation of State-owned Enterprises', concluded between the government, trade unions and employer organizations in 1993.[23] Its purpose was to gain trade union acceptance of the program for privatizing the state-owned enterprises. In exchange for their support thereof, they were granted certain wage guarantees, the right to a voice in the privatization process, free distribution to the workers of 10% of the stock in the newly formed companies, as well as being guaranteed one-third of the seats on the Boards of Directors of the same. In addition, the government agreed to submit legislative solutions to certain labour problems to the Polish Parliament, one of the primary of which was the aforementioned law on collective bargaining.[24]

Negotiation of the 'Enterprise Pact' constituted proof of the constructive role tripartite negotiations could play in overcoming social resistance and frustration arising out of the social costs associated with the implementation of economic reform. It also revealed the necessity for granting legislative recognition to the Tripartite Commission for Social and Economic Affairs, which was partly achieved by the 1994 law concerning negotiation of the growth in the average wage.[25] This particular law establishes that the Commission is a form of co-operation and co-ordination between the chief governmental administration organs, trade unions, and employer organizations. Its task is to establish the annual growth index of the average industrial wage, taking into consideration the prognosis for growth in the gross national product as well as the projected rate of inflation. The final determination takes the form of a tripartite agreement, the provisions of which are to be taken into account in negotiations regarding plant collective bargaining agreements.

The above-mentioned law limits the jurisdiction of the Tripartite Commission to regulating wage increases, omitting by silence other aspects of governmental economic and social policy that, according to initial plans, were to be included in discussions between the government and its leading social partners. Nevertheless, the law definitively sanctions tripartite agreements as a form of wage policy, and in doing so, expands the range of collective negotiations as a form of labour relations regulation. This is underscored by the legislative provisions granting to such tripartite agreements a normative character. This solution is also consistent with the overwhelming majority of opinions expressed regarding the future development of Polish labour law. The number of adherents to general agreements of a politico-social nature seems to be dwindling.[26] It seems, however, that the legal nature of the provisions contained in general agreements depends on the nature of the problem about which the negotiations were concerned and on the method used in formulating the stipulations.

C. Collective Negotiations

Prior to 1989 there were no legislative provisions concerning collective bargaining, *per se*. The trade union law of 1991 specifically enumerates the right of unions to conduct collective bargaining negotiations, alongside the provision authorizing unions to enter

---

23.   *See:* J. Wratny, *Pakt o przedsiebiorstwie panstwowym w trakcie przeksztalcania. Omówienie i dokumenty (Pact on State-Owned Enterprise During Transformation. Commentary and Documents)*, Bydgoszcz 1993.
24.   *See:* Sewerynski, *supra* note 18, pp. 475–476.
25.   *Dziennik Ustaw* No. 1, 1995, item 2.
26.   *See:* Sewerynski, *supra* note 18, pp. 474–475.

into collective bargaining agreements. A separate but complementary law concerning the resolution of collective disputes, passed the same day as the trade union law, also enumerates collective bargaining as a way of resolving such disputes. It however contains no provisions setting forth the appropriate forum and method for conducting such negotiations.

The rules and principles for conducting collective bargaining negotiations were not finally enumerated, then, until enactment of the 1994 law, which amended the provisions of the Labour Code regarding collective agreements generally. The amendments establish who may introduce and initiate collective bargaining; they bind employers to provide the union organization conducting such negotiations with the financial information on the enterprise's situation necessary to effectively conduct the same, while containing a corollary proviso that trade unions may not divulge confidential information; and they regulate the use of experts during the negotiations.

The provisions regarding initiation of collective bargaining are new to Polish labour law and deserve special attention. They provide that a party authorized to collectively bargain must negotiate with another such party at the other's demand, provided that the following conditions are met: the stated purpose of such negotiations must be to eliminate an existing gap in binding relations (either because an area is not included in an existing collective bargaining agreement or because the same has lost its legal effect); or it must be to modify an existing agreement due to a significant change in the economic circumstances of an employer or a significant worsening in the material conditions of employees.

A further important innovation is the provision of the law that such negotiations must be carried out in good faith and that both sides must respect the legitimate interests of the other. The act provides its own interpretation of the latter directive. Specifically, it provides that employers must attempt to meet those workers' demands that are justified by the employers' economic situation, and workers must refrain from demands that they know to be unrealizable based on the employer's economic situation. Moreover, both sides must respect the interests of those workers and employees who are not represented at the bargaining table.

It also should be emphasized that the law authorizes the parties to independently designate their own means of resolving those disputes that arise during the course of collective bargaining. If they reach an agreement as to a particular procedure for resolving such a dispute, then the provisions of the separate 1991 law regarding the resolution of collective disputes are not applied, unless the parties themselves agree to apply them in part. The legislative purpose underlying this grant of authority is undoubtedly the desire to extend the autonomy granted to both sides to collectively negotiate over substantive issues to include disputes over the negotiation process as well.

One cannot exclude the possibility, however, that various interpretations of both the law regarding collective dispute resolution and of the agreements reached between parties during collective negotiations will themselves lead to complicated procedural disputes.[27]

---

27.   *See:* Florek, *supra* note 20, p. 14.

VI.   COLLECTIVE LABOUR DISPUTES. STRIKES

A.   Collective Labour Disputes

The political and legal doctrines which prevailed in the communist countries excluded the possibility of social conflicts, including collective labour disputes. As a consequence, there was no established procedure for dealing with such disputes, and as a corollary the right to strike was of course not recognized.[28] This state of prevailing legal and political doctrine began to undergo change in some communist countries as the decline of the communist system became apparent by the 1980s, reflected by the appearance of legislative models for resolving collective labour disputes, including the right to strike.[29] The aim of such legislation was not simply the recognition of conflicting social interests and collective labour disputes in a communist system, however, but as well constituted an attempt to regulate by force of law the spontaneous mass workers' demonstrations that were then occurring.

In Poland, collective labour disputes were recognized by the trade union law of 1982, passed under heavy influence of the workers' protests that had swept the country in 1981. The provisions of this law were of a highly regulatory character, consisting of a significant network of obligatory procedures and far-reaching restriction on the right to strike.[30] This legislation remained in effect until modified by passage of the separate 1991 Act regarding the resolution of collective disputes.[31] The provisions of the 1991 act are based on international standards, as a result of which they are significantly less rigorous regarding both the procedures for resolving collective disputes as well as the right to strike.[32]

According to the 1991 act, the matters of collective disputes between employers and employees could be work conditions, pay, and benefits, as well as the rights and freedoms of trade unions. Representation of the collective rights and interests of workers rests with trade unions. According to the act, only unions are granted the right to initiate and conduct collective disputes, and to conclude agreements as a means of resolving disputes. In a workplace where more than one union organization legally functions, each has the right to initiate and conduct collective dispute, or they may agree to form a common representation for the purpose of carrying out such a dispute.

The 1991 act places certain limitations on the conduct of collective labour dispute. It prohibits disputes in support of the demands of an individual worker that are capable of resolution through the courts. In addition, it requires respect for social peace and order. A union cannot, therefore, commence a collective dispute over an area covered by an existing collective bargaining agreement to which it was a party. In the event of such a dispute, the same cannot be officially initiated until the day the existing contract expires. The effect of the requirement that the social peace and order be

---

28.   *See:* Sewerynski, *supra* note 12, p. 122.
29.   *See:* M. Sewerynski, 'Règlement des conflits collectifs du travail dans les pays de l'Europe de l'Est,' *Les modalités de règlement des conflits d'intérêt. XIIIème Congrès Mondial de Droit du Travail et de la Sécurité Sociale,* Athens 1991, pp. 16–28.
30.   *See:* L. Florek, 'Rapport national: Pologne XIIIème Congrès...,' *supra* note 28, pp. 387–394.
31.   *Dziennik Ustaw* No. 55, 1991, item 236. 'Documents de Droit Social' 1991 Pol. 3, Bit.
32.   *See:* T. Zielinski, 'Conflits collectifs de travail dans le droit polonais – période communiste et postcommuniste,' *Changements politiques..., supra* note 2, pp. 135–146.

observed not only underlies the aforementioned requirement regarding the initiation of disputes, but is especially evident as regards the right to strike.[33]

The 1991 act places two binding procedural requirements on the parties to a collective dispute: negotiation and mediation. Employers must agree to negotiate immediately upon the rejection of a union's demand, simultaneously informing the regional work inspector of the existence of a collective dispute. If the parties are unable to negotiate a resolution of their dispute, they must agree to submit the same to a neutral mediator, whom they choose jointly from an official list. Only if the matter cannot be successfully resolved by mediation does the right to strike present itself to trade unions. They may, however, choose not to exercise the right to strike, but rather submit the matter for resolution to a Board of Social Arbitration, which consists of a professional judge and six other members, chosen in equal numbers by each party. The Board reaches decision by a majority vote, and its decision is binding on the parties, unless one of them refuses in advance to be bound thereby. Thus the arbitrational procedure as well as the choice to be bound by its decision is optional. In the event the matter cannot be resolved by arbitration, unions are once again presented with the strike option.

B. Strikes

According to the act concerning the resolution of collective disputes, the right to strike is an individual right of each worker, which, in practice however, can only be exercised collectively, inasmuch as the act defines a 'strike' as a collective work stoppage by employees designed to resolve a collective labour dispute. The initiation and conduct of a strike is exclusively reserved for trade unions. A strike is a method of last resort, and therefore cannot be announced until all obligatory dispute resolution procedures have been exhausted. In order to announce a strike, a trade union must obtain agreement thereto by a majority of workers who are concerned. In undertaking the decision to strike, a union must measure the gains to be had therefrom against the losses incurred in connection therewith. As regards the specific forms strikes may assume, the act refers only to warning strikes and solidarity strikes. The latter may be organized in order to protect the rights and interests of workers not belonging to the union that itself undertakes the decision to strike.

Participation in a strike must be voluntary. If a strike is legal, participation therein does not constitute an abandonment by a worker of his or her obligations, and the worker may not lose his or her rights and privileges as a result of such participation, with the exception of the right to wages during the strike.

The limitations on the right to strike and the denial of the right to certain groups of workers is considerably less extensive than under the previous law. Essentially, the only justification recognized for limiting the right to strike or denying the same to certain groups of workers is if a strike is deemed to constitute a danger to life or health or threaten national security.

The law regarding the resolution of collective disputes is universally regarded as ineffective. In order to prove its D, one only has to look at the vast number of labour disputes and strikes which have taken, and currently take place in which the act's

---

33.   *See:* A. Swiatkowski, 'Social Peace Obligation During Transition Period from Planned to Market Economy,' *Yearbook of Polish Labour Law and Social Policy*, A. Swiatkowski (ed.), Vol. 4, 1993, pp. 111–123.

provisions are ignored. The primary reasons for this are social rather than legal. In the present state of affairs, most strikes are a spontaneous reaction on the part of workers to the losses they are suffering as a result of the transition to a free market economy. The government, on the other hand, shows toleration for illegal strikes and in fact negotiates with the strikers in order to avoid stirring up public discontent.[34]

However, the pathological nature of the current situation *vis-à-vis* collective labour disputes is also partly due to deficiencies in the 1991 act. It seems to prefer procedural solutions to substantive ones. Rather than concentrating on ensuring that the parties to a collective labour dispute have maximum autonomy and negotiating freedom over regulatory matters, thus opening the door to wide-ranging negotiation and agreements as a means of resolving collective disputes, the 1991 act offers a series of obligatory procedures. All of these procedures, with the exception of negotiation, should be optional. Rather than viewing them as a way to regulate and discipline the conduct of collective bargaining, they should be offered as an additional means to achieve a negotiated solution. In addition, judicial control of the legality of collective dispute, and especially strikes, should be established. Without such supervision, effective sanctions are difficult to apply in the event the same are necessary.

Some labour law scholars have also called attention to the lack of mutuality of remedy, especially that brought about by the failure of the 1991 act to acknowledge the legality of lock-outs.[35] In their defensive form they would offer employers a weapon to balance against strikes, and could be applied at least in the case where a court decides that a given strike is illegal. Polish employers and employer organizations favour the recognition of lock-outs. Trade unions are opposed.[36] In addition, the 1991 act offers no solution to those cases where a collective labour dispute becomes prolonged as the parties are not able to resolve it, and by its prolonged nature begins to constitute a threat to the public interest. In such cases it would seem that binding arbitration, subject to judicial review, should be made obligatory.

VII.   WORKERS' PARTICIPATION IN ENTERPRISE MANAGEMENT

In communist times, the principle of worker participation in management of the state-owned enterprise in which they were engaged was written into the constitution. Such was the case in Poland as well. The communist authorities, however, uniformly treated worker participation as an instrument to gain workers' approval for the tasks and projects each enterprise was saddled with from on high, and not as a method of introducing true democracy into labour relations.[37] Under the press of events in Poland in 1981, a law was enacted regarding the establishment of self-government by the personnel of state-owned enterprises.[38] The provisions of this law, patterned after the

---

34.   *See:* Szubert, *supra* note 14, pp. 150–151; and Florek, *supra* note 13, pp. 123–124.
35.   *See:* A. Swiatkowski, 'Strikes and Lockouts in Polish Society Heading Toward Industrialized Market Economy,' *Yearbook of Polish Labour Law and Social Policy*, Vol. 4, 1994, pp. 161 and 170.
36.   *See:* A. Baczkowski, 'In search of Optimum Solutions,' *Tripartism and Industrial Relations in Central and Eastern European Countries.* Ministry of Labour and Social Policy, Warsaw, March 1994, p. 37.
37.   *See:* M. Sewerynski, 'L'évolution de la législation sur l'autogestion des travailleurs en Pologne,' *Revue 4 Internationale de Droit Comparé*, juillet-septembre 1983, No. 3, pp. 463–495.
38.   *Dziennik Ustaw* No. 24, 1981, item 123.

Yugoslavian model, constituted a fundamental change in the legal framework of worker participation. They represented a compromise between 'Solidarity's' demands for complete socialization of the process of economic management by giving the same to the workers, and the position of the communist authorities who wish to retain for themselves control of the economy. The provisions of this law continue to remain in effect today.

The law recognizes the personnel of an enterprise as a legal entity legitimately entitled to participate in enterprise management. In the realization of its participation, the personnel as an entity is independent of governmental administrative organs, trade unions, and political parties. Its major organs are: a democratically elected Workers' Council, and a General Assembly of Workers (or Workers' Delegates). These personnel organs are simultaneously enterprise organs, existing side-by-side with the directors. The entire personnel also has the right to be heard via a referendum. The aforementioned provisions constituted a break with the previously existing system of management whereby worker participation was achieved exclusively through plant trade unions and communist party organizations.

The power of limited self-government, granted to the personnel, is implemented primarily by means of the issuance of resolutions regarding particular issues, resolutions which have obligatory force in the enterprise. In addition, the Workers' Council has the power to appoint and dismiss the enterprise director. This wide-ranging right is, however, partly restricted by the complementary authority granted to the so-called Governmental Founding Organs of each enterprise. The personnel organs also have the right to issue an opinion, the right of petition, and some supervisory rights. The decisions undertaken by both the personnel organs and enterprise directors are subject to mutual review and supervision. In the event of conflicts or disputes arising from such mutual collaboration, the same are to be submitted to a conciliatory committee based on parity of representation, and in the event the committee's efforts are unsuccessful, they are to be resolved by the courts.

The 1981 law does not clearly define the mutual relationship between an enterprise's self-government organs and the trade union(s) operating therein. While this is a significant flaw in the act, nevertheless its provisions are not in direct conflict with the rights granted to trade unions in other legislation.

The Round-Table Agreements of 1989 approved the model of workers' self-government found in the 1981 Act, and even envisioned its further strengthening. In the ensuing period, the role and prestige of Workers' Councils increased as they became engaged in the political changes taking place. This participation was short-lived, however. As the social costs of economic reform increased, the Workers' Councils more and more frequently opposed reform, hampering both the privatization of their own enterprises and the streamlining of employment practices. As a result, the Workers' Councils lost prestige and engagement in those political and social circles most closely associated with economic transformation.

The 1990 law on the privatization of state-owned enterprises[39] is of special importance to Workers' Councils, for it provides that following transformation of such enterprises into stock companies, the Workers' Councils undergo liquidation. Thus, the privatization of state-owned enterprises, the keystone to economic reform, will lead to the complete abolishment of worker participation in enterprise management in its present form. The law does provide, however, for another form of worker participation

---

39. *Dziennik Ustaw* No. 51, 1990, item 298.

in management of the newly-formed companies. This consists of a guarantee that workers will be granted one-third of the seats on the company's Supervisory Board.

The idea of eliminating Workers' Councils as a form of worker participation in management arose in the political circles most responsible for initiating economic reform in 1990. Their leaders, following a neo-liberal economic doctrine (or, in American terms, classic conservatism), were of the opinion that the Workers' Councils were necessary in communist times as a substitute for democracy, but in conditions of actual democracy the Workers' Councils are not only unnecessary, but even harmful inasmuch as they place roadblocks to economic reform and discourage foreign investment in Poland.

Not only in scholarly and legal circles, but also in political circles, the concept of Workers' Councils as a form of worker participation in company management is not without its adherents.[40] Even among them, however, the concept of worker self-government as expressed in the 1981 act, including the passage of binding resolutions and the appointment and dismissal of directors, is not appropriate to the new economic conditions. Thus they are seeking new legislative solutions to the problem of worker participation. They are influenced by the positive experience of some Western governments in this regard as well as the formulations of worker participation in company management contained in documents of the European Union.

In discussing the present state of Polish law regarding worker participation, to consider some of the provisions of the collective bargaining act of 1994 is also necessary. This act grants trade unions the possibility of participating in company management together with the directors thereof via the inclusion of such provisions in plant collective bargaining agreements. In other words, the regulatory provisions of the act concerning the substantive scope of collective bargaining agreements permit issues concerning management of a plant to be negotiated and solutions thereto to be included in the final collective bargaining agreement.

Also, the 1990 law on the privatization of state-owned enterprises establishes the principle of workers' *capital* participation in the creation of new companies. Its provisions envision granting workers the right to obtain up to 20% of the newly issued stock of such companies on preferential terms. The final form of such capital participation, however, will only be determined when the so-called 'Common Privatization Program' is fully worked out.

VIII.   CONCLUSION

The process of adjusting Polish labour law to the principles of a new political and economic system is not yet finished. Even if the projected amendments to the Labour Code are passed as expected, the process of recodification of labour law will continue. In addition, an all-encompassing law on industrial relations is presently being prepared.

---

40.   *See:* M. Sewerynski, 'Évolution et perspectives de la participation des travailleurs à la gestion de l'entreprise en Pologne,' *Changements politiques..., supra* note 2, pp. 172–177.

The Development of the Right to Work in Romania after the 1989 Revolution

Sanda Ghimpu and Alexandru Ticlea

I. INTRODUCTION

A. The Stages of the New Legislation

The 1989 December Revolution brought great changes in legislation, including the right to work. The judicial norms are now in accordance with the economic and social realities; likewise the juridical framework, which is essential for the further development of the society, is being established. The changes in the legislation mean that the legislation is adjusted to the new requirements of the market economy. In the first stage, a number of legislative measures were considered in order to remove the restrictive measures of the centrally planned economy. In the second ongoing stage, new normative acts have been adopted, with totally different orientations and content from the ones of the past system.

B. Distinctive Features of the First Stage

The first changes regarding labour legislation were mainly concerned with:
- the elimination of certain inequities regarding the wage system;
- shorter hours, setting up a 5-day work week;
- granting of certain new wage rights;
- increasing the share of benefits and pensions from the social insurance funds.

One of the most significant normative changes that modified the wage system was Law Decree No. 35/1990. This law abolished the provisions of Law No. 1/1986 and Law Decree No. 161/1988 on wages based on the norms, conditions, and indexes of export achievement. Although the above-mentioned former laws stated that wages were not limited in the case of a production which is larger or smaller than planned, in reality wages were cut without securing a guaranteed income since the centrally planned economy did not take into consideration the material resources and the low level of technical equipment when setting the norms of the plan; these norms could not be accomplished. Wages were also decreased because the export tasks were not fulfilled due to the above-mentioned causes and due to the lack of relations between the producing company and the foreign partner.

    The same law (No. 35/1990) abolished the unlawful and incorrect measures that limited the number of employees who were entitled to receive wage increases for working in very bad and dangerous conditions. According to these measures, a great number of workers did not receive wage increases, although they worked in the same circumstances as others who could take the advantage of this right, only because the statistical figures indicating the number of people working in hazardous conditions were not realistic, and only this registered number of people were covered by the system.

Law 35/1990 also abolished the unlawful former measures that limited the number of employees in work groups I and II, where employment guaranteed advantageous pension conditions, e.g., the length of service was increased by three or six months per one working year, the retirement age was reduced, and so on.

The other provisions abolished by the same normative act were those which limited the number of workers who could be employed in the last class of the tariff system and the number of persons who could be promoted to grades 4, 5, 6 and 7.

A provision of high importance, which is intended to promote the career prospects of young employees, is Article 10 of Law No. 135/1990 according to which the minimum length of service stipulated by Law No. 12/1971 for promotion in grade and classification as well as the minimum length of service necessary for promotion to higher grades could be reduced by a maximum of 50%. Subsequently, Law No. 30/1990 on the employment of people according to their ability, abolished 'the legal provisions binding upon management positions, executions or any other kind of jobs, irrespective of their field, length of service or in the line...' (Article 5, paragraph 1).

Other inequities concerning the staff system of wages, the granted increases of wages and the employment in groups of work were removed by Law Decree No. 68/1990. This normative act abolished Law No. 1/1986 and the Decree No. 161/1981, which regulated remuneration in the collective agreement (Article 1) and granted certain rights to employees employed in work groups I and II (Article 2), to workers and trainers in the polygraph industry, and to drivers as well (Article 5). The act also stipulated higher wages, with bonuses and increases for uninterrupted length of service in the same company (Articles 7–12).

Law Decree No. 147/1990 modified or abolished a number of paragraphs of the Labour Code, of the Staff Rules in Civil Aircraft (approved by Decree No. 413/1979), of Law No. 12/1971 regarding employment and promotion of employees of state enterprises, and of Law No. 5/1978 (revised in 1981) regarding the management and functions of state socialist enterprises, as well as their operation by virtue of workers' self government and financial economic management. These amendments and abrogations aimed at eliminating some wordings and provisions which were no longer in harmony with the political, economic, and social situation of the country after 22 December 1989 (e.g. references to the former Romanian Communist Party, provisions meant to influence the freedom of labour or regarding the planned development of the national economy, to the improvement of the ideological and political training of the staff, to the attachment to the socialist system, to the role and function of trade unions in the socialist system, and to the system of reports on the behaviour of the would-be employees written by the trade union based on their previous place of work, which was a precondition of the new employment in an enterprise). Within the measures that were mainly meant to improve the legal relationship of the working people by removing certain provisions that hindered the freedom of employees' movement and deprived them of certain fundamental rights, the partial or total abrogation of other normative acts are being laid down.

We would also like to mention the rapid abrogation of the provisions of Article 64, paragraph 1, of Law No. 5/1978, a totally vague piece of legislation that violated the fundamental rights to have legal defence and to appeal and that, under certain circumstances, made it possible to deprive a person of the basic right to work without being entitled to defend himself or herself or to appeal against the measure already taken. In accordance with this text, there were other binding measures: e.g., the decisions of 'the general assembly of working people'; the management of an enterprise was to be released if found guilty of serious violations of the labour discipline of the people, or, of violating 'norms of socialist ethics and equities of being irresponsible for the fulfilment of the plan'. The labour contract for the other 'working people' was also cancelled if it violated these binding measures.

We would also mention the abrogation of Law No. 25/1976 on the employment 'in a useful labour' of people able to work by the Law Decree No. 9/1989, after these laws were declared contradictory with the conventions of the International Labour Organization on free and forced labour, ratified by Romania. This normative modification obliged people able to work, at or above the age of 16, to register themselves at the labour and social protection offices in the area where they reside and demand a job in the case that they do not attend any kind of educational institution, do not have any professional qualifications, or are not employed. In order to accomplish and observe the right to free labour and to meet the demands of the students, Decree No. 54/1975 on the system of day courses compulsory for higher education graduates was also abrogated.

Besides the above-mentioned changes, a new decentralized wage system was introduced that met the new requirements of the market economy. At the same time, the Wage Law No. 14/1991 came into force and abolished three laws: the Remuneration Law No. 57/1974 (republished in 1980) on labour quantity and quality (except for Article 75, paragraph 1 and Articles 196–197), Law No. 1/1983 regarding the basic principles of the improvement of the labour remuneration system and distribution of the incomes of the working people, and Law No. 1/1986 regarding remuneration in collective agreements and in the bilateral labour contracts of employees.

One of the greatest achievements of the employees that also appeared in a corresponding piece of legislation was the introduction of the five-day work week. It was stipulated by Law Decree No. 95/1990 that the five-day work week had to be introduced in all fields and branches of industry by 1 March 1990.

Another law of great importance adopted in early 1990 is Law Decree No. 31/1990 on paid leave for taking care of children for a one-year period; during this period the parent receives a benefit equal to 65% of her or his basic salary.

C.   Characteristics of the Second Stage

This stage is characterized by the adoption of several fundamental normative acts, i.e., the establishment of new legislation in Romania: Law No. 30/1990 regarding the employment of people depending on their ability; Law No. 2/1991 regarding holding more than one office; Law No. 13/1991 regarding collective labour agreements; Law No. 14/1991 regarding the wage system, Law No. 15/1991 regarding dispute settlements in offices; Law No. 31/1991 concerning the establishment of working days shorter than 8 hours a day for employees working in extremely difficult, harmful or dangerous conditions; Law No. 54/1991 regarding trade unions; Law No. 6/1992 regarding holidays and other leaves of the employees; Law No. 1/1992 (revised in 1994) regarding social protection and retraining of the unemployed, etc.

Law No. 13/1991 is of great importance regarding the right to work as it introduced the system of negotiations at the workplace. According to the stipulations of this law, the relations between the two social partners – owners and employees – are institutionalized; labour conditions and wage systems are established by them through collective agreement (Article 12). Under the new circumstances, due to this agreement the right to work ceases to be a nationalized right; it becomes a law of conventional nature, entirely different from the previous one. Law No. 14/1991 is also of tremendous importance regarding the establishment and development of the new right to work, which stipulates among others that wages are established by collective agreements, or under certain circumstances by individual contracts between legal or natural persons and the employers, or their representatives (Article 4, paragraph 2). Law No. 31/1991, which stipulates that the duration of working hours can be reduced and that the staff can take advantage of a labour program of less than 8 hours per day, can be utilized only on basis of the result of the negotiations between the owner and the trade unions (Article 3, paragraph 2); this is also the case for Law No. 6/1992, according to which, rules regarding paid and unpaid holidays, and paid days off, are established by collective agreement (Article 5, paragraph 1 and Article 10, paragraph 3).

This way, the right to work is gaining ground; it acquires valences by negotiation, that is by the dialogue between the employees organized in trade unions and employers, and it is becoming what it is already known to be in all developed countries of the world: a right to be negotiated.

Taking into consideration the great importance of the collective labour agreement and of trade unions, as well as the importance of collective bargaining, which was not regulated before 1989, we have decided to deal with these concepts in separate chapters of our study.

Another normative change that should be mentioned is Government Decree No. 503/1991; this stipulates the establishment of employers' organizations in Romania, in keeping with the exigencies of the market economy, in the case of municipalities and economic companies which are owned by the state. By virtue of this decree, trade companies partially or totally privatized, which employ at least 50 employees, as well as natural persons working as entrepreneurs, can join the employers' organizations of local municipalities and of the state-owned economic companies. According to the respective decree, within one branch industry more than one employers' organization can be set up at the national level of the owners' federations. Since 1924, in accordance with the law on legal persons, other employers' organizations, private in character, have been set up.

Another normative decree worth mentioning is Government Decree No. 349/1993 on the organizations of the Tripartite Secretariat for Social Dialogue, a political non-governmental and non-profit body. This body has an equal number of representatives from trade unions, from employers' organizations, and from the Government. The main purpose of the Secretariat is to provide the trade unions, the employers' organizations, and the Government with the technical assistance of the European Economic Community and with the support of the Co-ordination Union of the Phare Programme in order to promote social dialogue in Romania.

Of course, the legislative process in the field of law has not been concluded yet; other normative changes are to be accomplished in accordance with the new social and economic organizations in Romania.

First of all, a new Labour Code should be elaborated, as the 1972 Labour Code, which is still in force even today, is an outdated normative decree that – irrespective of its amendments – does no longer correspond with the present situation. Secondly there are certain fields which are not regulated yet, or there are poorly regulated ones, as is to be described in the following chapters.

D. Fields to be Regulated

1. Representations of Workers

There are no special regulations at present regarding workers' representation at the level of the enterprise, the election of their representatives, their participation in decisions, etc. The present situation is just the reverse of the situation before 1989, when the enterprises were organized and operated, according to Law No. 5/1978, by virtue of workers' self-governance. Before the revolution no decision could be taken, including the ones in the field of juridical labour relationship, without 'following the advice' or even 'the decision of the general assembly'.

Neither Law No. 15/1990 regarding the reorganization of state-owned economic units as self-governing administrations and economic companies, nor Law No. 31/1990 on economic companies, nor any other normative act, for that matter, stipulate the possibility of the employees' participation in the management of these units. At present, workers are taking part in decisions by means of trade unions under the terms stipulated by Law No. 54/1991, which we shall refer to in one of the following chapters.

Of course, this situation is not natural, and that is why the elections of staff delegates, the appointment of delegates or trade union representatives to the board of directors of these units (self-governing management, economic companies, etc.) and their duties and protection should be regulated as in other developed countries (e.g. France).

2. Labour Inspection

Although, in accordance with Government Decree No. 448/1994, the Labour and Social Protection Ministry is the specialized body which guarantees the uniform application of the legal provisions, the practice of the previous years has evoked the demand for the introduction of labour inspection, as it was instituted in the inter-war period.

An alarming negative fact is black labour, which is getting more and more widespread. Black labour means that employees work without concluding a labour contract and they are totally deprived of the rights guaranteed for employees within the present social protection network (wages, sick leaves, holidays, length of service, etc.). Among the 70,000 existing private companies in Bucharest, only 23,000 registered their employees at the Chamber of Labour. There is a draft law regarding certain protection measures for employees, but the observance of the legal provisions regarding labour relations could be ensured only by labour inspection – a specialized inspection body in this field.

3. Layoffs

Lay off, one of the measures employers use as a means for retortion in the event of strike, is also unregulated. Romania has not so far experienced a situation in which an employer should close down the enterprise because of a collective labour dispute. However, as we think that the present situation could warrant such retortion, the practice of lay-offs should be settled urgently in a similar way as strikes are regulated.

4. Labour Jurisdiction

After the 1992 abolishment of the jurisdictional bodies, the judicial committees that had general competence in settling labour disputes, the Common Law Courts, were also invested with competence to settle labour disputes. The Romanian juridical system includes Law Courts, Courts, Courts of Appeal and the Supreme Court of Justice.

The Court of Law is the Common Law Institution, which, according to Law no. 92/1992, is authorized to settle work disputes such as:
- financial disputes,
- appeals regarding the cancellation of the individual labour contract and labour reinstatement,
- disputes regarding the execution, amendment, and cessation of the collective contract (Article 17 of Law No. 13/1991),
- disputes regarding restoring of labour card (Article 8 of Decree No. 92/1976),
- disputes regarding unemployment benefit (Article 28 of Law No. 1/1991, republished in 1994).

We consider it extremely important that certain specialized institutions should be set up, Labour Courts of Law, with specialized judges for setting labour disputes, with a wide-range competence, with assessors appointed by professional organizations, and with the advantage of two jurisdiction grades. Romania had such a law, in 1933.

II. LABOUR POLICY, LABOUR ADMINISTRATION

A. Different Types of Training

1. Professional Training

In its first meaning, professional training is an activity carried out by a person before being employed at a job, with a view to acquiring general cultural and specialized knowledge necessary to practise a profession or a trade. As it has such significance, professional training is similar to professional skill.

Under other circumstances, in a broader sense, professional training can also mean improvement through training, i.e., acquiring fresh knowledge.

In view of its importance, professional training is unique as a continuous process, which is objectively determined by the progress of the society, by the continuous development of modern science and technique.

Professional training is firstly achieved by the national education system, the right to education being one of the fundamental rights of the citizens laid down in the Constitution (Article 32). However, the form of education that is carried out with the aim of employment, or carrying out other activities yielding an income, is called professional training.

In order to achieve the right to education and the participation of each citizen in a form of education, the 1991 Constitution and Government Decree No. 283/1993 stipulate provisions constituting important juridical guarantees such as:
–   citizens of Romania are entitled to education, irrespective of their social status, sex, membership of a party, religion, and without any other restriction that might contribute to the non-observance of the basic human rights;
–   primary and secondary education (grades I-VIII) is compulsory;
–   education is organized by the state, and is open to each citizen, with free admittance to all grades and forms of education, as well as the ability of transition from one type of school to another in order to acquire a sound, universal cultural and social-professional training organized at local and national scale and adjusted to international standards. The Constitution (in Article 32 paragraph 5) also stipulates the existence of independent education;
–   state education is free of charge;
–   the state secures protection and education facilities to children under the age of 16, by educating them in various forms of educational institutes;
–   education of all categories is carried out in Romanian, while the national minorities are simultaneously granted the right to education and training in their own languages. The Constitution also provides for the right of carrying on education in an international language (Article 33 paragraph 2);
–   the entire education system is co-ordinated by the Ministry of Education, which is in charge of its organization, contents, and the inspection of the instructional process.

In accordance with Article I of the Government Decree No. 283/1993, the education system in Romania includes: pre-school education; elementary education with grades I–IV; middle school education with grades V–VIII; secondary education with grades IX–XII or IX–XIII; vocational education with grades I–III or I–IV; continuing or apprenticeship education with grades I–II; practical trainers' technical education with grades I–II or I–III; post secondary school specialized education with grades I–II or I–III; higher education with years I–VI; post-graduate education; Ph.D. courses; etc.

2.   Vocational and Apprenticeship Education

According to Article 25 of the Government Decree No. 283/1993, vocational education is carried out by vocational schools with a duration of 3–4 years (day courses). These schools are organized under the leadership of the Ministry of Education, by school Inspectorates, Ministries, other central bodies, industrial companies, self-governing administrations, as well as local municipalities. Vocational schools can function by themselves or together, with secondary schools, technical schools for practical trainers and specialized post secondary schools constituting school group units. By the instructional process organized in these schools, both professional training and practical activity as well as universal training are carried out: the graduation degree in the trade in which their students are trained entitles them to practice the respective trade, in accordance with the classification list established by the Ministry of Education and the Ministry of Labour and Social Protection (Article 27).
        The continuing or apprenticeship system of education is organized by the local administrative boards, respectively by economic units appointed by the Ministry of Education, for promoted pupils of the VIIIth form (middle school), that have not been

included in the vocational or secondary form of education (Article 28). This form of education is organized in day courses with a duration of two years. It may function within school group units, high schools, vocational schools, or schools with grades I–VIII. Within continuation or apprenticeship education, general training, vocational training, and practical activity for a trade corresponding to local needs of co-operation, multiple service, and other departments are provided. The graduates of these schools earn degrees which entitle them to practise the trade they had been trained for on basis of the classification lists established by the Ministry of Education as well as by the Ministry of Labour and Social Protection.

The graduates of the continual or apprenticeship schools as well as of the vocational education can continue their studies in the high schools according to rules established by the Ministry of Education.

3. Technical Education for Practical Trainers

Article 32 of Government Decree No. 283/1993 stipulates that technical education for practical trainers is carried out at the request of the interested ministries, and of the economic units, by technical schools for practical trainers with a duration of 1–1.5–2 years (day courses), or 3–4 years (evening courses), on basis of the classification list for training.

Competitive examinations and entrance examinations as well as graduation examinations in the technical schools for practical trainers are organized in accordance with the rules in force by the Ministry of Education in co-operation with the interested ministries. The graduates of these schools get graduation degrees, which entitle them to practise their respective trade, in accordance with the classified lists established by the Ministry of Education and by the Ministry of Labour and Social Protection.

4. Post Secondary School Specialized Education

Article 35 of the Government Decree No. 283/1993 provides for the post secondary school specialized education to be organized by the Ministry of Education, at the request of the ministries and the economic departments, or of economic units other than central bodies.

High school graduates with a baccalaureate degree who want to be trained in order to practise certain professions in the field of technical, economic, social-cultural, and medical fields in accordance with the classification list for training, can attend these schools. The respective schools are organized with day and evening courses within school group units or together with secondary schools, under a one-man management.

The graduates of the post secondary schools are entitled, by virtue of graduation degree, to practise their learned profession in accordance with the classification lists established.

5. Higher and Postgraduate Education

In keeping with Article 39 of Government Decree No. 283/1993, higher education includes university and post-graduate education. University education, in its turn,

116

includes: short-terms university education – university colleges (2–3 years), long-term university education (4–6 years), and university education for elaborate studies (1–2 years).

Short-term university education (the first two years of studies) is organized simultaneously with long-term education and is devoted to training experts with high qualification, middle management with vocational and secondary level studies, and for long-term higher studies.

Long-term higher education is training for theoretical and practical experts. University education studies are achieved by day, evening, and partial attendance courses; in the case of the last two forms, the duration of the studies is one year longer than in the case of day courses.

Starting with the academic year 1993–1994, the higher education has been organized in stages (Article 41). The graduates of short-term higher education are given 'The Graduation Diploma,' those of the long-term higher education get 'Master of Arts,' and the graduates of the higher education with elaborate studies get 'The Elaborate Studies Diploma' (Article 44).

Higher education state institutions, starting with the academic year 1993–1994, admitted more students in the first year of studies than the number accepted for that year. These students pay an education fee (Article 46).

Post-graduate education is organized in: specialized post-graduate education forms, post-graduate courses (1–12 months), post-graduate schools (1.5 – 2 years), and doctorate courses. It functions within higher education institutions with full and part-time attendance.

The doctorate, which is stipulated by Article 52 of the Government Decree No. 283/1993, constitutes the higher form of scientific professional training of experts in different branches of science, technology, and culture.

6. Training Courses

Training courses represent a form of education that trains workers in a trade. They are regulated by Government Decree No. 360/1990 on skilled workers in state enterprises. The first-stage training courses and the second-stage training courses are also organized for unemployed persons – in virtue of Law No. 1/1991 revised in 1994 – by the territorial departments of labour and social protection.

In agreement with Article 1 of Government Decree No. 360/1990, state units can organize first and second stage training or multi-service training courses, with the consent of the local and central bodies and with the professional assistance of the Department of Labour and Social Protection, in order to meet the requirements of skilled workers to receive special training for specific activities.

The courses are organized according to trades, with or without theoretical education. As a rule the participants attending the courses have a full time work programme; the duration is 3–4 months, graded according to the difficulty of the trades (Article 2).

Workers who want to be trained for one or more trades that cannot be acquired without risks and evident hazards for the worker, workers who require authorization to practise a trade, or workers who are taking jobs at random can attend the courses. Courses can also be attended by workers who are trained on the basis of a contract that they have with other enterprises, as well as other categories of people who accept to train themselves for such trades (Article 3).

The following people can attend the training courses: people with normal age for work, middle school graduates, people in good health, people employed with a labour contract for an unlimited period of time, people who are not skilled in a trade, those who can no longer practise their trade or cannot be available for full time activity efficiently, and other categories of people who are willing to get trained in view of their reinstatement to work.

Graduates of the four elementary forms of education can also be admitted to training courses in simple trades that do not require theoretical knowledge (Article 14). Besides the above-mentioned measures, Government Decree No. 288/1991 (amended in 1994) has initiated the form of vocational training for unemployed people. Training and retraining in a trade for unemployed people is organized by the Labour and Social Protection Department and is carried out according to the circumstances, at their own enterprises or in other units (local municipalities, industrial companies, other economic units, authorized higher education institutes, authorized natural persons) by virtue of agreement (Article 1).

Training or retraining is effected for trades, specialized fields, positions, and activities adequate to the demands of the labour market (Article 2). The duration for this type of activity is 6 months maximum, depending on the complexity of the trade, profession, or kind of work (Article 4).

Persons able to work in the trades, the professions, or other types of activity can attend the course. They also have corresponding studies and have been selected and professionally oriented. Persons that have not finished their compulsory general education can also be admitted to the courses for easier trades or activities that do not demand theoretical education.

Article 11, paragraph 2 of Law No. 1/1991 stipulates the conclusion of an agreement between persons attending a training course (or retraining course) and the Labour and Social Protection department under which the person attending the course is obliged to repay the unemployment benefit (for the period of the course) as well as the education fees, should he or she refuse, without any serious reason, to accept a job offered to him or her at a respective enterprise.

7. Upgrading Professional Training

Employees have the right and duty to upgrade their professional training when they are employed or promoted to a corresponding classification of job (Article 13 paragraph 1 of the Labour Code; Article 97 paragraph 3 of the Collective Agreement of Labour, unique at the national scale for the year 1993, valid for 1994).

According to law, professional training is upgraded through refreshing courses (i.e. 'to refresh and enrich systematically the knowledge in the profession, to study thoroughly a certain field in the fundamental specialization, to have the ability to gain the most recent achievements of science, technique and culture in the specialized field or the related ones,' Article 2 paragraph 1 of Law No. 2/1971); through multiple service training (i.e., to achieve a further professional training besides the main occupation – Article 2, Part b); through retraining in another profession (when the previous profession does not meet the demands of the modern technique nor the pattern of the economy any longer, or it cannot be practised as a result of changes in the working capacity, Article 2, Part c); and through the adoption of some modern methods and procedures in the field of management.

In accordance with Article 3 of Law No. 2/1971, the different professional training upgrading courses can be organized at the respective place of work under the inspection of the main supervisor; as courses organized at the enterprise, as courses organized at another enterprise or at staff training centres, with regular inspection, as practical activities and specialization at the respective enterprise or at other enterprises in the country or abroad. If the person is employed, after having finished his or her education, he or she may attend graduate courses, which include post-graduate education and doctorate courses.

Professional training upgrading is directly related to labour legislation. The organization of this activity, and the control of the way in which the training is carried out, are the responsibilities of the management of the enterprises, as well as of the central and local bodies of state administration. Also, upgrading one's professional skills by training is an official duty of all employees (Article 21 of Law No. 2/1971).

8.   The Additional Provision of the Labour Contract regarding Professional Training

When employees are sent to school, or a training course, or when they are trained at the work place, an additional provision of the labour contract is necessary. This modification is mainly stipulated by Article 71 of the Labour Code, Article 21 of Law No. 1/1970, Article 33 of Law No. 2/1971 and by the national collective contract, which was put into force in the year 1993. This additional modification of the collective contract was stipulated by Government Decree No. 360/1990, which was already mentioned above.

According to Article 8 of the above-mentioned decree, the workers who participate at training courses during their working hours have to sign an additional provision of their labour contract before starting the courses, and in the case that they leave the enterprise without having the management's agreement within 3 years of graduation from the course, they are obliged to bear the tuition expenses proportionally with the full financial period concluded or with the period of 3 years.

As against the provisions of Article 71 of the Labour Code, referring only to 'the obligation of the person with a full time job to work a certain period stipulated by law in the enterprise after graduating from the respective school or course,' other normative measures include better corresponding forms, providing:
a.   the responsibility of the company to bear – directly or through another body – fully or partially, under the law provisions, the expenses for the training of that person;
b.   the employee's duty to work in the respective company a stated period of time, laid down in the contract, since the termination of the training course;
c.   the employee's duty to pay a compensation equal to the expenses borne by the company for the stated time, in the case that the employee is expelled from the school or training course for improper behaviour or the employee leaves school on his own volition.

B. State and Labour

1. Characteristics of the State's Involvement in the Field of Labour

The role played by the Romanian state regarding labour is far from being clear. The state doesn't participate directly, otherwise it should be considered a supporter of centralism.

It is obvious that in the market economy the manpower is a merchandise like all other goods. Job applicants are informed about the vacancies at different types of companies through different channels. From the point of view of supply and demand, the state is neutral when adopting a decision. However, the state is in favour of a situation where the demand meets the supply, so employment offices, the regional bodies of the Ministry of Labour and Social Protection, register both categories. But, the principle of freedom exists; the employer recruits independently the necessary manpower, and the job applicant can reject a certain job or he or she can totally refuse a full-time job; the individual labour contract is freely concluded. Of course, the state acts as a job offeror for its own companies (the local municipalities, state owned companies, organizations financed by state budget, etc.). Under such circumstances the state acts as an employer, and not as a state authority.

In view of setting up new jobs, the state supports the establishment of new companies and it grants certain facilities for the full-time employment of the graduates, as we can see in the chapters below.

2. Stimulating Economic Development

According to Article 1 of the Government Decree No. 25/1993, in view of creating new jobs and promoting productive activities in the field of industry, construction, tourism and services, and research and development in the private sector, the state supports the establishment and development of small-scale and large-scale enterprises, providing a network of advantages and facilities for their benefit.

These advantages and facilities are the following: manpower training, granting of production fields and grounds, allowances for starting investments, and development and modernization granting available new jobs (Article 8 of Decree No. 25/1993).

The system of advantages and facilities is granted to the small-scale and large-scale enterprises, set up according to Law No. 31/1990, which defines the concept of small- and large-scale companies by the number of employees and turnover in the following way:
- the number of 5 to 25 employees for small-scale enterprise;
- the number of 26 up to 200 of employees for the large-scale enterprise;
- a yearly turnover between 2 million and 10 million Lei for both types of enterprises.

The co-operative societies with above-mentioned turnover as well as private enterprises and family enterprises are also covered by the system of advantages and facilities.

Law No. 1/1991, revised in 1994, on social protection and occupational reinstatement of the unemployed stipulates, the process of granting credits under advantageous terms, with an interest rate at 50% of the normal bank interest rate determined in every quarter year, and it stipulates the process of setting up and developing small and large-scale enterprises, with the purpose of creating new jobs available especially for unemployed people (Article 24, paragraph 1 of Part d).

3. Promoting Full-time Employment of the Higher Education Graduates

In order to secure the employment of graduates of higher education, of secondary, post-secondary schools, vocational and apprenticeship schools, Article 1 of Government Decree No. 32/1994 stipulates the obligation of economic units and state companies to inform yearly the labour and social protection regional offices, before the 30th of June, about vacancies for graduates.

The economic units with state or private capital, as well as the authorized state institutions employing graduates with individual labour contract for an indefinite period of time, receive for each graduate employed in the above-mentioned way, for 9-month's employment, the amount of the minimum wage in the case of employees with academic education all over the country, or 60% of the monthly minimum wage in the case of the other categories of graduates. These amounts are paid by the Ministry of Labour and Social Protection from the unemployment benefit fund.

According to Article 5 of the Government Decree No. 32/1994, graduates of the education institutions can get an employment in the above-mentioned terms one time within the year following the graduation.

If within the 9 months period the graduates employed have their labour contract cancelled through no fault of their own, they can get a new job at other economic units or state authorized institutions, for the full period of employment not exceeding 9 months.

C.   Protection of Unemployed

1. The Concept of Unemployed Categories of Persons Taking Advantage of the Protection

Article 1 of Law No. 1/1991 regarding social protection of the unemployed and their professional reinstatement (revised in 1994), stipulates that people capable of work taking the advantage of unemployment benefit and some other forms of social protection, are considered unemployed because they cannot be employed as a result of the lack of available vacant jobs suitable for their qualification and training.

The unemployed – depending on the circumstances – take the advantage of the unemployment benefit of professional transition or, after the period of this benefit expires, a special allotment.

The unemployment benefit is given to persons who have already had a job, with the following conditions:

a. persons whose contract of labour has been cancelled at the initiative of the enterprise, and persons whose employment as a member of an artisan co-operative society has ceased due to unforeseeable reasons;

b. persons whose contract of labour has been cancelled at the initiative of the enterprise, if the decree or decision of the competent body declared the measure taken by the enterprise unlawful due to the fact that the person in question did not commit any fault and if the reinstatement of the person in a job is no longer possible at the company where he was previously employed, or at the company that is the legal successor of the original company;

c. persons whose labour contract has been cancelled at their own initiative, according to law, if their re-employment does not interrupt the length of service;

d. persons already employed with a labour contract of a fixed length of time.

Natural persons authorized to carry out an individual entrepreneurial activity and members of family enterprises who effect an activity, by virtue of Law Decree No. 54/1990, are also regarded unemployed and may take advantage of the unemployment benefit when they conclude their activity and return their licence, if they contributed to the unemployment benefit fund for a duration of 12 months in the last two years prior to the registration of the application (Article 2 of Law No. 1/1991).

The occupational transition benefit is given to persons who have never been employed in a full-time job i.e.:

a. graduates from secondary level education institutions with the minimum age of 18 whose own does not exceed 50% of the national minimum wage and who – within the period of 60 days following their graduation – could not find a job in accordance with their professional training;
b. graduates of education institutions with the minimum age of 16 who can prove by legal evidence that they are not under legal custody or paternal care, which is a legal obligation in the case of person who are under the legal age;
c. young boys who, before effecting their military service, had not concluded a labour contract with a company and who, within the period of 30 days after their discharge, could not find a job (Article 3).

2. Persons not Taking Advantage of the Unemployment Benefit or Professional Transition Benefit

In accordance with Article 6 of Law No. 1/1991, the following categories of people may not take the advantage of the unemployment and professional transition benefit:

a. people who, together with their families, possess agricultural lands with an area of minimum 20,000 m² in the hilly regions and in the plain, or agricultural lands with the area of minimum 40,000 m² in the mountainous regions;
b. persons having their own income or acquiring income as a result of performing authorized jobs against law provisions, and who, in this way, can obtain an income equal to a minimum of 50% of the national minimum wage minus the fee provided by the law;
c. persons having been offered a job corresponding to the level of their training and qualification, which is not dangerous to their personal and health condition, and which is within the distance of 50 km from their dwelling place, or persons having been offered to attend training, retraining or upgrading courses or any other form of occupational training and have unreasonably rejected the offer or the recommendation;
d. persons entitled to retire, according to their length of service and age limit;
e. graduates of secondary schools attending higher level institutions of occupational training, irrespective of their type and duration.

3. Conditions of the Allotment of Unemployment or Professional Transition Benefit

In order to take the advantage of the unemployment or the professional transition benefit, the persons interested should meet the following requirements:

a. they must be registered at the employment offices and social protection offices in the county districts, or at the Department of Labour and Social Protection in

Bucharest, wherever they reside or as the case stands, were they are domiciled, if they had their last job in that locality;
b.   their health condition, proved by the evidence of a medical record, which would otherwise entitle them to be employed in a part-time job (Article 5).

Applications for the payment of the unemployment and the professional transition benefit are submitted to the labour and social departments in the country districts, and to the Labour and Social Protection Department in Bucharest (Article 9).

4.   The Share of the Unemployment and Occupational Transition Benefit

The amounts of the unemployment benefit, and the occupational transition benefit, are calculated in a differentiated way, according to the classes of qualification of the persons concerned and their length of service, as follows:
a.   60% of the national minimum wage out of which the fee – in accordance with the legal provisions – is subtracted in case of occupational transition beneficiaries, being recruited from the ranks of the pre-university, vocational and apprenticeship school graduates, aged 18 or in special cases 16;
b.   70% of the national minimum wage out of which fee stipulated by the law has been subtracted, in case of the beneficiaries of occupational transition benefit recruited from the ranks of higher education graduates;
c.   50% of the average of the real minimum wage of the last three months, out of which the fee stipulated by law has been subtracted, for the unemployment benefit beneficiaries with a length of service of 5 years, but not less than 75% of the national minimum real wage, minus fee stipulated by the law;
d.   55% of average minimum wage of the last 3 months minus the fee stipulated by the law, for the beneficiaries of unemployment benefit with a length of service from 5 to 15 years, but not less than 80% of the minimum wage, minus fee provided by the law;
e.   60% of the average minimum wage of the last three months, minus the fee stipulated by the law, for the beneficiaries of the unemployment benefit with a length of service of minimum 15 years but not less than 85% of the national minimum wage, from which the fee stipulated by the law was subtracted;
f.   40% of the average monthly income, left after the payment of the fee stated according to law, for the last 12 months, for the persons defined in Article 2, paragraph 4, who contributed to the unemployment benefit fund for up to 5 years, but not less than one year;
g.   50% of the average monthly income left after the payment of the fee according to law, for the last 12 months, for the persons defined in Article 2, paragraph 4, who contributed to the unemployment benefit fund for a period over 5 years.

The unemployment benefit calculated as mentioned above cannot exceed the amount of a maximum of two minimum wages at the national level, out of which the fee stipulated by the law has been subtracted (Article 6).

5.   Acquiring the Right to Unemployment and Occupational Transition Benefit

The right to an unemployment benefit is acquired at different stages depending on the categories of beneficiaries.

Therefore, persons who have been employed with full-time jobs are entitled to receive the unemployment benefit from the date of the cancellation of the labour contract, as are persons who have been employed as a member of a handicraft co-operative, if they have registered at labour offices within 30 days following the cessation of their employment or following the date they registered at the labour office, if the application was submitted later than this date.

Persons who have been reinstated in a form of activity are entitled to unemployment benefit from the date of the final decision of reinstatement, according to the decree, if they were released from criminal procedure or released from prison or acquitted, and if they registered at the labour office within 30 days after the respective date or after the date they registered at the office, if this took place after the expiration of the period of 30 days.

Women who have ceased work in order to care for their children, as well as people whose status as pensioners has ceased, are entitled to receive unemployment benefit from the date of their registering at the labour offices.

The right to occupational transition benefit is determined as follows:

a. after a period of 30 days in the case of graduates of pre-university and university education, following their application at the labour offices and departments or at other competent bodies, in accordance with the law that stipulates that people are to be employed at a job which corresponds their training and qualification;

b. after a period of 30 days following the date when the persons finished their obligatory military service, in the case that they have submitted their application for employment to a job corresponding with their training and qualification at the labour departments (Article 9).

Unemployment and occupational transition benefit are paid for a period of at least 270 working days. If the labour and social protection department organizes training, retraining, and upgrading courses meanwhile, or, as the case stands, any other professional training, the unemployed persons and the occupational transition beneficiaries are obliged to attend them (Article 10).

6. Allotment of the Aid

In keeping with Article 12 of law No. 1/1991, paragraph 1, people who have taken advantage of the unemployment or occupational transition benefit and who do not have any possibility to make a living, can further take advantage of special aid until they are employed at a job, but not for longer than the period of 18 months after the expiration of the legal period of the allotment of the unemployment benefit, or the occupational transition benefit.

Persons meeting the following requirements, cumulatively, are considered not to have any means of supporting themselves:

a. persons who do not possess agricultural land with a minimum area equal to the area stipulated by Article 6, paragraph 1, Part a, together with the members of their family;

b. persons who do not achieve, together with the members of the family, an average monthly income, for one family member, of at least 60% of the minimum wage, out of which the fee stipulated by the law has been subtracted (Article 12).

The aid is an amount equal to 60% of the minimum wage, out of which the fee stipulated by the law has been subtracted. While receiving aid, the unemployed can attend training and retraining courses in order to learn another profession, or they can take upgrading courses, or as the case stands, other forms of occupational training whose period does not exceed the period of the allotment of the aid.

The occupational training of the unemployed, which started within the period of the unemployment benefit or occupational transition benefit, can be continued within the period of the aid, by forms of education stipulated by law, in trades and specializations whose duration does not exceed the time for which the aid is granted.

7. Cessation and Cancellation of the Unemployment Benefit Payment, of the Occupational Transition Benefit or the Aid

Article 20 of Law No. 1/1991 stipulates that payment of the unemployment benefit, of the occupational transition benefit, or of the granted aid ceases under the following circumstances:

a. on fulfilment of the terms for which it is granted, e.g., for a licence for practising an entrepreneurial activity of his own;
b. on engagement in full-time work of the bearer or 30 days after obtaining an authorization to practise an activity on his own;
c. in case of unjustified refusal to accept employment at a company, with a labour contract for a definite or indefinite period of time in a job which corresponds to the qualification, level of studies, personal record, and health file of the unemployed person;
d. on the date of his or her unjustified refusal to attend a course or another form of occupational training (paragraph 3) or, as the case stands, on the date of interrupting the course, or in case of failure to graduate for reasons chargeable to the beneficiary.

Payment of the unemployment benefit, the occupational transition benefit, or the aid is also cancelled in these cases:

a. if the beneficiary does not fulfil his requirement to go to the labour department every month;
b. during the period of the beneficiary's military service;
c. during the period for which the bearer is residing abroad;
d. during the period when the bearer is under preventive arrest or during the execution of a punishment that deprives the person of his liberty;
e. during the period when the bearer is employed with a labour contract for a stipulated period of less than 6 months.

8. Other Rights Granted to Unemployed People

Law No. 1/1991 stipulates that persons receiving the unemployment benefit, occupational transition benefit, or aid, have the advantage of other rights.

Hence, they may take advantage of an allotment for their children as well as medical care free of charge. The family members, supported by the respective person, also have the advantage of free medical care (Article 14).

The beneficiaries also hold the right to maintain their official quarters for the whole period of receiving unemployment benefit or aid, except for the case when the official quarters are situated inside the company, or the case when these quarters are needed for securing permanent service or continuation of the service rendered by the company, or in the case of eviction; however, a similar residence should be provided for the unemployed.

The duration for which a person is entitled to receive the unemployment benefit or the occupational transition benefit depends on the length of the service at the same company (Article 15).

Persons who lost wholly or partially their working ability during the period in which they are entitled to the unemployment benefit, the occupational transition benefit or the aid, or during the period of a professional training course, or other forms of occupational training, are entitled to the same social insurance benefits and disability pension as people employed at a job (Article 16).

D.   Bodies with Competence in the Labour Department

1.   The Ministry of Labour and Social Protection

In accordance with Government Decree No. 448/1994, the Ministry of Labour and Social Protection is the specialized institution of the central state administration that ensures the uniform application of labour legislation and social protection and that supervises activities regarding labour and social protection (Article 1).

The ministry mainly has the following competence:
In the field of unemployment:
–   it evaluates the resources and labour demands of the society and elaborates programmes regarding employment;
–   it organizes activities of social-professional integration and reintegration;
–   it applies active measures for social protection of the unemployed;
–   it administrates the unemployment fund.

In the field of social protection:
–   it applies legislation in the field of social security, also in the case of farmers; it elaborates methodology and controls the management of the social security;
–   it administers the budgets of social security and of the one for farmers; it supervises the revenue of the state's social security system and the revenues of the farmers's fund;
–   it organizes, co-ordinates, and supervises the services rendered by the social security to support families or people of disadvantageous social situations;
–   it organizes the system of medical and holiday resort centres financed by the state budget for pensioners and employees.

In the field of wages:
–   it suggests strategies and measures regarding the system of wage distribution in the local municipalities and industrial companies wholly or partially owned by the state;
–   it elaborates draft proposals regarding the salaries and wages of employees in the budget sector and supervises the compliance with the legislation in this field;

- it co-operates with social partners and grants specialized assistance in this field.

In the field of labour protection:
- it elaborates the methodology, the norms, the standards, and the indicators regarding labour protection;
- it authorizes the economic units to organize safety at work; it controls the technical equipment, and supervises and controls safety conditions; it controls the individual safety equipment; and it works out the normative regulation concerning employment in groups of work and controls the observance of regulation;
- it checks the application and observance of legislation in this field.

In the field of labour legislation and social protection:
- it co-ordinates and secures improvement of legislation in the field of labour and social protection;
- it elaborates projects and normative documents including draft proposals concerning legislation in the field of labour and social protection;
- it discharges its legal duty of making contracts and collective agreements;
- it controls the activity carried out by the employees of the economic units with private capital, of non-profit associations and organizations, as well as natural persons employing employees.

The following departments operate under the Ministry of Labour and Social Protection:
a. Social protection and labour district departments, the social protection and labour department in Bucharest, and the decentralized state departments;
b. The Labour Office;
c. The National Institute of Medical Survey and Recovery of Working Ability;
d. The Territorial State Inspectorates for Labour Protection;
e. The Romanian Management Institute;
f. The Scientific Research Institute in the field of Labour and Social Protection;
g. The Scientific Research Institute for Labour Protection;
h. Central Office for Pension Payment;
i. Social Assistance Units.

An important competence in the field of labour is held by the labour power departments and the Labour Chamber within the territorial departments of labour and social protection, as well as by the Labour Office.

2. Labour Power Offices

The main competencies of these bodies are the following:
- the evaluation of existing labour resources at the level of their territorial competence, considering age, sex, level of qualification, level of classification, and access to the labour market;
- co-operation with economic units in view of acquiring information about vacancies;
- analyses of the situation of job creation by developing the private sector;
- following the changes in the vacancies at the level of each enterprise and informing the interested persons;
- proposing measures in view of avoiding unemployment and achieving a decrease in the unemployment rate;

- promoting the employment of unemployed people;
- occupational orientation of graduates with a baccalaureate diploma or of those who want to change their job;
- taking measures to avoid social tensions due to the further reduction of the economic activity of some enterprises.

In order to retrain unemployed people for one or more new trades, the labour power offices deal with:
- drawing up plans and strategies concerning the training and retraining of workers;
- elaborating the one-year syllabus of the training, retraining, and upgrading courses held for unemployed people so that they can acquire one or more new skills;
- co-operating with economic units and school units in view of training the unemployed;
- organizing training courses for the unemployed so that they can acquire a skill in a new trade, in another trade or in more trades.

3. Labour Chamber

The Labour Chamber is a section in the Social Protection and Labour Department which ensures that the labour legislation is correctly put into force in the units that are organized and function by virtue of free initiative. It has the following main tasks:
- to ensure that employees of these units (units which are organized and function by virtue of free initiative) have concluded individual labour contracts in written form;
- to be responsible for charging and paying the social security and the additional pension contribution of employees;
- to set up, register, and keep the labour cards of the employees who work at the units that are organized and function by virtue of free initiative;
- to inspect whether the whole staff working in a unit is legally employed, whether the employees have concluded individual labour contracts, and whether the regulations of the contract are complied with.

4. Labour Office

Established by Government Decree No. 434/1990, the Labour Office regulates the activities of Romanian citizens at diplomatic establishments and authorized offices located in Romania. At the request of these diplomatic establishments and authorized offices, it secures and is responsible for ensuring that the conclusion and cessation of working relations between companies and Romanian citizens is carried out with the strict observance of Romanian legislation.
    The Labour Office has the following tasks:
a. it keeps a record of the work carried out by the Romanian employees employed by virtue of individual contracts.
b. it observes whether the parties negotiate all rights and duties stipulated by the Romanian labour legislation, in the framework of the individual labour contracts.
c. it sets up, registers, and maintains the labour cards of the above-mentioned employees.
d. it pays the income fee and social security contribution corresponding to the salaries agreed upon between the parties.

e. it is in charge of making payments towards a third party employed by the office on
    behalf of the employees.
f. it controls whether the employees have paid all of their social security contributions.
g. it issues different documents, e.g. documents on the length of service that serve as
    legal evidence of the employment.

Labour Law of Russia in the Transition from the Planned to the Market Economy

Semian A. Ivanov

I. GENERAL TRENDS OF RUSSIA'S LABOUR LAW CHANGES

For me it is quite obvious that the market economy in Russia does not exist for the time being; at most, the first steps are being made and some prerequisites to it are being created. Years or even decades will pass before the actual transition to market relations takes place. So, on elaborating a new concept of labour law, one should be a realist and try to adapt law to the period in question and be oriented towards it. Labour law is undergoing significant changes related to the transition to the market economy. The changes concern, above all, labour law extension and its bargaining fundamentals. While the Soviet Labour Law related to workers and employees employed, as a rule, at state enterprises, various departments, and organizations, labour law now applies to 'all employees' (Article 1 of Labour Code). True, this is rather vague. So, the extension of the labour law sphere should be considered only as a trend and not as a *fait accompli*. The extension of the fundamentals of labour law bargaining must be viewed in the same vein: the individual labour contract and the collective contracts should acquire their true meaning. Unlike the labour law of the Soviet period, Russia's labour law stipulates that the individual agreement be based on more liberal command of the parties concerned and be filled with wider content. At the same time labour contracts concluded for a definite period of time have been given wider recognition. This has led to greater instability in the employment sphere. Legislators have made an effort to halt this tendency and corresponding amendments were introduced into the labour law. In practice, however, temporary labour contracts are concluded more often than not despite the law.

In the following I shall dwell upon the collective contracts, but first it should be mentioned that while in the Soviet period the collective contracts as instruments of labour regulation were of a formal nature, nowadays they tend to be made into real tools.

Along with the above-said trends, other important changes are taking place in Russia's labour law. They can be divided into two groups: the first group includes radical changes relating, above all, to wage regulation, as well as to the rules governing labour contracts. In the past, labour legislation stipulated the procedure for only settling individual labour disputes; today it deals also with collective conflicts. Particular stress should be placed on the recognition in principle of the right to strike. Changes relating to control over implementation of the labour legislation should also be listed in the first group, in particular the return of the Labour Inspection to the jurisdiction of the state. In the early 1930s it was taken from the state and placed under the jurisdiction of the trade unions. The second group comprises changes in the status of trade unions, their pluralism, freedom of action and non-interference on the part of administrative bodies in their internal affairs. It also includes changes in employment and protection against dismissals.

Other changes have also occurred, among them the appearance of norms concerning social partnership and trilateral cooperation: in particular, the President's decree of 15 November 1991 on social partnership and the settlement of labour disputes. Today these norms tend to have a stronger foothold in the labour legislation. Not all changes have been fixed in a proper way; many of them are still waiting for essential adjustments. Some of these will be examined below. Before going into detail, I would like to draw attention to regrettable facts accompanying the labour law reforms in the present transitional period on the path to market relations. I am referring to an unbridled, at times flagrant and cynical, violation of labour legislation and citizens' labour rights. In their efforts to gain as much profit as possible, employers disregard workers' rights, as well as their own duties for the respect of these rights.

Today these violations related to gaining maximum profit are no less, and even more, numerous than those that occurred in Soviet times when they were justified by the need to fulfil the production plan. The motto 'Profit by every means' overshadows the Soviet slogan 'The plan above all else'.

Violations of labour rights are especially flagrant at non-state firms, though state enterprises have nothing of which to boast, either. Having offered their employees comparatively higher wages, leaders of co-operative enterprises, joint-stock companies, and joint ventures ignore the labour legislation, which is actually helpless in guaranteeing employees normal and decent conditions of work. Under the circumstances, solutions that would protect employees from their employers' arbitrary actions are especially timely. In essence they boil down to the following two aspects: first, to carry out a reform in legislation that would be in a position to challenge the transitional period on the path to market relations, and secondly, to start a secure mechanism for its practical realization. In this connection, a novelty introduced, by the Constitution of the Russian Federation (RF), into labour law is of considerable interest. In the RF Constitution adopted in late 1993 (in the period of reforms), a number of labour rights referred to human rights categories: the freedom of labour and the ban on coercive labour, remuneration of labour without any discrimination and not below the minimum level, the right to labour safety and protection against dismissals, the right to individual and collective labour disputes, including the right to strike, the right to leisure (Article 37), as well as the right to set up trade unions to protect employees' interests (Article 30). These refer to only a part, albeit considerable, of labour rights; however, the Constitution has secured the direct connection between labour rights and human rights, which has already been incorporated into various international documents, contributing to a more reliable application of labour rights in various countries. Time will prove the value of this novelty in the legal regulation of labour and labour relations, as well as its influence on the substance of Russian labour rights now undergoing reform, and its influence on securing labour rights of Russian citizens. The market economy under political democracy, as is evidenced by the experience of Western countries, cannot by itself ensure either social justice or social security for the majority of citizens. The transition to it, as our own, Russian, experience demonstrates, tends to sacrifice them. Hence in the transition to the market, employees' labour rights must be most carefully considered, especially in introducing amendments into labour legislation. Greater attention to protective measures is probably more important in the transitional period than afterwards when this period is finished and stabilization is achieved in the economy and social spheres.

II. DECENTRALIZATION OF THE LEGAL REGULATION OF LABOUR AS AN IMPORTANT FACTOR OF REFORMS IN LABOUR LEGISLATION

Transition to the market economy by necessity dictates decentralization of the legal regulation of labour. Both scholars and practicioners dealing with labour and labour relations agree with this thesis. The problems are how far will centralization go and whether it should remain the same in the post-transitional period. Decentralization should certainly differ in scope: in the transitional period it must be on a lesser scale, in the post-transitional period it must be greater. In the transitional period it should proceed gradually and not go too far, because taking into account a relatively low level of legal culture in Russia and her weak trade unions, decentralization could encourage exploitation and would benefit only entrepreneurs and not employees. In a federated state like Russia, decentralization may have two aspects: the first relates to the transfer of the legislative regulation competence from the federation to its subjects, the second one is the transition from legislative regulation to regulation by means of contracts and collective bargaining.

Aspect one. The Constitution of the Russian Federation gave rise to decentralization of the legal labour regulation. Though still vague, the general view is as follows: according to the Constitution, many labour law institutes are within the competence of the Federation since they fall under the Constitution's articles regulating the securing of freedoms and rights of man and citizen: i.e. the freedom of labour and the ban on coercion to it, the right to work and labour remuneration, setting a minimum wage, the right to individual and collective disputes, including the right to strike, setting working hours, and the right to a weekly rest and annual leave. Also within the competence of the Federation are: the ban of any form of discrimination, equal labour rights of men and women, as well as the right to organize trade unions. At the same time, according to the Constitution of the Russian Federation, labour legislation is within the 'joint' competence of the Federation and its subjects; that is, all institutes of labour law not belonging to the Federation are within the joint competence, in particular the institutes of labour and collective bargaining, labour discipline, and labour of young people. In general the model of joint competence is rather vague and inadequate. In practice this model has already caused discontent and created difficulties in the legal regulation of labour since according to the Constitution, republics, regions, areas, and even some cities may adopt laws and various regulations.

Aspect two. This aspect of decentralization is expressed in enhancing the role of collective bargaining over working conditions at enterprises, in different branches of the economy, and at the state level. The collective contract may become an important instrument in settling problems of remuneration and working conditions at enterprises. Although this enhancement has just begun, today we may say that labour regulation is carried out in two ways: adopting legislation and concluding collective contracts. Legislation remains of primary importance: it stipulates the setting of minimum wages and working conditions that can be improved in collective bargaining. The Law of the Russian Federation of 11 March 1992 greatly contributed to enhancing the role of collective bargaining adjusted to the conditions of transition from the planned economy to the market. It stipulates the conclusion of collective contracts not only at enterprises as was previously the case, but also at the level of a branch of industry and even on a national level. Along with the collective contract, a special appendix may be attached to it in which employees have a right to condition their particular professional interests. This appendix, being of an equal power with the collective contract, is, in turn, indicative of the decentralization of labour regulation. Collective bargaining may be conducted on a wide range of socio-economic questions. A collective contract may include the employer's obligations concerning wages, working time and a weekly rest or annual leave, working conditions and labour safety, medical and social insurance, economic security, and so on.

Remuneration occupies an important place in collective bargaining. While in the past this issue was settled in a centralized way, today this is the case only for budget enterprises. As far as the non-budget sphere is concerned, labour remuneration questions are settled on the level of branches of the national economy and at enterprises. For a long while, delays in payment have been a weak point in the new legislation on remuneration. Though the Labour Code obliges employers to pay their employees at least once every fortnight, in fact many employers delay payment of wages for many months. Delays in payment are widespread in many cities and regions of Russia, and at numerous enterprises. It is only natural that this has aroused discontent among the working people who then put the blame for such a state of affairs not so much on their employers, since they are at times insolvent, but on the government. Reasons for delays in payment lie not so much in the realm of law but rather in the economic sphere, and the delay as such is one of the difficulties, or rather paradoxes, of the transitional period.

At present, collective agreements and the Law of 11 March 1992 on these agreements are far from perfection. What is the most striking is the lack of experience in collective bargaining and the conclusion of true collective contracts. Though the above-mentioned Law opens vast vistas in collective bargaining, in practice new collective agreements remind one of their predecessors, that is, Soviet-era contracts. I believe that it will take some time to acquire the necessary experience and knowledge to make these possibilities provided by the Law a real practice. Already some shifts have occurred in concluding agreements at the level of some branches of the economy and at the national level, but not always. For instance, the General Agreement between All-Russia Trade Union Associations, All-Russia Associations of Employers, and the Government of the Russian Federation for 1994, concluded in April 1994, is for the most part just a declaration, and has not had a noticeable influence on the improvement of the population's socio-economic conditions, working conditions, or in securing employees' labour rights. Collective agreements are an important element in the establishment and development of market relations. The labour law of the transitional period must give them priority, not putting them off till some indefinite future. In general, the challenge consists in combining a streamlined legislation with know-how and perseverance in the collective bargaining practice.

III. EMPLOYMENT AND PROTECTION AGAINST UNEMPLOYMENT

In the transition to the market economy, the problem of employment has been from the very beginning a complex problem. Let us consider it not from the practical but from the philosophical point of view, which we have been faced with while approaching the economic reform. The fact is that many researchers, especially economists, having predicted mass unemployment, began to consider it as an exceptionally positive and inevitable phenomenon inherent in the market economy, which can only be hailed and even encouraged. Thus, one economist declared that unemployment is not only an unavoidable disadvantage, but also quite a recognized advantage. Moreover the serious negative consequences of unemployment for individuals and the society as a whole were passed over in silence.

The views on unemployment under review must have a negative impact on the legal regulation of labour. Though the Law of the Russian Federation of 19 April 1991, on employment of Russia's population, proclaims the guarantee by the state of citizens' rights to full, productive, and freely chosen employment (Article 5), nothing of the kind can be found either in the Code of Labour or the Constitution of the Russian Federation. And these are fundamental laws, especially the Constitution. As a result, the content of the right to work is devoid of its core, that is employment. In the Constitution it seems rather to be a right to the protection of labour, since it speaks about the right to work under decent working conditions, safety, and hygiene (Article 37).

It would be expedient to preserve the right to work in the Russian legislation. But not in the form it used to be in Soviet laws; it should be changed accordingly and must directly connect the concept of the right to work with the policy of full and productive employment of the population, approximately in the same way as had been done in the International Convention on Economic, Social, and Cultural Rights, where such a policy is viewed as a measure for ensuring the right to work (Article 6). As regards the actual practice, more attention should be paid to the rise of unemployment among the population, the loss of jobs, and closure of enterprise. By 1 December 1994, the Federal Department of Employment had registered 1,820,000 citizens not engaged in labour activities, among them 1,549,600 unemployed. On the whole, out of an able-bodied population of slightly more than 70 million, only 5 million are fully employed. Women are in the majority in the structure of officially recognized unemployment and comprise about 70% of unemployed. It is expected that by 1998 the number of unemployed will amount to 14 million. The state of affairs is aggravated by latent unemployment: the number of enterprise forcing their employees to take unpaid leave is growing. This happens when enterprises stop operating due to the lack of raw materials necessary for their production or to a drop in sales.

Under the circumstances, several measures have been taken in order to improve the regulation of employment and protection against unemployment, as well as some legal acts, in particular the above-mentioned Law of 1991 on employment with amendments and addenda introduced by the Law of 15 July 1992. Both the Law of 1991, and the Constitution of the Russian Federation, proclaim freedom of labour, define rights of citizens in employment, their guarantees, the way public works are organized and participation of the unemployed in them, conditions and terms of unemployment benefits, etc.

Though there are many shortcomings in the law, the very fact of its adoption is an important step forward for Russia in the regulation of labour, since unlike the previous legislation the new law recognizes unemployment as a socio-economic phenomenon and creates mechanisms for protection against it. The unemployed are able-bodied persons who have neither work nor earnings, they are registered at employment services with a view to search for a suitable job, and are ready to take it. For a period of 12 months, an unemployed person is paid benefits equivalent from 75 to 45% of the person's average annual wage at his or her last place of work. Along with this, the legislation stipulates a compensation in the case of collective dismissals, that is, the reduction of the number of workers or staff at an enterprise, or at its closure (Articles 33 /1/ and 40 /3/ of the Labour Code). Employees are entitled to a dismissal benefit amounting to an average monthly wage, as well as to an average wage for the period of searching for a new job (but not for more than two months, or in some cases three months). Thus, at collective dismissals the terms of material support for those who lost their jobs have increased by 2–3 months as compared with the terms stipulated by the Law on Employment. Norms regarding vocational training and retraining occupy an important place in regulating employment. Their application, however, leaves much to be desired. The inadequate development of measures on vocational training and retraining intended to lessen unemployment and contribute to greater employment is striking. As a result the number of persons involved in retraining is less than 5% of the overall number of unemployed.

IV.   REGULATION OF COLLECTIVE LABOUR CONFLICTS AND STRIKES

The setting up of the system for settling collective labour conflicts and recognition of the employees' right to strike are among the most noticeable changes in Russia's labour law in the transitional period. The 1993 Constitution of the Russian Federation recognizes this right as a human right. But long before the adoption of the Constitution, the right to strike had appeared in the USSR Law of 1989 on the procedure for settling collective labour conflicts and strikes, which is applied today with some amendments. According to this Law, the basis of peaceful resolution of collective disputes consists of two organs: a conciliation committee and a labour arbitration court to which employers and employees alike may apply in the case of a labour dispute. Pursuant to the Law of 11 March 1992 on collective contracts, which is intended to settle contradictions arising in the course of collective bargaining, mediatory services are not forbidden. As far as the strike is concerned, according to the Law it is an extreme way of settling a collective labour dispute: before going on strike, employees must go through the prescribed procedure for a peaceful settlement of the conflict. Any deviation from the prescribed procedure makes the strike unlawful with all the consequences involved. Consequently, the procedure for settling collective labour conflicts is based on coercion. The subject of collective labour conflicts may be disputes over the introduction of new measures or changing the existing socio-economic or working and living conditions, or the conclusion and implementation of collective agreements. It is in these connections that strikes may arise.

The problem of the sphere of the right to strike is a worldwide issue, since no state can allow strikes at absolutely all enterprises, nor can it give the right to strike to all categories of employees without exception, without affecting to lesser or greater measure the population of the country concerned. So a problem of setting limits to strikes and harmonizing interests of strikers and the society arises. Its solution differs from country to country. In Russia this problem is still awaiting solution, since the legislation applied today can hardly offer a proper solution to the problem under study. Pursuant to the 1989 Law, work stoppage is not allowed, if it endangers the life and health of people. This, in principle, is a correct norm, adopted under ILO pressure, but it is rather vague and may cause abuses in the sense of setting limits to the right to strike.

In addition, work stoppage is banned at enterprises and organizations of the railway and public transport (underground included), civil aviation, communications, power, defence industries (in sub-departments directly engaged in the production of defence-related goods), at state bodies, enterprises and organizations ensuring the defence capacity, law, order, and security of the country, and at continuously operating enterprises, the stoppage of which may cause serious and dangerous consequences. The list is not only rather long but also unclear, which may also lead to various abuses. Even if abuses are absent, these norms deprive the majority of employees of the right to strike. Moreover, all political strikes are also banned, including those that oppose the government's socio-economic policy. Obviously, the ban on political strikes has its roots in the past. However, in our day and age there is a worldwide tendency to narrow down the concept of 'political strike,' and to outlaw only particular types. Thus, the Freedom of Association Committee, previously the Committee of Experts of the International Labour Office, believes that purely political strikes do not pertain to the principle of trade union freedom. As a rule 'purely political' strikes include strikes in no way connected with economic, social, or professional demands of employees. From this point of view, strikes aimed against the economic and social policy of the government could hardly be considered unlawful. At the same time, I would like to note that the regulation of strikes includes one of the most complex and unclear problems, namely political strikes, since there is no clear demarcation line between a political strike and a strike caused by employees' socio-economic demands that has acquired a political colouring. In the present rather tense situation in Russia it would be expedient to ban not political strikes in general, if ever, but purely political ones. Moreover, the strike's nature could be specified in every particular case on the basis of types of unlawful strikes.

Employees participating in a legal strike enjoy the right to keep their general and uninterrupted work record, their right to the state social insurance and their jobs secure. However, their wages are not paid during strikes. In other words, the labour contract is not abrogated, but only suspended. What are the legal consequences of participation in an unlawful strike? The participation in it may be considered as a breach of discipline and should entail disciplinary measures. Pursuant to the Law, some additional measures, implied by collective contracts, may be applied too. Another consequence may be the imposition of a fine. There are many indications to this, but almost all of them are rather valued, which allows fines to be imposed widely. The 1989 Law stipulates the responsibility of a work collective, in case of an unlawful strike, to pay damages to the employer, as well as the trade union, which pays damages out of its own means. In all cases the imposition of fines and payments of damages should be done pursuant to the court decision. What is, then, an unlawful strike? Strikes are treated as unlawful if they are governed by political motives, as mentioned above, as well as strikes declared without passing through the procedure of peaceful settlement of collective disputes, or at enterprises where they are banned or for some other reasons. The decisions to outlaw a strike is adopted by the court on the application lodged by the enterprise's administration, self-governing body, or by a public prosecutor. The decision makes it mandatory to stop the strike and return to work. Many courts adopt unfounded decisions.

There are no official statistics but the impression is that today most strikes are outlawed by courts. It seems obvious that legislators, in regulating the right to strike, were pursuing the aim of setting limits to the right and applying sanctions for unlawful strikes. This, however, does not rule out strikes, though it is not an easy matter to go on strike today. Since coercion does not work, a new tendency towards introduction of the notion of 'lock-out' into the labour legislation has appeared: moreover it would be applied as a means of mass dismissal of strike participants. One can understand the government as trying to do its best to avoid strikes in a crisis-stricken situation. But this is hardly tenable when the measure is based not on negotiations entered at the free will of the conflicting parties, nor on co-operation and search for a compromise (both of which are considered beneficial throughout the world), but on coercion. It is mistaken to think that coercion can settle all or almost all complex problems of working relations. Fines, deprivation of various benefits, dismissals, etc., may for a while somehow suppress a conflict, but they cannot eliminate it. It is most important to set up a truly democratic, flexible, and trustful procedure for settling conflicts and for the use of strikes. They are resorted to in extreme situations, when living and working conditions are becoming intolerable, and employers and the government are deaf to employees' demands to improve them. So instead of placing all hopes on coercion and punitive sanctions against the strikers, an effort must be made to find ways for a compromise to settle collective disputes and come to co-ordinated decisions.

Labour Law in the Slovak Republic, Present Situation and Future Trends

Helena Barancova

I. MAIN FEATURES OF LABOUR LEGISLATION IN THE SLOVAK REPUBLIC

A. Labour Legislation before 1989

Like in other totalitarian countries, the legal system in Slovakia was derived from the central planning of the national economy. Directives prevailing in the economy corresponded also with labour legislation. Most significantly, the Labour Code contained numerous coercive provisions, as well as provisions based on limited freedom of parties to contracts of employment and reliance on administrative methods. Consequently, statutory regulation of employment contracts and also of collective agreements had comparatively little meaning. Under the administrative approach, extensive discretionary and disciplinary measures of employers prevailed. There was, in reality, no collective labour law and collective agreements were only formal acts.

Compared to current employment policy, under the conditions of full, though inefficient, employment, governmental authorities had different responsibilities. In the circumstances of exclusive state ownership, the state being the sole employer and owner of the means of production, the governmental authorities were primarily concerned with mandatory allocation of jobs through administrative procedures.

B. Labour Legislation after 1989

Following the radical political changes in the country, transformation of the legal system had also begun. The first stage began in 1991 when three important laws were passed. Act No. 1/1991 was the first to introduce regulation of the labour market and the terms and conditions of material assistance for the unemployed. The Collective Bargaining Act No. 2/1991 provided for the procedures of collective bargaining, including settlement of collective disputes and the use of lock-outs and strikes.

(Theoreticians in the field of labour law extensively criticize the absence of provisions governing collective agreements at the national level in the public sector concerning the employers on governmental budget).

Act No. 3/1991 is an extensive amendment to the former law enacted in 1965, reducing in particular the extent of mandatory provisions of the Labour Code and thus establishing the basis for the development of a market economy. Since 1981, the

Employment Act and the Labour Code have been amended on several occasions. The Collective Bargaining Act has remained unchanged.

The second stage of reforms in Slovak labour law should begin after the adoption of the new Labour Code, as a response to the requirements of the market economy. Extensive reforms are being introduced in Slovakia so that the new Labour Code, the new Employment Act, and the Civil Service Act will soon be passed.

Both stages of the transformation of labour law in Slovakia can be best characterized as the process of extending the authority and rule of labour law and increasing the independence and autonomy of parties to employment contracts and collective agreements. Labour law has become more liberal and more open to collective bargaining and collective agreements; the processes of deregulation, liberalization and of increased flexibility of labour law are the most typical features of the development in the last five years in support of further development of the market economy. Growing liberalization, however, also has a negative impact. The effort to maximize autonomy of the parties often goes against the interests of employees, the weaker side. Moreover, as a result of liberalization, the powers of trade union bodies have decreased since 1989.

1.   The Role of Governmental Authorities in Labour Legislation

The most important guarantors of the new quality of labour legislation are the Slovak Parliament and the Cabinet. The Ministry of Labour, Social Affairs, and Family, having the power to pass regulations (i.e., laws of lesser force than the acts of parliament), is responsible for the co-ordination and development of labour legislation. The employment policy of the government is the main responsibility of the Employment Services Administration and its subordinate administrative agencies.

When compared to the pre-1989 situation in the labour market, the position of administrative agencies has changed substantially, with the major focus on assistance to job seekers and placement of the unemployed.

2.   Social Partnership under New Legislation

Social partnership operates on the tripartite system in Slovakia. When preparing new labour laws and employment relations, central government authorities are obliged to consult all matters with the appropriate central union and the appropriate organization of employers. With the progress of the transformation of ownership, the organizations of employers are now gradually becoming a more important factor influencing labour legislation and national collective agreements. Experience shows that the tripartite system has had a positive impact on social peace. On the other hand, it prolongs the legislative process, which has become cumbersome and less practical, obstructing the passage of some new laws.

II.   LEGAL ASPECTS OF LABOUR MARKET REGULATIONS

A.   General Characteristics

As a result of changes in ownership of property and privatization, the approach to the right to work has also undergone legislative changes, although it is still defined by the

Slovak Constitution as one of the fundamental social rights. The emphasis on freedom, the major principle of a market economy, is reflected also in the legal meaning of the right to work which is now regarded as the freedom to choose employment without any discrimination.

The government is legally responsible for an active employment policy but its implementation has been insufficient in recent years even though, within the system of instruments of employment policy, the creation of new jobs is a priority which is hard to fulfill because of difficult problems accompanying the economic transformation.

B. Regulation of the Labour Market

The new quality of employment relations has been provided by the Employment Act No. 1/1991. Following the transition from centrally directed to market economy, it lays down the fundamental functions of the labour market and provides for unemployment benefits. Employment rights can be exercised through local labour offices, which assist in job placement and provide information and consultation services.

The Employment Act, revised and amended on several occasions since 1991, is based on the state monopoly in providing a free service for job seekers and fixing the conditions in which paid services are also possible. These services must not be profit-oriented.

1. Application in Individual Cases

The Employment Act operates on territorial jurisdiction, applying basically to the citizens of the Slovak Republic. Aliens or persons other than the nationals can be employed only upon the receipt of residence and work permits from the appropriate authorities.

2. The Right to Employment

The Employment Act defines the right to employment as the right of unemployed persons who are willing and qualified to work, i.e., a right based on objective and subjective criteria. The right of employment covers the right to find a job through the assistance of the labour office, the right to seek retraining as a necessary job qualification, and the right to receive unemployment benefits before a new placement or after a termination. These rights are guaranteed by the corresponding governmental labour offices responsible for job placement, retraining, and material assistance.

3. Appropriate Employment

The right to employment comprises an important element, i.e., the adequacy of the job sought through the agency of a labour office.

Under Section 2 subsection 2 of the Act, an appropriate job must be adequate to the health conditions of the individual job seeker, considering also his or her age, qualifications, abilities, and accommodation circumstances.

The legal definition does not cover occupational protection, explicitly recognizing the qualification for a job only as auxiliary criterion. Similarly, the legal construction of adequate job disregards previous standard of pay and the distance between the offered placement and permanent residence of the unemployed person. Refusal of a job offer defined within these limits of adequacy has important legal consequences. Where an unemployed person refuses to accept the adequate job or retraining without a reason, the labour office is obliged to strike the person off the register and warrant a new registration only after six months have elapsed.

The only legitimate excuse for the refusal of the job offered can be justified by reasons concerning pre-school or compulsory school attendance of a minor child (or children) whose care would otherwise be difficult for a single parent or one of the parents in relation to the location or nature of the job.

Persons whose names have been deleted from the register of job seekers are not entitled to unemployment benefits or any social assistance even when in need, as explicitly precluded by the Social Hardship Regulation No. 243/1993. In addition, the mandatory requirement to delete disqualified job seekers from the register for no less than six months also means that the statistics provided by the labour offices – by excluding disqualified jobless persons – do not reflect factual unemployment. Because of the current restrictive law governing employment in terms with the narrow definition of appropriate job, it is very difficult to anticipate the long-term employment trends, a pressing problem threatening to result in serious political tension. The restrictions relating to appropriate job placement and rigid legal consequences of a refusal of an appropriate job were enacted in 1993. They were necessary for the prevention of widespread misuse of unemployment benefits, and in order to cut some expenses off the very limited unemployment budget.

Nevertheless, there are objections to these legislative measures on the grounds that they are not fair. In practice, the unemployed person is forced to accept any job meeting his or her health conditions with no regard to certain other criteria widely enacted and applied in other countries. The broad formulation of appropriate employment does not encourage governmental labour offices to find, especially in the initial stage, a job placement according to the original qualification of the unemployed person who could make better use of his or her training or educational skills, in full or at least in part. Consequently, the application of appropriate job may result in disproportionate waste and loss of the high educational standard and potential of the work force in Slovakia, and thus also in devaluation and depreciation of costs relating to different forms of education still fully borne by the state.

4. Unemployment Benefits

Financial assistance in unemployment, not based on any insurance system, is governed by the Employment Act No. 1/1991, also amended later. New legislative proposals on unemployment benefits based on insurance policies are now extensively discussed. Employers pay a mandatory contribution equivalent to 3% of the total monthly amount paid in wages, with the employees contributing a monthly 1% of taxable income to the Employment Fund. Self-employed persons contribute monthly the equivalent of 4% of their taxable incomes.

Unemployment benefits are funded from the Employment Fund.

a.   Terms and Conditions of Unemployment Benefit

To quality for unemployment benefits, a person must satisfy the requirement of the
minimum length of employment (12 months) during three years preceding the
application for a job. For the purposes of unemployment benefits, the period of
employment covers also the time during which the person received training or
education designed for handicapped persons, and also the time during which the person
received disability benefits prior to its termination.

b.   Duration and the Amount of Material Assistance

Under current legislation a person is eligible for unemployment benefits amounting to
60% of the average net wage received from the previous employer in the first three
months, and 50% of the same in the next three months. The same terms apply to
unemployed persons participating in retraining programs.
     Compared to the period following immediately after the enactment of 1991, the
Act was subsequently revised to disfavour the recipients. Experience in other post-
communist countries is similar; after originally copying the patterns applied in the
European Community, gradually more rigorous measures were taken. There are
numerous reasons for this development occurring in different post-communist countries.
Generally, during the initial transformation processes, the active employment policy
failed, mainly the so-called macroeconomic employment policy implemented by
major industrial sectors. Thus, due to limited economic growth in Slovakia in general,
unemployment benefits gradually became the main instrument and thus a serious threat
to the economic stability of the country. On the other hand, because of the slight
differences in workers' compensation and the amount paid as an unemployment
benefit, the motivation to seek a job was low.
     Through stricter rules imposed later, both the amount and duration were cut,
and maximum rates were introduced. The maximum assistance was reduced from 1.8
times the minimum wage in 1989 to 1.5 times the minimum wage. The general opinion
is that it has been unfortunate to link unemployment benefits to minimum wages. The
maximum amount should be linked to the average income or the minimum living
standard fixed by law. Similarly, the amount of assistance for those under retraining
programs, and its duration, were also changed. In addition, such stricter rules were
introduced in the circumstances of high inflation in which the real value of unemployment
benefits originally fixed by law steadily decreased.
     Another typical feature of unemployment policy in Slovakia is the uniform rate
of unemployment benefits received regardless of the previous income, age, and
employment history of the unemployed person.
     Uniform rates paid to unemployed persons, or to those participating in retraining
programs, have in practice reduced the number of applicants interested in retraining;
now more and more unemployed persons opt for the financial assistance alone. The
present situation can be best characterized by the relatively small interest in retraining
and relatively limited possibilities of retraining programs offered by labour offices.
This unfavourable situation corresponds to the existing level of economic transformation
in Slovakia which provides few prospects even after retraining. The majority of state
enterprises are in their pre-privatization death throes, with very little or no expectations
of productive development. Partly this is also the failure of macro-economic planning.

The uniform rate in unemployment benefits is held to be a weakness and mistaken policy of the existing legislation.

Only the material assistance paid to unemployed handicapped persons, in the form of different allowances, is more favourably provided under the Employment Act.

C.   Other Instruments of Employment Policy

The current legislation encourages employers to create new jobs. Any newly created job is rewarded with a non-refundable governmental subsidy of Sk 100,000. The employer is bound to maintain the position for no less than two years or to pay back all or a part of the amount granted.

D.   Quota System for Physically Handicapped Persons

This system is governed by the Employment Act and Governmental Regulation No. 256/1992, under which employers with more than twenty employees are obliged to hire at least 4% of handicapped persons out of the total number of their workers. For the purposes of job placement, any person with a major physical handicap equals five persons with a minor handicap. The main objection to the current regulation in relation to the quota system is that no extra payments or contributions to the Employment Fund for Handicapped Persons are prescribed for those employers who have failed to meet the statutory requirement and provided no jobs for such persons over a long period of time. This situation will be improved by the new law currently under preparation.

III.   EMPLOYMENT RELATIONS

A.   Employment Contracts

The new Labour Code will bring a revival of employment contracts, a policy generally designed to expand the autonomy of parties to the contract. Appointment to a position as a method of hiring, previously often criticized by legal theoreticians, will be reduced to a minimum. This method, together with contract and election to a position, used to be misused for political reasons. Compared with employees who had a valid contract, it was easier to terminate the employment of an appointee with a fixed notice because no other condition was prescribed by the Labour Code in the case of such removal. Executive officers can be discriminated through the provisions of Section 65 of the Labour Code, providing for a just cause and lawful notice by reason of redundancy where the parties cannot agree on a transfer to a different position. This provision of the Labour Code was misused by employers in order to justify a dismissal with reasons other than the performance of professional duties, particularly political ones.

It should be noted here that employment contracts do not compete with any other hiring contracts in Slovakia. Even though the current law allows for the employer's subcontracting an employee to a third party, or the employee's out-of-job contracts (agreement of authorship, contract of work), these are only complementary in nature.

1.   Essential Elements of Employment Contracts

A contract must include the following data:
1. description of work to be performed;
2. place of work;
3. commencement day.

The data included in the employment contract cannot be changed by option of one party except subject to Section 37 of the Labour Code, which expressly enumerates the reasons for which an employee may be transferred to another job should the employer choose to do so. The new Labour Code will provide for the mandatory indication of the amount to be paid for the job. In addition, the lawful reasons for transfer to another job by the employer will be significantly reduced.

2.   Fixed-term Contracts of Employment

Just like in the legislation in other countries, fixed-term contracts of employment are limited on various lines as set by law in force in Slovakia.

Fixed-term contracts of employment cannot exceed three years. Renewal of such contracts can be made on no more than two subsequent occasions under the terms and conditions fixed by law. The following categories of persons are excluded from entering into employment under fixed-term contracts: young persons, partially disabled persons and misfit persons (such as persons discharged from prisons). Under the new Labour Code the categories of persons excluded from fixed-term employment contracts will be expanded. The prohibition may be disregarded only where a person submits a written application explicitly requiring the contract to be made for a fixed period. The categories of persons banned from entering into contracts for a fixed period may not be hired subject to any probation period; the purpose of this provision is to increase the protection of these workers against arbitrary dismissal by the employer during a trial period or against a short-term employment.

Since the legal restriction of fixed-term contracts as a protection for certain categories of persons has been justified and confirmed by practice, it will probably also apply in the future. But on the other hand, this protection may also encourage discrimination against these persons who are often rated as less attractive manpower, and thus worsen their position in the labour market.

Under the new Labour Code due consideration will be given to justification of the reason for the exclusion from fixed-term contracts, as well as to the time limits. The new legal construction will, however, result in liberalization and negotiation of conditions of employment for a fixed term. Based upon a lawful reason, the employer will be allowed to make a number of subsequent contracts signed for a fixed term.

B.   Probation Period

Determination of the probation period for a newly hired worker is now affected by relatively strict rules. Although the parties may agree on the length of probation period as they please, the Labour Code provides for a maximum trial period not exceeding three months.

C.   Part-time Contracts

Part-time contracts are possible also under the current legislation but the new Labour Code will follow the principles set forth by the ILO Convention on part-time jobs under preparation. Legal protection of those working part-time will be equal to the protection guaranteed in full-time jobs, provided the working time is not shorter than one third of the statutory weekly hours. Should the time be shorter than one third of the weekly hours set by law, legal protection will be reduced accordingly. The legislation in force does not provide for combining part-time employment with unemployment benefits.

D.   Working Hours and Holiday Rights

The Labour Code sets a 43-hour weekly working time for adult workers and 33 hours for minors. Under the present regulation, meal breaks are included in the working time. The new Labour Code will provide for a 40-hour week for adult workers and 31-hour week for young persons. Following the principles used in other countries, meal breaks will not be counted.

It is a typical feature of the transition period that working time is generally increasing in Slovakia, which is a result of free choice of employees to engage in extra part-time activities. Although no worker can legally enter into more than one employment, he or she can be involved in part-time activities amounting to 99% of full working time. The real length of working hours is increased also by overtime. Extra pay for overtime work is a significant incentive for the workers, no matter how detrimental it may be to their health. The Labour Code limits overtime work to 150 hours annually, but the appropriate governmental departments have the power to increase the maximum overtime limit. The steady increase in overtime work also has a negative impact on the unemployment rate in Slovakia.

The annual vacation is basically three weeks. After fifteen years of employment the employee has the right to a four-week recess. A five-week vacation is provided for those working in the public sector. Under the collective agreement the vacation period can be extended by one week by any employer. The new Labour Code will prolong the basic annual vacation to four weeks without any requirements in relation to the length of previous employment. In addition, it will be possible to add one extra week through collective agreements.

E.   Working Conditions

Working conditions have deteriorated in the transformation process. The main cause of lower health and safety standards is the lack of incentive of small business owners who opt for higher profit rather than environmental spending. Another cause is the decline in the number of union members. As there are no other elected representatives, employees not organized in trade unions are not effectively protected against their employers.

F. Stability of Employment Relations

The stability of employment relations is safeguarded by the current legislation, particularly by means of the following:
- stating reasons for which an employee can be transferred to another job;
- the prohibition on transferring an employee to a different site of work without the previous consent of both parties;
- stating just cause of dismissal for immediate termination of the employment of an employee;
- the trade union intervention in the case of dismissal or immediate termination of the employment of an employee;
- previous consent of the union in the case of a dismissed or terminated union member (such consent is a substantive legal condition of a lawful dismissal);
- previous consent of the appropriate labour office in cases of dismissal of a handicapped employee (such consent is a substantive legal condition of lawful dismissal);
- a fixed period of protection during which no employee can be dismissed: according to Section 48 of the Labour Code, under certain circumstances the employee cannot be dismissed (e.g., during temporary sick leave not longer than twelve months, during pregnancy, if providing care for a child under the age of 3, during performance of public or military service);
- the prolongation of the period of notice in specific circumstances (Section 47 of the Labour Code).

Another type of employment relations and eligibility to unemployment benefits is to be found mainly in the termination of employment. The Employment Act provides for material assistance only if the termination of previous employment was justified by a serious reason. In practice, however, this may give rise to termination, in which, through mutual agreement of both parties, no reason need to be given under the present Labour Code, but in which the employees push their employers to state a reason defined as serious by the Employment Act in order to be eligible for unemployment benefits. Through fabricated reasons, the Employment Act is often violated.

G. Termination of Employment

Legal grounds for termination of employment, including immediate dismissal without previous consent of both parties, are expressly enumerated in the Labour Code. A dismissal must be consulted with a trade union body, and in relation to handicapped persons, previous consent of a labour office is necessary.

The rights of the employer as owner of the means of production are considerably limited by the existing legislation, which, according to some labour and employment theoreticians, is considered a significant obstacle to labour mobility. When compared to dismissal legislation in force in the EC countries, Slovak rules provide for greater rights of employees whose social security will, under given circumstances, be safeguarded at the same level also in the future. Some legal constructions relating to dismissal based on a just cause are too broad and too open to misuse by employers (e.g. Section 46 subsection (1)(c) of the Labour Code relating to redundancy). The new Labour Code will also provide for collective dismissal in accordance with the directives adopted by the European Union.

147

1. Legislation Governing the Civil Service

Employment in the civil service sector will be governed by a new regulation to be adopted soon. The Civil Service Act will be limited to a relatively small group of people, those working in central governmental departments. Apart from the new act, employment of public prosecutors and police officers is governed under separate law. A law governing employment in the public sector, i.e. railway workers, teachers, physicians, and Post Office workers is also anticipated.

IV. COLLECTIVE LABOUR LAW

Collective labour rights are currently regulated by the Collective Bargaining Act No. 2/1991 and the appropriate provisions of the Labour Code. The Collective Bargaining Act lays down the procedures by which collective agreements can be made, including provisions relating to strike and closure.

Other sources of collective labour law are Act No. 120/1990 covering some relations of trade unions and employers, the Employment Act No. 1/1991, and the Wage Act No. 1/1992 providing for payment for emergency work and average earnings.

A.   Collective Agreements

1. Types of Collective Agreements

The Collective Bargaining Act defines two types of collective agreements: collective agreement at the company level and those made at higher level. The relatively slow process of the establishment of employers' organizations, corresponding to the slow process of transformation of property and ownership relations, means that there is no party to national collective agreements to be concluded with the national trade union bodies.

The Collective Bargaining Act does not provide for the priority of a collective agreement made at company level over that made at a higher level. Under Section 8 subsection 2 of the Collective Bargaining Act, a collective agreement made at company level or a part thereof shall be ineffective if the scope of rights for the employees is less extensive than the rights included in the collective agreement made at a higher level. Similarly ineffective is any collective agreement made at company level or a part thereof if it guarantees higher pay for the work than the maximum amount granted by the collective agreement made at a higher level, namely the portion by which the pay exceeds the admissible amount. In addition, any collective agreement contradicting any of the current laws will also be ineffective.

Apart from what has been mentioned, the Collective Bargaining Act contains no other provisions governing settlement of conflicts arising from a collective agreement and contract of employment. An exception in this respect can be found in compensation for work in the private sector for which the principle of the priority of the employee's interest applies under Act No. 1/1992.

2. Parties to Collective Agreements

Under the Collective Bargaining Act, the parties to collective agreements are the employers on the one hand and the company trade unions or higher union bodies, on the other hand.

Collective agreements at company level can be made by any trade union organization registered at the Ministry of Interior. A higher-level collective agreement must be made between and by the appropriate trade union body and the organization of employers.

There are no provisions governing the powers of trade unions to conclude agreements in the same range as is lawfully granted in other countries. At the company level, any trade union organization can conduct collective bargaining. National unions based on industrial branches are entitled to make national collective agreements. Under the Collective Bargaining Act, however, national collective agreements are practically excluded in the public sector funded from the state budget. This relative drawback will be removed by the new Labour Code under which collective bargaining and collective agreements will apply also to the public sector. The idea behind the new provisions of the Labour Code is based on the principle that the State is not only a party of public law and a legislator, but also a party of private law when acting as the employer.

Under current legislation, the exclusive power of collective bargaining is vested in the trade union bodies. In this respect, no changes are expected in the new Labour Code. There are not a great number of trade unions in the Slovak Republic, or in the Czech Republic, although Act No. 120/91 provided for plurality of trade unions. The Christian unions that have been established are not strong enough to be a real force.

Even though social partnership is a basic requirement for the development of a market economy, some practical problems exist in identifying social partners of collective agreements. Due to the slow privatization, state-owned companies or governmental joint-stock companies predominate. Since these companies will be soon privatized, such employers are not motivated to act as conventional social partners. Private businesses, mostly small firms, cannot be involved in national collective agreements, either; thus the national union bodies have no partner at the level of nation-wide employers' organizations.

3. Collective Agreement – the Content Framework

The content of collective agreements is only roughly framed by the Collective Bargaining Act and by Section 20 of the Labour Code, thus regulating the individual and collective relations of employers and employees and the rights and duties of the parties, i.e. the union and the employer. The Collective Bargaining Act does not prescribe what should be included in collective agreements. Many practical problems result from the absence of such detail.

It may be mentioned here that a collective agreement can deal with any matter in which either party may be interested unless it contradicts rule contained in the Labour Code or other statutory regulation. The Collective Bargaining Act does not set any limits to rules or obligations. The relations of collective agreements and employment contracts are regulated by the Wage Act No. 1/1992 for the purposes of compensation of workers in the private sector and partly also the workers employed in the public sector. The principle underlying these relations is that of priority of the employee's interest.

The Wage Act had a positive impact on the development of collective agreement and collective agreement made at higher levels.

The guarantees of more favourable employees' rights exceeding the scope provided for in the Labour Code vary with different employers. More favourable rights can be generally granted by employers in the private sector.

4. Collective Agreements as Generally Binding Instruments

The Collective Bargaining Act provides for making collective agreements mandatory instruments through which legislation can be controlled through state intervention. Under Section 7 of the Collective Bargaining Act, the Ministry of Labour, Social Affairs, and Family can decree the national collective agreement to be binding on the employers not unionized in the same organization of employers. A collective agreement made at a higher level can be binding on employers involved in similar economic activities or similar social and economic conditions provided they are based in the Slovak Republic but not bound by another collective agreement made at a higher level.

Such broader applicability of collective agreements made at higher levels has recently had a favourable impact on the growing number of employers in the private sector with no union organization where the employees are legally disadvantaged. Quite often the employers are not willing to be associated in any organization solely because they do not want to be bound by a collective agreement made at national level.

B. Collective Bargaining Procedures

The main purpose of collective bargaining is to make a collective agreement. The procedures relating to collective bargaining are governed by the Collective Bargaining Act No. 2/1991.

1. Obligation to Negotiate

The Collective Bargaining Act No. 2/1991 prescribes for the employers the obligation to negotiate before the collective agreement is made. In addition, collective agreements can be made if so decided by a mediator.

2. Obligation to Reach 'Peace'

Apart from the obligation to negotiate, the Collective Bargaining Act also contains the so-called 'conciliation' requirement, a duty to reach social peace after the collective agreement has been made. The current law lays down an obligation for the parties to resolve disputes by means of a mediator.

3. Collective Disputes

Under the Collective Agreement Act No. 2/1991, collective disputes comprise conflicts of interests (arising before the collective agreements are made) and conflicts of rights (involving non-fulfilment of any obligation fixed by the collective agreement) in which individual employee's rights are not in issue.

a. Conflicts of Interest

Such conflicts arise where the parties fail to agree as to the contents of the collective agreement. The first step is to use a mediator, which is a mandatory procedure. The decision of a mediator does not replace the agreement. Mediation is unsuccessful if the parties do not accept the recommendations made by the mediator.

The next step is neither mandatory nor uniform in nature. The parties may try to settle the dispute through an arbitrator. If the parties do not choose to handle the dispute by an arbitrator whose decision results in making the collective agreement, a strike action may be chosen.

Arbitration is non-compulsory and can be instigated only with the consent of the parties. However, it can be an obligatory procedure for employees who are exempted from the right to strike by law. A decision of the arbitrator is final and cannot be appealed. The collective agreement is deemed to have been made upon the delivery of the decision reached by the arbitrator.

b. Conflicts of Rights

The first step in conflict resolution over non-fulfilment of the collective agreement not affecting individual rights is to bring the action before a mediator. If this is unsuccessful, the next step is arbitration. Here, however, no option is possible because strikes are not allowed in the case of non-fulfilment of collective rights.

Unlike in conflicts of interests, decision by the arbitrator is not final and can be appealed to the appropriate court. A decision of an arbitrator can be enforced by courts.

C. Strikes and Lock-outs

Strikes and lock-outs are governed by the Collective Bargaining Act No. 2/1991. Since the conditions for taking a strike action are laid down in great detail, the public considers it to be anti-strike. The act provides for mandatory mediation before beginning a strike. This final resort can be legally used only in conflicts of interests provided a collective agreement has not been achieved by mediation and the parties do not seek arbitration as a form of conflict resolution.

Strike actions, however, are possible only where provided for by the collective agreements. The Collective Bargaining Act does not enumerate conditions in which strikes can be held, but the issues have to deal with making or changing the collective agreement. Thus it can be said that after the collective agreement has been made, both parties are obliged to seek labour peace.

A strike action must be announced by a union. The Collective Bargaining Act limits the right to strike by excluding certain groups of employees. On the other hand, the Act provides for solidarity strikes. A solidarity strike can be declared unlawful by a court in cases where the employer, having regard to non-existing economic or production links with the units in support of which the action has been taken, cannot influence the course and results of the strike.

1. Legal Status of Employees participating in Strikes

No employee participating in a strike action is entitled to any compensation or pay. Participation in a strike action prior to a court ruling on unlawfulness of such action constitutes unexcused absence from work. Participation in a strike after the court rules on its lawfulness is an excused absence as provided by law. Compensation during a strike can be paid only to those employees who could not work but did not take part in the strike.

No employer can legally dismiss an employee solely because of his or her participation in a strike. Thus, compensation and pay are suspended in the same way as the contract of employment, which also becomes suspended.

During a strike, the employees are not entitled to sickness benefits, or allowance for taking care of a sick child. Eligibility to these benefits and allowances is renewed on the day immediately following the strike closing day when all other conditions have been fulfilled. Their term cannot be prolonged by the days during which the strike was held. For the purposes of retirement plans, the days during which the strike was held, save for unlawful strike, are counted in the working time. Low pay as a consequence of a strike is not a justification for social assistance to those in need.

2. Lock-outs

The Collective Bargaining Act provides for lock-outs. Like strikes, lock-outs are permitted only in cases of a conflict of interests before the collective agreement is reached or after an unsuccessful mediation where the parties have chosen not to go before an arbitrator.

Under Section 28 of Act No. 2/1991 a lock-out cannot be used against employees who are excluded from the right to strike. Otherwise a court will declare such lock-out unlawful.

Unlike strikes when the employees are not entitled to any compensation, the employer is obliged to pay a compensation in the amount of 50% of the average wage to all employees during a lawful lock-out. Sickness benefits and social security rights remain unaffected during a lock-out. For the purposes of retirement benefits, the time of lock-out is not calculated into the average-pay period. Where the pay is reduced as a result of a lock-out, the employee in need can be considered for eligibility to an assistance allowance.

3. Resolution of Individual Labour Disputes

Under current legislation, individual conflicts are dealt with by courts. In the near future Slovakia intends to introduce labour tribunals.

D. Participation of Employees

In Slovakia, the participation of employees has not developed into the plurality of forms known in other countries with an advanced free market. Such participation is only through trade unions. Unlike in other post-totalitarian countries, new trade unions were constituted on the structural basis of the former union organization. Currently, there is only indirect participation of employees, who are represented exclusively by the unions. Legally, the organization of workers' participation is through the channels consisting of information, consultations, decisions, participation in decision making, and controlling.

1. Information

Under the current Labour Code, particularly its basic provisions of Article VI, employees have the right to be informed of the activities of the employer relating to economic and developmental matters, through the trade unions.

Article VI, having the nature of the basic principle of Slovak labour law, has been often criticized by labour theoreticians as discouraging employees from participation in decision making. Another drawback is the absence of plurality of workers' representation; such plurality is strongly opposed by the trade unions which do not want to risk their monopoly position.

2. Consultations

Employers are obliged to consult with the union on such matters as dismissal, job transfer, unbalanced working time, the beginning and the end of working hours, etc. Although the employer is not bound to respect the union recommendations, the matter must be consulted before a final decision can be made.

3. Decision Making

This channel has undergone most significant changes since 1989. Separation of trade unions from the state has resulted in shifting former trade union powers to governmental authorities. Trade unions have retained some decision making only in occupational safety and health protection at work (Section 136 subsections (1) (c) and (d)).

4. Participation in Decision Making

Here participation is guaranteed by the previous consent of an appropriate trade union body or a concurrence with the proposal of the employer. Coordinated decision making of employers and trade unions is obligatory in cases specified by the Labour Code, e.g., in dismissal of a union office-bearer, night shifts for women, rules of the company, absence from work, etc.

5. *Control*

Control through which they can enforce compliance with labour laws, rules governing compensation and pay, fulfilment of obligations under collective agreements, and safety and health standards is crucial for the appropriate union bodies. The rights to control are set forth in Section 136 of the Labour Code.

E. Current Problems of Workers' Participation

In addition to unions, the new Labour Code will also introduce new types of representatives of employees' interests. This novelty has been heavily criticized by trade unions, traditionally the sole representative of workers.

The new forms of representation will include works councils, and also representatives in charge of safety and health matters and handicapped workers. The main thrust behind the introduction of the plurality of workers' representatives is the constantly falling number of union members found among those who have lost confidence in the unions of the former type. More and more private employers, at the same time, discourage their employees from union involvement by means of a complex system of incentives, particularly by higher pay or more favourable working conditions. In this way, the number of legally unprotected employees is growing, especially situations wherein employers use illegal discouragement against union membership. Through the works councils it will be possible to guarantee fully free coalition as provided by Article 37 of the Constitution of the Slovak Republic, the section defining the privilege of the employees to defend their economic and social rights and interests through trade unions. In this context it should be mentioned that Slovakia formerly had a very effective system of works councils before 1950. Their re-introduction, despite strong opposition comparable with anti-union resistance of the beginning of this century, is a crucial measure.

Under the new Labour Code, trade unions will retain the right of collective bargaining and the power to see that the labour laws be implemented.

It is anticipated that the former traditional powers of trade unions in human resources or personnel policy, programs of in-service training, or in economic matters will be vested in the works councils consisting of union representatives, representatives of the handicapped, those charged with responsibilities in occupational safety and protection of health, and those representing minor or female employees.

The new Labour Code, particularly the part dealing with works councils (the main objection of the union bodies), has become a subject of political struggle for the monopoly influence of trade union bodies in Slovakia. Although Act No. 2/1991 can be positively evaluated, it is quite clear that the parties to company-level collective agreements or collective agreements made at a higher level cannot obtain and maintain their autonomous positions under the current Labour Code which abounds in mandatory provisions. By reducing the number of rigorous provisions in the new Labour Code, the autonomy of the parties in the collective bargaining will be achieved.

CONCLUSION

The present development of labour laws, in particular the anticipated legislative changes, emphasizes harmonization of the legal systems of the Slovak Republic and the European Union, especially after the signing of the Association Agreement. Its recommendations are taken into consideration in preparing and passing new laws, including labour laws. The preparation of the new Labour Code will be in harmony with the EU regulations and directives. Such matters as collective dismissal in the case of bankruptcy of the employer and the transfer of rights to the succeeding employer have been only partially regulated.

Through the new Labour Code, labour law will retain its relative independence, despite some criticism of this codification, which, however, is in the minority.

Changes and Adaptations of Labour Law and Industrial Relations in Slovenia

Polonca Koncar

I. SOME BASIC FEATURES OF LABOUR LAW IN FORMER YUGOSLAVIA AND IN SLOVENIA

The system of labour law and its changes in Slovenia need to be studied from the standpoint of the introduction of a market economy and general democracy – a process going on in other Eastern European states as well - and from the standpoint of the secession of Slovenia from former Yugoslavia.

During the period before the independence of Slovenia in 1991, the Yugoslav Federation and the republics shared the responsibility of regulating labour relationships in accordance with the Constitution of the Socialist Federative Republic of Yugoslavia (SFRY) 1974 and the Constitution of the Socialist Republic of Slovenia (SRS). The constitutions of the federation and the republics regulated a considerable number of socio-economic rights on which the federal labour law system was founded, as well as the labour law system of the republics and autonomous provinces. Former Yugoslavia ratified 70 ILO conventions, which significantly influenced the national labour law.

Labour relationships were regulated on the federal level by the Law on Associated Labour, 1976. In 1977 Slovenia adopted the Law on Labour Relationships which has been amended several times since then. Both laws have two typical tendencies:
1. restriction on federal legislation in favour of the republic's legislation;
2. restriction of state interventions in favour of self-management regulations.

The legislation was quite comprehensive, but it also included many implementing provisions. The consequence was that the general self-management enactments on labour relationships were executive regulations and not genuine enactments adopted by the workers. The aim of the legislation was to expand employment possibilities and to attain a more productive working time. Legal regulation should also be a prerequisite to ensure greater discipline at work.

The introduction of a category of social ownership without a titular in self-managing socialism influenced the legal nature of labour law relationship based on the principle of reciprocity. The labour relationship was not a relationship between two parties, the employer *ante* employee, but between the workers themselves working with socially owned resources. The system was not based on a minor relative conflict between the interests of work and the interests of capital. That is why individual labour law was emphasized while collective labour law was not known, except for the small private craft sector. Trade unions therefore did not perform the task they have in a

157

market economy (collective negotiations, protection of workers' rights, and representing workers in firms). Collective agreements were negotiated only for workers employed by private craftsmen. Trade unions played an important role in adopting self-management enactments, ensuring protection at work, settling individual disputes at work within enterprises, and in disciplinary proceedings.

Individual disputes at work were not settled only in firms. A labour court system was introduced in 1974.[1] Courts of associated labour were a kind of self-managing body and not a part of regular courts. This dualism in jurisdiction was established by the Constitution of 1974. Courts of associated labour administer justice in accordance with the Constitution, laws, self-management enactments, and, towards the end, collective agreements as well.

The Yugoslav self-management socialist system was in many ways different from the system in other socialist countries,[2] but inefficient nevertheless. In 1986 the process of economic and political reforms was initiated and transition to a market economy, democratization and pluralization of the political and other relations was accepted as one of its most important aims.

In order to carry out the reform, certain amendments to the Constitutions of the SFRY and the Socialist Republic of Slovenia had to be adopted and the questions of incorporation had to be regulated. A law on enterprises was passed,[3] which made a distinction between socially owned, mixed, and private enterprises. This should logically be reflected in the various stati of workers employed in different types of enterprises. Labour legislation was not adjusted to new types of enterprises. There was a dilemma whether or not to introduce the system of collective agreements to all enterprises regardless of the type of ownership. At the same time, the equal position of enterprises was emphasized, regardless of the ownership relationship. Answers had to be found for how to solve the problem of unemployment and how to attain an equilibrium of the power of capital and labour. Last but not least, the new role of trade unions had to be defined.

The development of labour law could take different directions:
1. neo-liberalism;
2. labour law should preserve its protective character exclusively;
3. a combination of the first and the second.

The last of these directions was taken and in 1989 when the Law on Basic Rights of Employment Relationship was adopted.[4] Its main characteristics are as follows.

The law covers the individual as well as the collective labour law, with insufficiently and inadequately defined collective agreements.[5] The law has retained the principle of unity in regulating labour relations, which means that it covers all types

---

1.   'Zakon o sodiscih zdruzenega dela' ('The Law on Courts of Associated Labour'), Ur. 1. SFRJ (*Official Gazette*) No. 24/74; 'Zakon o sodiscih zdruzenega dela' ('The Law on Courts of Associated Labour'), Ur. 1. SRS (*Official Gazette*). No. 24/74.
2.   For instance, the system was not so centralized; the enterprises were more autonomous than in other plan-oriented economies.
3.   'The Law on Enterprises', Ur. 1. SFRJ (*Official Gazette*) No. 77/88, 40/89.
4.   'Zakon o temeljnih pravicah iz delovnega razmerja', Ur. 1. SFRJ (*Official Gazette*), No. 60/90, 42/90.
5.   The law at first provided for obligatory collective agreements on the level of the federation and the republics. The principle of voluntary collective bargaining was established only with changes and amendments of the law. Such a change did not occur in the Law on Labour Relationships of the Republic of Slovenia.

of organized labour regardless of the type of ownership. It does not distinguish between the economic and non-economic sector either. Some of the provisions of the new law promote greater mobility of workers, and define more authority for directors regarding the decisions on workers' rights; at the same time they reduce the authority of the self-managing organs and give new authorizations to the trade unions' representatives. The new law, one of the links of the economic reforms, thus reflects the needs of the labour law reform.

The federal Law on Basic Rights of Employment Relationship represented a new legal basis for the republic's legislation. In 1990 a Law on Employment Relationships was passed.[6]

The reform period after 1985 was a period of searching for new solutions to regulate employment relationships. And during this period the right to strike was acknowledged as a constitutional right. That was a time of a real strike movement. Reality thus refused the opinion that it is almost impossible in socialist countries for collective labour disputes to emerge between the parties to collective agreements. Such disputes in Yugoslavia were considered almost incredible.[7] The 1974 Constitution of the SPRY in Article 47 determined the so-called disputes which could not be settled by regular means. The content of the provision was repeated word for word in Article 636 of the Law on Associated Labour. But in theory the opinion prevailed that such an unclear constitutional text does not represent legal regulation of strikes in Yugoslavia. The strike movement contributed a great deal to strengthening the idea of adapting trade unions, even though it was not yet clear then that collective agreements could in time become an important autonomous source of labour law.[8] The frequency and severity of strikes showed the necessity for strikes to be regulated. Two amendments were adopted: amendment No. XXVIII to the Constitution of the SFRY and amendment No. XLII to the Constitution of Slovenia,[9] which promoted the right to strike to the level of a constitutional right. The amendments defined the right to strike under conditions determined by federal law. The Constitution was the legal basis for adopting the Law on Strikes.[10]

These beginnings of the transformation of labour law in former Yugoslavia have been described to emphasize that its process started before the independence of Slovenia. It is important to know that the Yugoslav legislation in this field is still valid temporarily pending the adoption of new Slovene legislation.[11] Following the independence of Slovenia, the process of adaptation is continuing. Some new laws have been passed in the field of individual as well as collective labour relationships, and some laws are in proceedings. There is much impatience and some would like to

---

6. 'Zakon o delovnih razmerjih', Ur. 1. SR (*Official Gazette*), No. 14/90, 5/91m 71/93, 2/94.
7. *See: World Labour Report*, 2, ILO, p. 49. It was taken into account that in the states with centrally-planned economies, the global interests of society were identical to the partial interests of its individual parts and also with interests of individual workers. The strike is therefore not possible in the socialist system, because the entire system (including the system of collective bargaining) is oriented towards co-operation between workers and directors of enterprises. Collective disputes therefore could not emerge.
8. It would be more logical to form the concept of strike taking into account the existing relations between the social partners, especially the role and the power of trade unions in the system of collective bargaining.
9. Ur. 1. SFRJ (*Official Gazette*), No. 70/88: Ur. 1. SRS (*Official Gazette*), No. 32/89.
10. 'Zakon o stavki', Ur. 1. SFRJ (*Official Gazette*), No. 23/91.
11. 'Ustavni zakon za izvedbo Ustave Republike Slovenije', ('The Constitutional Law on Implementation of the Constitution of the Republic of Slovenia'), Ur. 1. SR (*Official Gazette*), No. 33/91.

establish overnight a new labour law system suitable to the market economy, forgetting that ownership transformation has not yet been completed. Labour law, on the other hand, is not only a compilation of state regulations on labour relationship. Equally important are autonomous sources that depend very much on the strength of the employers' and the employees' organizations and on realization of the workers' right to participate in management of enterprises. This is the field of social relationships which evolves gradually according to the nature of economic and social conditions. Time is needed and the role of labour legislation, which can be only the basis or the promoter of industrial relationships, is limited. In connection with the implementation of legislation a change of mentality and understanding of the role of social partners is needed in the field of collective relationships. It must also be taken into account that labour legislation, like any other branch of law, is being shaped to function in the framework of social, economic, and political reality. The implementation of labour law depends especially on certain special factors, not only the employers' and the employees' organizations. In implementing individual labour law, the representative organs of workers can be an important factor in enterprises. The role of labour courts and supervising institutions, for example labour inspection, should not be regarded as less important.[12]

The following section examines the transformation of labour legislation and the development of industrial relationships in the Republic of Slovenia.

II. THE STATE AS A FACTOR OF LABOUR LAW AND INDUSTRIAL RELATIONS

The Slovene state has a triple role, like any other state: as labour administrator, legislator, and social partner.

A. Labour Administration

The Ministry of Labour, Family, and Social Affairs is in charge of questions related to employment relationships, wages policy and regulation of the wages system, collective bargaining and relations of social partners, policy on employment in the country and abroad, unemployment insurance, status and social care of the disabled, the young, children and the family, scholarships system, vocational training, pension and disability insurance, safety at work, family and demographic policy, social protection and social assistance, veterans protection, etc.[13]

The Labour Inspection of the Republic of Slovenia and the Office for Safety and Health at Work function within the Ministry of Labour, Family, and Social Affairs.

The Law on Labour Inspection, passed in June 1994,[14] places labour inspection under the supervision of a central authority. In the past labour inspection was organized on the national level and on the level of communes. The inspectorate controls the

---

12.   P. Koncar, 'O novi delovni zakonodaji in delovnem pravu' ('On New Labour Legislation and Labour Law'), *Podjetje in delo* (journal), Ljubljana, 5 June 1993 XIX, p. 399).
13.   'Zakon o organizaciji in delovnem podrocju ministrstev' ('The Law on Organization and the Work Area of Ministries') Ur. 1. RS (*Official Gazette*) No. 71/94.
14.   'Zakon o inspekciji dela', Ur. 1. RS (*Official Gazette*) No. 38/94.

implementation of laws and other regulations, collective agreements and general acts regulating labour relationships, wages and other income deriving from the labour relationship, safety at work, employment of workers at home and abroad, implementation of the law on participation of workers in management, and strikes.[15] The inspectors have greater authorization under the new legislation. They have the power to issue an order requiring the implementation of regulations, collective agreements, etc., by the employer, through taking or abandoning action, or through an act. Inspectors can order the employers to stop the process of work or the use of certain resources until the deficiencies are rectified. In some cases (grey economy) prohibition is obligatory. The inspectors have the right to seal certain resources for work, work premises, as well as to order that the supply of electricity, water, gas, and telecommunications to an employer be terminated or interrupted.

The law prescribes stricter conditions regarding the qualification of inspectors. At present the number of inspectors at the Labour Inspectorate is insufficient, in view of its many tasks and an increasing number of violations.

B. The Normative Role of the State

The question of the role of the state in forming labour law is closely connected to the question of the relation between the state and the autonomous sources of labour law. The question is whether in a given social environment a system with strong state regulations (detailed and extensive), or a system of labour relationships regulated mainly by collective agreements, would be more appropriate.

In systems in which the normative role of the state is strong, legislation can be codified on one hand, while on the other hand labour relations can be regulated by a number of separate laws and other provisions.

Regarding the labour legislation in force, Slovenia can be classified among the countries where labour law is state directed. However, many law provisions are not directly applicable. The Slovene legislation extensively imposes the questions that should be negotiated 'in detail' by social partners. This is why the autonomy of social partners is actually still less important, especially regarding the contents of collective agreements. We are well aware from the former self-management system that the creativity and initiative of social partners can be very negatively affected if the autonomous law is strongly directed.

At the beginning of the so-called period of transition to a market economy, certain theories appeared stating that codification of labour legislation should be prepared simultaneously with the implementation of all political, economic, and social changes. But since the conditions for such codification do not exist,[16] the idea of codification was rejected. The result is that certain questions which have in the past been regulated by one law are now regulated by several laws. Such fragmentation of legislation has some positive sides (e.g. better adaptability to changes, or a possibility for faster regulation of the most urgent new questions), but there are also negative sides.

---

15. The court is conferred jurisdiction of the legality of strikes, and not the inspectorate.
16. *See*: e.g., *The Codification of Labour Law, 9th International Congress, Reports and Proceedings*, Munich, 12–15 Sept. 1978, Band II/2, Verlaggeselschaft Recht und Wirtschaft mbH, Heidelberg.

A greater number of various regulations may sometimes be a reflection, or even a cause, of non-systematic and partial regulation.[17] A danger also exists that due to an increasing number of the state and the autonomous sources of labour law, as well as the international ones, these are not harmonized. Such a situation can in turn endanger the legal security of workers.

As far as the normative role of the state in the future is concerned, no reasons justify, in my opinion, the state to withdraw from certain fields and leave them to autonomous regulation. The degree of power and ability of the employees' and the employers' organizations to negotiate is not yet sufficient. At the same time, the workers' lack of rights has spread in this transition period due to many reasons. Consequently, it remains appropriate for the state to regulate the most vital questions connected to the conclusion of the employment contract, the rights and duties arising from the employment relationship, and the determination of employment. These are the fields where a minimum of rights should be guaranteed to all workers whether the collective agreements have been signed or not. The state should retain an important role in restoring institutions that will have the power to regulate labour relations autonomously, taking into account regulations of fair play. The state should however withdraw from regulation of wages and/or its role should be limited to defining only the minimum wages.

The Law on Employment Relationships from 1990 is still in force in Slovenia and the Law on Basic Rights of Employment Relationship[18] is still applied. It could be concluded that little has been done to change labour law in Slovenia. However, such a conclusion cannot be accepted since a number of important laws in the field of individual and collective law have been passed since the adoption of the constitution in 1991: the Law on the Representativeness of Trade Unions,[19] the Law on the Employment of Foreigners,[20] the Law on Participation of Workers in the Management of Enterprises,[21] and the Law on Labour Inspection. The Law on Collective Agreements and the Law on Safety at Work are in the drafting procedure.

Slovenia is bound by 66 ILO conventions.

III.   NEW PRINCIPLES OF LABOUR LEGISLATION AND THE MAIN CHANGES INTRODUCED TO DATE

Although the labour legislation dates from the period before the independence of Slovenia, the entire process of changes is based on the new constitution of the Republic of Slovenia adopted at the end of 1991.[22]

---

17. This statement could be confirmed by examples from our everyday life, in my opinion. Therefore, separate regulation of collective agreements and strikes has been announced, while for the time being peaceful resolution of disputes has not been mentioned often. It is also interesting that the legislator decided to regulate the legal basis for collective bargaining first, while the legislation of individual labour relationships is to be revised later.
18. On the basis of Article 4 paragraph 1 of the Constitutional Law on the Implementation of Constitutional Charter on the Independence and Sovereignty of the Republic of Slovenia (Ur. 1. SR (*Official Gazette*) year I, 1/91), this law is applied in Slovenia until the adoption of a new labour legislation.
19. 'Zakon o reprezentativnosti sindikatov'. Ur. 1. SR (*Official Gazette*), No. 13/93.
20. 'Zakon o zaposlovanju tujcev', Ur. 1. SR (*Official Gazette*), No. 72/93.
21. 'Zakon o sodelovanju delavcev pri upravljanju', Ur. 1. SR (*Official Gazette*), No. 42/93.
22. 'Ustava SR', Ur, 1. SR (*Official Gazette*) No. 33/91–I.

The constitution of the Republic of Slovenia is intended to be a modern and rational constitution and its main objective is the protection of human rights and freedoms. In addition, one of the most important principles of the Slovenian Constitution is the principle of separation of powers. The chapter on human rights provides for the following rights and freedoms: the freedom of work (Article 49), the right to social security (Article 50), the right to medical care (Article 51), and rights of the disabled (Article 52); Slovenia is 'a democratic and social state' according to the constitution. The principle of social state is confirmed also by some provisions of the chapter on economic and social relations.[23] The Constitution thus provides that the state creates the possibilities for employment and work and ensures their legal protection (Article 66) and that the workers may participate in management of the business and agencies (Article 75). Freedom of association (Article 76) and the right to strike (Article 77) are also guaranteed. Foreigners employed in Slovenia enjoy special rights as defined by law (Article 79).

Among the new principles and novelties in the Slovenian labour law system, the following should be mentioned:

1. in the field of individual labour law the employment contract has been introduced;
2. the so-called monopoly on posts has been abolished and dismissals due to techno-logical, organizational and structural reasons have been allowed;
3. a system of collective bargaining and collective agreements as autonomous sources of labour law has been introduced;
4. participation of workers in the management of enterprises has been introduced;
5. the jurisdiction has been reformed and new specialized labour and social courts became a part of state courts.

It is interesting that no solution has yet been found for the dilemma of unity or dualism of labour law. Formally at least, the principle of law unity is still valid.[24] In 1991 and 1992 the law on civil servants was much discussed, the consequence of which would be elimination of the mentioned principle. The preparations of the new law have been slowed down. Recently some theses appeared, which, on the basis of comparative law analyses, drew attention to tendencies towards a more unified regulation of the labour law status of all kinds of dependent workers when the nature of a given activity, or particularity of some types of work, does not dictate a special regulation. Some authors[25] advocate uniform regulating of labour relations in the public and the private sector, taking into account that a modern state is less and less authoritarian and that the administrative systems are changing in essence. The basic rights and duties of a labour relationship, including the right to participation, should be valid for all workers. At the same time, there should be a possibility to regulate the labour relationship with special provisions. Regarding the rights that exceed the legal minimum standards, voluntary collective and individual bargaining should be possible. Administrative law should regulate only the status of a narrow circle of people, namely the officials of the state administration.

---

23. It has been maintained that the so-called economic and social rights should be integrated in the chapter on human rights and freedoms.
24. Even though both laws on labour relationships are regarded as basic laws for all employed persons, examples of implementations of dualism have appeared. Special provisions, for example, regulate the labour relationships of state administration employees and officials almost completely.
25. *See:* e.g., T. Dobrin, 'Enotnost ali dualizemv delovnopravni uredcitvi' ('Unity or Dualism in the Regulation of the Labour Law'), *Podjetje in delo* (journal), August 1994 XX, pp. 1164–1172.

IV. INDIVIDUAL LABOUR LAW

A. Employment Contract

The principle of mutuality of labour relationship was abolished in favour of labour relationship between two parties based on an employment contract.

It has to be emphasized that the employment contract is not regulated by civil legislation in Slovenia.[26] The employment contract is mentioned only in both laws on employment relationships. Legal regulation is very meagre and deficient. It is a great problem that the regulation on rights and duties has not yet been adapted to a contractual employment relationship.

The Law on Employment Relationships defines the employment relationship as a two-sided voluntary relationship between a worker on one side and an organization or employer on the other. At present two conditions have to be fulfilled to begin the labour relationship: conclusion of an employment contract[27] and starting to work. The contract theory is therefore not valid. It is widely held that the future system of individual labour relationships should be built on this theory.

The constitution provides freedom of work and forbids unjust discrimination in work opportunities.[28] Nobody should be discriminated in concluding an employment contract. Exceptions to this rule are two examples laid down by the law. A priority right to employment is reserved for the disabled and for redundant workers whose last employer starts to hire again within a legally prescribed period. Their priority right means that these persons have an individual claim against the employer to be employed.

An employment contract requires a written form according to legal provisions. An employment contract is not a contract of civil law, but it is nevertheless necessary to take into account general requirements of civil law for a valid contract. Case law on defects of employment contracts does not yet exist.

According to Article 11 of the Law on Employment Relationships, the organization, or the employer, and the worker agree, through the employment contract concluded in accordance with the collective agreement of the general act, on those rights and particularities regarding the post for which the worker signed the contract. The parties to the employment contract are basically free to decide on the content of the employment contract. As employment contracts are relatively new in our legal system, soon after their enactment, their content was found to be vague. Practically all collective agreements now define an obligatory minimal content of the employment contract.[29]

---

26. *De lege ferende* - a new regulation of employment contract in the Law on Obligation Relationships is not foreseen. It appears that the contract will remain a contract of labour law, while general requirements for contracting civil law contracts will have to be replaced.

27. When a worker starts to work without having an employment contract, we can speak about a *de facto* employment relationship. In such a case the case law acknowledges only indemnities against the employer.

28. Article 49 of the Constitution of the Republic of Slovenia.

29. The following are some obligatory elements of the employment contract: commencement of work and the duration of the labour relationship, the post, probation work if required, the location of the work, working time, breaks, vacations, measures for special protection of workers, training, basic wages, allowances, compensations, premiums, the manner of changing the contract, competition clause.

The basic problem of the legislation in force is that it re-introduced the employment contract as an instrument of employment relationship, but the regulation of individual institutes was not adapted to that. Thus we continue to speak about types of employment relationships instead of special types of employment contracts. There are no legal regulations or case law regarding the change of employment contract. The laws regulate cases of termination of the employment relationship instead of the termination of employment contract or dismissals. One of the basic tasks in the future in changing individual labour law will be adaptation of legislation to the fact that the employment relationship is based on an employment contract.

B. New Employment Policy and New Legal Measures Related Job Security

Growing unemployment[30] in Slovenia, due to an increasing economic stagnation, loss of the former Yugoslav market, changes related to the introduction of an integral market, and to some extent to development of technology, dictated a redefinition of employment policy in the country. Instead of the former full employment, a productive employment on the enterprise level and an optimal employment of all for the able-bodied population was set as a goal. This goal should be realized also by means of an active employment policy. The Law on Employment and Unemployment Insurance[31] has enacted concrete elements of a modern regulation of the labour market, including the intervening function of the state and public institutions.

In the framework of the active employment policy, measures of assistance to enterprises or employers as well as to individuals are foreseen.

The Employment Agency mainly assists enterprises or employers with the following measures: co-financing of new productive posts; compensation for part of the expenses for preserving productive jobs; loans for new production investments; co-financing of fostering whole-year employment of workers in seasonal activities; assistance in training of the newly employed; co-financing retraining and other educational programmes; co-financing adaptation of technical equipment in work posts for disabled persons; co-financing retraining and additional training of redundant workers and purchase of additional insurance periods for redundant workers; and programmes of public works.

The following measures applying to individuals may be *inter alia* included in active employment policy programmes: covering expenses of implementing informative, training and educational programmes for vulnerable groups of the unemployed; compensating a part of the wage for workers on probation; loans to purchase equipment for self-employment; covering expenses for retraining due to new employment possibilities, etc.

The following relatively successful measures have been implemented in the past three years in Slovenia: direct payment of unemployment benefits (in capitalized amount) to enterprises which are ready to employ redundant workers; seminars on possibilities for self-employment; training and retraining programmes; compensating part of probationers' wages; and co-financing the severance pay to redundant workers.

---

30.   The unemployment rate was 4.7% in 1990, 12% in 1992, and it reached 13% in 1994. It started to decrease slightly in the second half of 1994.
31.   'Zakon o zaposlovanju in zavarovanju za primer brezōpselnosti', Ur. 1. SR (*Official Gazette*), No. 5/91, 12/92, 71/93, 38/94. The law regulates the compulsory unemployment insurance scheme and provides for insurance on a voluntary basis. It also introduces measures of active employment policy.

The growing unemployment in Slovenia was closely connected with the phenomena of redundancy. The main reasons for redundancies were the reduction of the volume of production (also because of the lost markets in former Yugoslavia) and various internal measures for the rationalization of work.

The Law on Employment Relationships was amended twice, in 1991 and in 1993. The amendments of 1991 mainly regulated the status of workers whose work is no longer needed due to urgent operative reasons. Urgent operative reasons are defined by the law as technological, organizational, or structural reasons that add to greater effectiveness of enterprises, and economic reasons.

The law was passed in accordance with the ratified ILO Convention No. 158 Concerning Termination of Employment on the Initiative of the Employer, 1982, as well as some comparative analyses of legal systems in other European countries including the EEC Council Directive of 15 February 1975 on approximation of the laws of member states related to collective redundancies.

The law distinguishes between temporarily redundant workers (workers who temporarily, up to a maximum 6 months, cannot be given work) and permanently redundant workers (workers whose work becomes redundant for more than 6 months).

Temporarily redundant workers cannot be subject to termination of employment unless they become permanently redundant. The manager or employer can choose, after seeking the opinion of the trade union, one of the following legally determined measures:
1. temporary transfer within the enterprise;
2. temporary transfer to another enterprise;
3. retraining or additional training with the right to compensation of wage up to the amount fixed by the collective agreement;
4. lay-off with the right of compensation of wage in the amount fixed by the collective agreement; and
5. introduction of part-time work.

In the case of permanent redundancy the law provides for the following measures to avert termination of employment:
1. transfer;
2. retraining or additional training on condition that it is possible to qualify the worker for another job in 6 months; and
3. introduction of part-time work for all workers.

The law also provides for measures to mitigate the adverse effects of termination of employment. These are:
1. the right to a period of 8 months notice during which the worker may work, or if he does not work he is entitled to a compensation wage;
2. the right to 6 months compensation of wage in one instalment in lieu of the 6 months notice period;
3. the right to a severance allowance.

Additional rights are provided for certain categories of workers: the disabled who do not fulfil conditions for a disability pension; older workers lacking 5 years of insurance period but also lacking guaranteed employment benefit; workers with less than one year of service, etc. The employment of these categories of workers may be terminated only with their consent.

The Slovene legislation seems quite progressive and flexible even from the standpoint of some of the western systems, since it provides for different schemes.

These try to cope with redundancy and unemployment and mitigate social tensions while promoting industrial restructuring. But on the other hand, life confirms the well-known fact that it is impossible to substitute economic initiative and the laws of the market with legal norms. The transfer of workers or any other measure is not possible if the entire economy is faced with over-employment, while there is not enough capital available to create new jobs, or when the state has no means for the realization of social programmes.

V. COLLECTIVE LABOUR LAW

A. Trade Unions and Employers' Associations

The Constitution of the Republic of Slovenia defines freedom of establishing trade unions and joining them (Article 76). Since the constitutional provision relates only to freedom of association of workers (according to the European understanding), it has to be emphasized that Slovenia is bound by some important international norms as well – the UN International Convention Civil and Political Rights, and the International Convention Economic, Social and Cultural Rights of 1966. Some ratified ILO conventions are also important, especially the following: Freedom of Association and Protection of the Right to Organize Convention, 1948 (No. 87), the Right to Organize Collective Bargaining Convention, 1949 (No. 98), and the Workers Representation Convention, 1971 (No. 135). Slovenia has also ratified the European Convention on Human Rights of the Council of Europe.

The democratization and pluralization of political and other relations in Slovenia resulted in trade union pluralism. It may be useful to mention the four principal trade union organizations in Slovenia:
– the Federation of Free Trade Unions of Slovenia;[32] Independence;
– the Confederation of New Trade Unions;[33] Pergam;
– the Confederation of Trade Unions of Slovenia; and
In addition, there are also more than a hundred trade unions for various branches and professions (sailors, journalists, doctors, dentists, casino workers, etc.). The existing pluralism is reflected in a variety of political orientations and in the co-existence of different types of trade unions (craft, enterprises and industry unions).

The Law on Representativeness of Trade Unions was passed in 1993.[34] According to the law, a trade union becomes a legal entity on the day of issue of the decision, upon the placement in safe-keeping of its statute at the authorized administrative organ. Under the law, to be regarded as representative a trade union must meet the following conditions:
1. it must be democratic and respect the principle of freedom of association;
2. it must have been active for an uninterrupted period of at least 6 months;
3. it must be independent of state organs and employers;
4. its number of members must comply to the law.

---

32. The successor of the former trade union with about 430,000 members; the membership was not automatically inherited, because all members had to fill in a new declaration of accession.
33. With about 140,000 members.
34. 'Zakon o reprezentativnosti sindikatov', Ur. 1. SR (*Official Gazette*), No. 13/93.

Regarding employers' organizations, there are three known business organizations in Slovenia. The Chamber of Trade of Slovenia is still the association that signs collective agreements on behalf of employers as a legal representative of their interests. In February 1994 the Association of Employers of Slovenia was established at the initiative of the Chamber of Trade. This is a voluntary membership association. Since the process of privatization is not yet completed, the membership of the new association is mixed. The third, exclusively private employers' organization, the Employers' and Industrialists' Association, was founded in Maribor in 1991. For the time being it is not formally engaged in industrial relations and collective bargaining.

There are no regulations defining how to establish employers' organizations. Nevertheless demands to regulate this field have emerged in Slovenia. This would be needed to alleviate difficulties in connection with registering employers' organizations, the representativeness of which should also be regulated.

B. Tripartitism

Since 1992 we have been witnessing attempts to introduce social partnership. A belief prevails that the co-operation of all three social partners can contribute a great deal and that Slovenia will become a social state in fact. In the past few years there have already been certain cases of institutionalized tripartite co-operation of social partners (e.g. in the management board of an employment agency; co-operation of the employers and the trade unions' representatives in the Second Chamber of the Parliament). Employers and trade unions also adopted an agreement on wages policy for 1994. This is intended to represent a separate social agreement that has not yet been reached. It is important also because with this agreement a tripartite economic and social council has been established. The council is authorized to deal with all questions regarding economic and social policy and collective bargaining.[35]

C. Collective Agreement

Both laws on labour relations are the legal foundation for collective bargaining. They have reintroduced collective agreements as so called autonomous sources of labour law.[36] The laws indicate the contents of collective agreements (the part covering the rights and duties of the parties, and the part setting legal norms) and determine the parties and the levels of collective bargaining (national, branch, and enterprise level). Under the legislation in force the so-called advantage principle applies not only to the relation of law *versus* collective agreement or to the relation of collective agreement

---

35. Trade unions advocate that the council should be established by law.
36. In the past, between the two world wars, and a very short period after World War II, collective bargaining was practised on Slovene territory. The Law on Labour Relations of 1957 introduces collective agreements to the so-called private sector (craft) in which they have remained an important source of labour law right up to the present.

versus employment contract, but also when the relation between different levels of collective agreements is concerned.[37]

General collective agreements for the economic and the non-economic sectors, as well as for the branch collective agreements, are obligatory, while collective agreements are not obligatory on the enterprise level. The legislator referred to the fact that labour legislation is incomplete in defining minimum rights and duties of the workers and should therefore be supplemented by compulsory collective agreements. Due to the same reason it should be stipulated that the collective agreement is valid for all workers who perform their job on the territory of Slovenia, and not only for the members of the parties to the collective agreement.

Collective agreements may be concluded for a limited period of time (a maximum of five years) or for an indefinite time. They are contracted in writing. The legislation provides that general collective agreements and collective agreements for relevant branches of industry enter into the register kept by the Ministry of Labour, Family, and Social Affairs.

We are all aware that the legislation is deficient and is not in conformity with the international standards that define the principle of free and voluntary collective bargaining. The practice of collective bargaining also shows deficiencies.[38] The interference of the state in the field of wages is a special problem. It is conditioned by the opinion of macro-economists that in comparison to the economic situation, wages are too high. Under a permanent threat that the state will intervene and 'freeze' wages with a special law, partners to general collective agreements try to limit themselves in such a way that bargaining *in melius* is not possible on the level of branches and enterprises due to certain adopted mechanisms.

To abolish various formal and substantial deficiencies, a new Law on Collective Agreements is in the process of being drafted. It will be based on the principle of free and voluntary collective bargaining and will no longer make it obligatory to conclude collective agreements. It will not explicitly mention the levels of collective bargaining either. The parties to collective agreements will, in the future, be voluntary associations only. The collective agreements should, in the future, become an autonomous source of law and should not only supplement laws. The new law should regulate the following questions as well: the contents, the procedure of conclusion, the form, the validity, the termination, the friendly resolution of collective disputes, the collective agreement register and the control.

D.   The Strike

The Constitution of the Republic of Slovenia of 1991 gives the workers the right to strike. But in contrast to the former constitutional regulation, the right to strike may be restricted by law when such a restriction is in the public interest according to the type and nature of the enterprise or agency affected (Article 77).

---

37.   But in fact we already know some exceptions, for example: the general collective agreement for the economic sector limited maximum wages and prevented negotiations *in melius*.
38.   Stated only as an example: all attention is paid to wages, and thus the problems of working conditions are neglected; bargaining about wages is limited due to various interventions of the state: solving disputes related to the bargaining is not effective; the employers or the state as parties to collective agreements cannot fulfil their obligations arising from valid agreements, yet there are no suitable sanctions for the breach of the collective agreement.

According to the constitutional concept, the right to strike is an individual right exercised by workers collectively. This means that the so-called organic concept, known in Germany, was not accepted.

The law on strikes adopted in the former SFRY[39] is temporarily in force in Slovenia pending the adoption of the law. On the basis of the constitutional regulation of the possibilities of restricting the right to strike, some laws have already defined types of work that are to be performed even during strikes.[40] This means that in fact some workers have been denied the right to strike.[41] A new Law on Defence[42] stipulates that the military do not have the right to strike, while for other employees in the army the same regulations are applicable as for civil servants. Types of work which have to be performed even during a strike are identified.

The Law on Strikes defines the strike as an organized cessation of work to obtain economic and social rights and interests. According to the law a strike may be organized on the level of an enterprise or a part of it and on the branch or industry level. The right to general strike is also recognized. The decision to strike can be taken by trade unions or by the workers themselves. The law contains provisions requiring at least a five-day notice of the intention to go on strike. The waiting period is provided for a possible peaceful settlement of the dispute. For all vital services, maintenance of a minimum service is required in order to avoid danger to life and property and to ensure the conditions for life and work and functioning of other enterprises. Engaging in a lawful strike may not incur disciplinary sanctions and corresponding civil action. The Slovene system of industrial action does not recognize the lock-out.

E. Workers' Participation

The Constitution of the Republic of Slovenia provides for participation of workers in the management of enterprises and public agencies in such a manner and under such conditions as may be determined by the law (Article 75).

---

39.   The law was adopted, by a special decree of the Slovene parliament in 1991, into the Slovene legal system since it was believed that a bad law is better than none. It may be of interest that the legislator took into account many solutions from the Guidelines for the Conduct of Strikes, adopted by the trade unions in Slovenia even before the law was passed.
40.   'Zakon o notranjih zadevah' ('The Law on Internal Affairs'), Ur. 1. SR (*Official Gazette*), No. 28/80, 38/88, 8/90, 19/91, 58/93; 'Zakon o izvrsevanju kazenskih sankcij' ('The Law in Implementation of Penal Sanctions'), Ur. 1. SR (*Official Gazette*), No. 17/78, 8/90, 12/92, 58/93; 'Zakon o carinski sluzbi' ('The Law on Custom Service'), Ur. 1. SR (*Official Gazette*), No. 1/91-I, 58/93.
41.   The laws have already been brought to the Constitutional Court of the Republic of Slovenia, which has decided that the laws are not inconsistent with Article 77 of the Constitution of the Republic of Slovenia. The Constitution supposedly concedes to limit the right to strike by objective criterion (limitation according to the type of activity), while it does not allow limitations by subjective criterion (denial of the right to certain categories of workers): U-I-193/93, Ur. 1. SR (*Official Gazette*), No. 35/94.
42.   'Zakon o obrambi', Ur 1. SR (*Official Gazette*), No. 82/94.

The Law on Participation of Workers was passed in 1993.[43] It should fill the gaps after the gradual abolishment of self-management.[44] It should provide for the attainment of ethical, political, social and economic goals pursued by the system of participation elsewhere in Europe as well.

The law applies to commercial companies, co-operatives, public commercial services, and partly to institutions. It emphasizes collective and indirect participation with a possibility for an individual and a direct participation. It provides for a strict separation between the participation of workers in management and the trade union activities. The law determines participation through works councils and/or the workers' representatives as a basic model. The workers may also participate in management through the workers' assembly and in the company's organs (supervisory board, labour director as a member of the management board). The works council is an optional organ.

The law allows for the following forms of workers' participation in management: the right to an initiative and to a reply to it; the right to information; the right to give opinions and to demand explanations from the employer; the duty of the employer to inform the works council; consultations between the employer and the works council; mutual decision making; and the works council's right to withhold the employer's decision.

The law is a typical example of an uncritical adoption of foreign regulations, concretely of the German system of codetermination, regardless of the existing trade union organization and the collective bargaining system. Therefore difficulties are expected in the implementation of this law. Due to the inconsistency of the law with other regulations, especially with the Law on Commercial Companies, the law will have to be changed and amended.

VI.   JURISDICTION IN LABOUR AND SOCIAL SECURITY MATTERS

The Slovene labour court system was changed in April 1994 when the Law on Labour and Social Courts[45] was passed. Some important new features are as follows.

The courts are no longer defined as a sort of special self-management courts. They are now included in the framework of state courts thus forming a uniform judicial power. In comparison with the earlier regulation, their jurisdiction is essentially extended. In addition to individual labour disputes and disputes in connection with social security, the jurisdiction of the labour and social courts also includes the collective labour disputes (on existence or non-existence of the collective agreement; on competence to engage in collective bargaining; on conformity of the collective agreement with a law; on legality of strikes; on implementation of the right to participation; on representativeness of trade unions). Jurisdiction on labour and social security matters has a three-level structure, and the third level is the Supreme Court of Slovenia. As to the structure of the courts it should be mentioned that professional judges work together with assessors who are elected on the list drawn up by the

---

43.   'Zakon o sodelovanju delavcev pri upravljanju', Ur. 1. SR (*Official Gazette*), No. 42/93.
44.   The implementation of the law will be possible after the transformation of ownership of enterprises and when these are organized in conformity with the Law on Commercial Companies ('Zakon o gospodarskih druzbah'), Ur. 1. SR (*Official Gazette*), No. 30/93.
45.   'Zakon o delovnih in socialnih sodiscih', Ur. 1. SR (*Official Gazette*), No. 19/94.

representative trade unions and by the employers' associations. The peaceful resolution of disputes has been newly introduced as an essential part of pre-trial proceedings. A special fixed term for amicable settlement is provided in collective disputes. The law contains some provisions on proceedings, while provisions on civil procedure are used subsidiarily.

The court proceedings on an individual dispute, as a rule, are not possible before it has been decided upon in an enterprise.

VII. FINAL REMARKS

The description of developments in the field of labour law and industrial relationships in Slovenia shows that the political, economic, and social changes are reflected in the field of labour law as well. The changes are of course a long-term process and some time will be needed to adjust labour law to these changes.